Beethoven, Sibelius and the 'Profound Logic'

Beethoven, Sibelius and the 'Profound Logic'

Studies in Symphonic Analysis

by
LIONEL PIKE

With a Foreword by
ROBERT SIMPSON

UNIVERSITY OF LONDON
THE ATHLONE PRESS
1978

Published by
THE ATHLONE PRESS
UNIVERSITY OF LONDON
4 *Gower Street London* WC1

Distributed by
Tiptree Book Services Ltd
Tiptree, Essex

U.S.A. and Canada
Humanities Press Inc
New Jersey

British Library Cataloguing in Publication Data
Pike, Lionel
  Beethoven, Sibelius and the profound logic.
  1. Beethoven, Ludvig van. Symphonies
  2. Sibelius, Jean. Symphonies
  I. Title
  785.1′1′0922   MT130.B43
  ISBN 0 485 11178 0

Set in Monotype Baskerville by
GLOUCESTER TYPESETTING CO LTD
Gloucester
Printed in Great Britain by
WHITSTABLE LITHO LTD
Whitstable, Kent

For Jenni

FOREWORD

To a composer analytic writing on music tends to get less and less appetizing as he gets older and learns to depend more and more on his instincts and experience, and when Professor Ian Spink suggested I might care to read a large unpublished work by one of his colleagues at Royal Holloway College, my pulse did not at once begin to race. On the other hand the book was about two of the composers who have meant most to me in my life, and I had just met Lionel Pike for the first time and received an instant impression of quiet intelligence and acute musicality. Reading the book proved far more than mere confirmation of this impression—it became steadily plainer that here was an exceptional mind, one from which it was exciting to learn, as much so as at any time since I was a schoolboy, when I first encountered Tovey.

Pike considers the two great symphonists on various different levels, coherently related, and when he remarks that his aim is to discover the nature of 'the profound logic' by comparing them, he does not mean that they are comparable in any crude sense. You cannot compare incomparables, but you can make use of your attempts at understanding them to discover common factors that satisfy certain deep requirements you feel you need from organic works of art. I am not sure that I would follow Sibelius in verbally associating music with any kind of logic; all the same, his finest music has long ago deeply explained to me what he meant, and Lionel Pike has put much of it into words. Whether one defines this essence as logic or not, it is certainly profound, and is present in all the greatest music. So the 'comparison' of Beethoven and Sibelius amounts to a search for it. I have found Pike's thinking both absorbing and revealing, even where our estimates have differed (about the finale of the *Eroica* or the slow movement of the Pastoral Symphony for instance); and perhaps the most positive way I can express that is to say it has stimulated, in some indefinable way, my own creative efforts—not by filling my head with theories, but by illuminating the sort of mental activity he has been able to perceive in two great masters, and showing much of what makes them both great.

There are many unexpected things in this book, even disconcerting things—but everything is fresh and clear, unexaggerated (there is no hyperbole) and expressed as directly as possible. It is not a book to browse through, or to use for quick reference; it is one to study, absorb, agree or disagree with, over a period of years. If, as Dr Pike suggests, a few of my ideas have somehow influenced him, these are but a drop in an ocean in which I shall be happy to swim for a long time to come.

Robert Simpson

ACKNOWLEDGEMENTS

Several portions of the book have already appeared in print, and I am grateful to the editors and trustees of *Music and Letters* and *Soundings* for permission to incorporate material from articles which first appeared in those periodicals: 'Sibelius' Debt to Renaissance Polyphony' (*Music and Letters*, July 1973) is the basis of a section of Chapter VIII, and 'The Tritone in Sibelius' Symphonic Music' (*Soundings*, 1975) is reproduced virtually unaltered as part of Chapter V. Naturally, the works of other authors have been consulted. These are referred to in the notes, where appropriate, by means of abbreviated titles, which are listed in the Bibliography. The extracts from Sibelius' *Tapiola* and Symphonies numbers 1, 2 and 4 are printed by permission of Breitkopf & Härtel, London, on behalf of the copyright owners; the extracts from that composer's 5th, 6th and 7th Symphonies are reproduced by permission of Edition Wilhelm Hansen, Copenhagen; and quotations from Sibelius' 3rd Symphony are included by permission of Robert Lienau, Berlin.

I am particularly grateful to Professor Ian Spink for his encouragement and for suggesting that I might present my lecture material on Beethoven and Sibelius in this form; and to Royal Holloway College for granting me sabbatical leave in which to complete my work on this book. My students have also helped me in many ways, chiefly by their questions and comments. My thanks are due to Mr Peter Costello for his care in setting the music examples. As will be very evident, Dr Robert Simpson's ideas have influenced me greatly: I am deeply grateful to him for his continued interest in the project and for the time he has spent in discussing it with me. My greatest debt of all is acknowledged in the dedication: without the loyal support and encouragement of my wife I could never have undertaken the writing of this book, nor, without her editorial help and criticism, could I have hoped to finish it.

Royal Holloway College (University of London)   L.J.P.

CONTENTS

'. . . a succession of clearly conceived, closely linked events in which every note has its organic function and its proper place, just as every word has in a well-built sentence and every sentence in a well-reasoned paragraph.'

Hans Gal, definition of Music

Introduction

The title of this book refers to a remark made by Sibelius during a well-known conversation with Mahler. Talking of the symphony, Sibelius said that what interested him in the form was 'the profound logic that created an inner connection between all the motives'. Mahler disagreed, saying that the symphony must be like the world, and thus should include everything. In this book I have tried to give some idea of the nature of the 'profound logic' which was so much admired by Sibelius. It is too easy to imagine that a composition, like a good performance, is something spontaneous. But in order to achieve a musically expressive work, the composer has to obey the formal dictates of the musical material he has chosen, just as in his turn the conductor must pay heed to the minutiae of playing technique in order that the effects intended by the composer shall be realized. It is with the labour of composition that this book is concerned. Just as the composers discussed have developed their material in musical terms, so I have tried to trace that development in words and, wherever possible, indicate the structural (not necessarily thematic) links by which a composer has integrated his music so as to make it intelligible to his listeners.

This book is therefore not intended to be a collection of programme notes: it will not say simply, 'The second subject begins at bar 54 and is in the dominant'; nor will it describe the music in naturalistic terms: it will not tell the reader whether 'the opening conjures up the snow-clad slopes of northern fjords'. Nor shall I attempt to deduce the state of Beethoven's emotions from his music. Such treatments of the music of Beethoven and Sibelius are in plentiful supply elsewhere. I shall assume that the reader already has some knowledge of the basic principles and terminology of symphonic form; and, since the symphonies of these two men are so popular as to make it likely that study scores will be readily available to everyone, I have referred freely to such scores as a means of reducing the number of musical examples.[1] Reference to the scores is in any case essential to a full understanding of the argument. It follows that the book is not an armchair companion to the symphonies of Beethoven and Sibelius, but is intended for the serious student—professional or amateur—of symphonic music. It is therefore unlikely that any value will accrue from an attempt to read it at a single sitting.

In order to demonstrate what Sibelius understood by 'profound logic', it seemed essential to analyse his symphonies in some detail. In addition, it seems evident that his remark was intended to apply not only to his own works in this form, but to the *idea* of the symphony as an art form generally. He obviously regarded 'the profound logic that created an inner connection between all the motives' as the highest ideal of symphonic writing. To measure how far he succeeded in realizing this ideal, it seemed necessary to compare his achievements in symphonic writing with those of the composer who is generally acknowledged to be the greatest of all symphonists, the more especially since Sibelius, like most composers after 1820, had immense admiration for Beethoven. Two tests must thus be applied to Sibelius' symphonic music. First, since Beethoven's symphonies are generally regarded as the finest works in the form, the excellence of Sibelius' can best be assessed by comparing them with those of the earlier master. Second, though it is easy to talk or write glibly about 'profound logic'—it is a phrase which rolls very impressively from the tongue or the pen—it is rather more difficult to define precisely what it *is*, since each composition, if it is to be recognized as an original and individual piece of music, and not merely the-same-piece-with-different-notes as something else, must put forward its own distinctive formulae for the development of its inherent logic. Thus it became necessary to attempt to define 'profound logic' closely in relation to each of the symphonic works of Sibelius. The question then inevitably arises: if we are to judge the excellence of Sibelius' symphonies by comparing them with those of Beethoven, the acknowledged master of the form; and if Sibelius, who admired 'the profound logic that created an inner connection between all the motives' in symphonic music, also admired and was influenced by the works of Beethoven, is it not possible that Sibelius held them in such high esteem because they, too, have this 'profound logic'? It seems more than likely that an understanding of Beethoven's compositional processes can help us to understand what Sibelius felt about symphonic form, and an understanding of the works of both men—one a great early exponent of 'the profound logic' and the other a great 20th century one—can help us to gain an insight into the changes and developments in the handling of the classic symphony. Since these relate to different aspects of compositional technique rather than to one composer or the other, I make no apology for changing from the examination of the works of the one to those of the other (and, perhaps, back again) within a single chapter.

I have tried as far as possible to confine my discussion of each symphony to one section of the book: nevertheless, the various facets of composition dealt with in those sections are so interdependent that it is virtually impossible to isolate them from one another. Thus the treatment of Sibelius' Fourth Symphony in Chapter V—ostensibly about tonality—is also a discussion of its rhythm. In the arrangement of the material I have tried to begin with simple concepts which are easily discernible, and then work towards those which are more complex or less immediately obvious. I have tried to follow this plan both in the ordering of the chapters, and in the discussions within each chapter. In addition, I have tried to work from the general to the particular; and I have called the first chapter 'Exposition', since it introduces in general terms themes which are developed later in the book.

The term 'symphonic' occurs many times in this book: while I use the word to refer to symphonies in which 'the profound logic' is evident, I do not wish to deny that other forms of symphony may be equally viable.[2] Such terms as 'exposition', 'development' and 'recapitulation' are also used even when the works discussed contain almost continuous development—as in the first movement of Sibelius' Second Symphony—since no other terms give quite the same help as these in referring to the position and function of particular sections in a movement. 'Motif', a word given different meanings by different analysts, I take to refer to a short melodic or rhythmic figure of, say, three or four notes. The designation x is given to such a figure when it seems to me to be of paramount importance to the work: each symphony may thus have a motif x, and I trust that this will confuse no-one. Finally, any confusion over such phrases as 'modal tonality' may be avoided if I state here that it seems inadequate to refer to the application of modal colour to the classical tonal schemes as either simply 'modality' or 'tonality'. It will readily be understood that certain expressions, if used in a musical context, can lead to ambiguity: the necessity for avoiding such statements as 'There are sound reasons for the major part of a movement to be in the minor, for this plays a key role in the development' will immediately be apparent.

CHAPTER I

Exposition

This book is an attempt to describe symphonic development—not only the organization of large-scale works by various compositional processes, but also the development which can be seen by comparing the works of an early master of such processes with those of a great 20th century writer in the same field. I hope to show how Beethoven and Sibelius have approached the problems set by one of the most demanding forms in all art,[1] and to demonstrate that each work evolves a different solution to these problems. Neither composer was content to write the same symphony several times with different notes.[2]

What are these problems which every composer of symphonies must solve? In order to answer this query I have taken for discussion a series of further questions which have often been posed: How does a composer ensure that the separate movements or sections of a work belong together, so that they cannot be interchanged with portions of other works? How is it that the themes of a symphony cannot be played in any arbitrary order and still achieve the desired result? How does a composer manage to weld the diverse types of music required of a symphony—scherzo, slow movement, and so on—into a logical whole? These are not the only problems involved, but they are basic to symphonic form.[3]

The discovery of Beethoven's and Sibelius' manner of working has been most exciting. Unfortunately, the process of writing out one's listening in prose inevitably destroys some of this excitement. When trying to explain music in cold prose, it is not easy to avoid writing something approaching a catalogue: furthermore, if any composer could adequately express in words the feelings he wishes to communicate, it would not be necessary to write music. Sibelius, as well as other composers, himself made this point.[4] The fact that music does so much more than words must, of course, mean that a great deal is lost in the process of trying to describe it.

It is not my purpose here to explain everything in the symphonies of Beethoven and Sibelius: it would indeed be a brave, if not a foolish, man who pretended to know everything about them. Great music exists on several levels—the two most obvious are those of the pure 'sound of music' and what Tovey called 'intellectual construction'. Recent analysts have referred to *foreground* ('the opening theme conjures up the snow-clad slopes of northern fjords . . .') and *background* ('the work is built on two inter-locking intervals of a fourth . . .').[5] It is with background alone that this book is concerned, but this is not to deny the existence of the foreground areas, which are very appealing in the music of both Beethoven and Sibelius. The processes described here are not the sole prerogative of the symphony, though they are perhaps more characteristic of this form than of any other. A great musical work will have both foreground and back-ground interest: works which survive the test of time do, as a rule, have both. A piece which has only intellectual interest will no doubt fascinate the scholar but fail to attract the majority of the musical populace, whereas a piece which has little 'background' interest and relies primarily on the 'sound of music' (as I believe Sibelius' First Symphony does) is less likely to prove a lasting success than one which has plenty of both foreground and background interest (Sibelius' Fifth Symphony, for example). The greatest symphonies contrive to strike a balance between these two areas.

Until the second half of the present century the majority of commentators on musical works concentrated on the foreground area: this is more difficult to capture in prose than the background. Because music is less precise than words it is often open to various interpretations, as Alan Walker has shown in his comparison of analyses of the same work by Hadow, MacPherson, Tovey and Prout.[6] The concentration on back-ground—which is what most musicians now think of as analysis—is a relatively recent phenomenon, and it has sometimes failed to see the proverbial wood for the trees. There is a tendency to look ever deeper into the music, using more and more complex analytical techniques, yet often missing the most obvious features of construction simply because the listener's response is not sufficiently taken into account. One's own response is bound to be subjective; but since musical art (of the type with which this book is concerned) is intended to communicate, some kind of response, common to all listeners, must be envisaged by the composer: this response need not be in the nature of a 'dramatic' experience, but may exist simply in the fact that all listeners hear the same musical events in the same order. This common response (as opposed to the individual response, which has more to do with the character of the responder than that of the music) should be the proper business of criticism: the kind of criticism which reduces a musical structure to a set of formulae, leaving out of account any response on the part of the listener, neglects the main business of music—communication between the composer and his audience.[7] (Especially prevalent is the type of analysis which concentrates on melodic construction and ignores other facets of composition.) A corollary to the view that the listener's response is important is the opinion that music exists in performance rather than on paper. Music exists, therefore, in time—the time it takes in performance. The way in which this time is filled up is of such significance—and has been so little discussed—that considerable space is devoted to it in this book.[8]

Background analysis raises various difficulties and temptations. When one has discovered some kind of structural device in a work, there is perhaps a tendency to impose it inappropriately upon earlier works. One has also to counter the tendency to mistake elements of style for structural devices: it is nevertheless a fair comment that a composer will obviously choose from the common stock of stylistic devices such unifying elements as suit his own purposes. All music (with the exception of that currently termed 'avant-garde') can, of course, be reduced to the formulae (with its inversion), (with its inversion) and (with its inversion) if you stretch it far enough.[9] As I have hinted already, thematic analysis by itself is not sufficient, though it is clear that symphonic writing of the type employed by Beethoven and Sibelius started with thematic devices as the main means of achieving unity and only later (with the symphonies from the 'Eroica' onwards) began to integrate other devices more extensively.[10] One does not get a unified symphony (at least, not in the Beethoven and Sibelius sense) by writing four totally unrelated movements and then imposing upon them a 'motto' or *idée fixe*, or by adding an introduction which announces all the main themes together. Symphonic growth and logical argument are important as well.[11] The unity of a work is often hidden: it is not necessary for the ordinary listener to know *why* the Finale of a symphony 'sounds right'—but it is very important that he should feel its rightness. Even professional musicians have not always understood the forces working for unity: Berlioz did not understand the reason for the loud dissonant passage at the opening of the Finale of Beethoven's Ninth Symphony, yet a brief examination of the tonality of that work would have shown him the thinking that led up to it: Spohr considered that Beethoven's Fifth Symphony was not a classical whole.[12] Weber thought that the Introduction to Beethoven's Fourth Symphony was 'a few notes spread over several pages'—and the end of Sibelius' Seventh Symphony has been likened to *Valse Triste*; but these opinions show a lack of understanding of the music. Sibelius himself, though he admitted following the 'compulsive' policy of Beethoven, yet remarked that 'Beethoven's works have many failings, especially from the period of his total deafness.'[13]

It follows from this that the unity of a symphonic work must be audible so that the sense of its 'rightness' will be created in the listener, even though he may not be *consciously* aware of it: mere counting of notes—paper analysis—does not show what it is in the music that makes for such an impression. It has been suggested[14] that the ideal listener is the one who remembers every detail and can relate each one to the later events in a symphony: this ideal listener presumably ought also to have perfect pitch. No such ideal person exists, yet with thorough knowledge and frequent hearing of the symphonic repertoire one can become aware of devices which on casual acquaintance might pass unnoticed. I hope that all the devices discussed in this book are audible ones—none of them has been noted by 'paper analysis'—since music is written essentially to be heard, not looked at.[15]

An ideal starting point for an investigation of the kind undertaken in this book is to assume that mature symphonists do not do things by accident: after all, if a work is thoroughly unified, every event within the music must have some compelling logic to explain its presence. The loud C sharps in the Finale of Beethoven's Eighth Symphony are a perfect example of this: they have long been explained away as an example of Beethoven's 'rough humour'—yet the discovery of the reasons for their presence shows that they are in fact an integral part of the overall scheme of the work. It follows, too, that if a work is thoroughly unified, the very opening notes—however insignificant they may seem—will be an important part of the total design: a splendid example may be found in the opening G stroke on the timpani in Sibelius' Seventh Symphony. It will be made plain in this study that both Beethoven and Sibelius announce their intentions at the outset in such a way that the attentive listener cannot but be aware of the relevance of the opening to the whole.

The fact that such a highly musical argument as is suggested here can only take place on its own terms raises the question: Can a programme be used as the basis of a symphonic work without destroying the purely musical logic of that work? This is a difficult problem, and there is no easy solution. The answer seems to be that too detailed a programme can easily upset symphonic logic. This is not to imply that symphonic music may not be descriptive: the 'Eroica', 'Pastoral' and 'Choral' Symphonies plainly are. But it was perhaps the realization that too detailed a programme would be bound to conflict with the requirements of purely symphonic logic that prompted Beethoven to make the 'Pastoral' 'more an expression of feeling than painting'. Provided, therefore, that the programme is controlled, it need not upset the purely musical logic of a work.

There are many ways of approaching and analysing a symphony. Sir Donald Tovey's strictures about thematic analysis are too well known to need repetition,[16] and in this book such analysis is dealt with briefly. There are many other contributory factors which help to make a work a unified whole and which are quite audible to the attentive listener: these elements are given more thorough treatment. The symphony succeeded the fugue (and the even earlier motet) in being regarded as the highest form of music-making. It thus has the most complex form of organisation, and in a great work everything is carefully planned so as to contribute to the logical development of musical ideas—harmony, rhythm, tonality and thematic material all play their part in this development, and none is neglected at the expense of others.[17] The symphony is a struggle between tonalities, between thematic materials and other elements of composition. It has been described as 'unity created out of diversity'; a set of movements and themes which on the surface appear to be completely diverse are yet drawn together in a logical way.

Up to a point thematic analysis has been useful in explaining the phenomenon of unity. It is quite clear from Rudolf Reti's studies that Beethoven's works are thematically unified even if the notion is more questionable when applied to earlier works in more than one movement.[18] There were, however, historical precursors of thematic integration in the Pavane and Galliard pairs, in the head-motif techniques, in masses (and other choral works in several sections) based on a plainsong or on other pre-existent material, in the monothematic early symphony and in the late works of Haydn and Mozart. When Sibelius made his now famous remark that what attracted him to the symphony was the profound logic that created an inner connection between all the motifs, he obviously included thematic means of unification. Hans Keller[19] has pointed out some Mozartian examples of the technique, but he fails to mention that the original slow movement of the 31st Symphony (K.297), rejected by the conductor Le Gros, and Mozart's replacement slow movement[20] have identical underlying shapes, though the resulting sound is quite different. This goes far towards suggesting that the use of that particular thematic shape was of importance to the work as a whole. Naturally, a correspondence of material is not evident in every instance in which a movement has been replaced: the lack of thematic unity in a first version may well have been the reason for the change, even if the composer was only subconsciously aware that this was so.

The objection might be raised that pre-existent material, which is sometimes incorporated in symphonies (in the 'Eroica', for example), must surely weaken the feeling of unity. For instance, Schubert's mature works (avowedly less tightly organized than Beethoven's) make wide use of pre-existent material; though a thorough study of them shows that the composer was always careful to borrow thematic material that was compatible with the remainder of the work, or else to develop it into a form in which it became compatible. Beethoven's own sketches, too, demonstrate that, even in their most primitive form, the themes show signs of unity with other motifs from the work to which they belong: they are then polished and developed into their final form, while maintaining the same underlying shape. An excellent example of this manner of working is to be found in the sketches for the Trio of the 'Eroica' Symphony. Another example is the Trio of the Ninth: in many early sketches, Beethoven used the theme of the Trio of his Second Symphony, which has some obvious points of contact with the thematic material of the 'Choral'. Beethoven clearly felt that the Trio of the Second Symphony fitted into the Scherzo of the Ninth very well, and, so far as the thematic shape is concerned, it does: the Trio he eventually wrote was similar to it in some respects.

Few composers—if any—have ever surpassed Beethoven in the writing of variations. When one bears this fact in mind, and also considers the immense number of sketches, the amount of care and polishing, rejecting and experimenting that went into the making of each symphony, it is surely naïve to suggest that he would not apply techniques of variation to his themes. His strict training in fugue, with its inversions, augmentations, diminutions and stretti, would also have suggested to him the use of techniques of thematic metamorphosis. Yet, even in recent writings, one still finds statements such as

Much has been made of the resemblance of the first phrase in the second group [of the Ninth Symphony] to the choral theme of the Finale. This can mean nothing in the first movement, as the latter theme is still unknown and the whole point of the drama preceding its entry is the total rejection of the earlier movements, a sequence of events in which such a thematic reminiscence would be a distracting irrelevance.[21]

On the contrary, the whole point of thematic unity (and other types of unity as well) is surely that the listener will be subconsciously aware of the rightness of each event within a given work; and the rightness depends upon the relationship of these events with each other. It is because the theme of the Finale of the Ninth Symphony is developed from previous material—heard and subconsciously remembered by the audience—that it 'sounds right'.[22]

'Heard and subconsciously remembered by the audience': even if we admit that unity exists, we may still speculate as to whether it is felt by the composer subconsciously, or whether he is aware of the processes involved.[23] Sibelius must have been conscious of a profound logic, or he would not have mentioned it; likewise his hint that in the Sixth Symphony analysis would reveal that several interesting things were going on suggests an awareness of the logic of construction. Yet he could also say, 'When a work of art which is intuitively created is scientifically analysed it reveals amazing requirements. Yet the artist works entirely instinctively.'[24] The acknowledgement of the existence of profound logic does not necessarily involve acceptance of the view that every detail of a work is arrived at by a conscious intellectual process: composition is not merely a technical exercise. It is clear that certain passages gain acceptance for no other reason than that the composer's instinct tells him that they 'sound right', and that others are rejected because they 'sound wrong'.

It may perhaps be somewhat uncharitable to suggest that the great composers did not understand what others (or, indeed, they themselves at times) were doing or why they were doing it; and yet it is clear that some of them did not. I have already pointed out the lack of understanding of Beethoven by Spohr, Weber and Berlioz; and it was not until the 20th century that any discussion in depth of the principles of thematic construction took place. Surely, if composers were aware of such techniques, they would have taught them to their pupils, or written about them? They are there, for all to observe, in their works: why was it that, even if they themselves considered the writing of new works more important than the explanation of the procedures they had already used, lesser composers (who, it has been said, make avid theorists) and critics have not mentioned them? Were the devices a closely guarded professional secret—a mystique of awe surrounding the processes of composition which was to be maintained with care? Very few commentators, indeed, mentioned the processes;[25] the writers who did appeared not to understand those of Beethoven.[26] André, a great admirer of Mozart, in 1825 told Hiller and Spohr about Beethoven's Seventh Symphony:

The worst fault that André could allege against him was the *way* in which he composed. André had seen the autograph of the A major symphony during its progress, and told us that there were whole sheets left blank, to be filled up afterwards, the pages before the blanks having no connection with those beyond them. What continuity or connection *could* there be in music so composed?

Tomaschek, though writing of the year 1798, likewise remarked

his frequent daring deviations from one motive to another, whereby the organic connection, the gradual development of idea was put aside, did not escape me. Evils of this nature frequently weaken his greatest compositions, those which sprang from a too exuberant conception.[27]

Sibelius doggedly refused to discuss his own techniques of composition, as many of his biographers make quite clear. Indeed, in his 'Author's Postscript' Simon Parmet[28] suggests that, in common with many composers, Sibelius was made uneasy by 'relentless dissection—even vivisection' of his works, preferring to forget the technical processes involved once a work was completed, in order to concentrate on the 'poetry'. Here a parallel might well be made with literature: 'George Eliot, like most great novelists, intentionally avoided either referring to or speaking of her own works. She took the attitude of letting her books speak for themselves.'[29] Although we cannot prove positively whether composers work entirely consciously or unconsciously, Alan Walker[30] writes interestingly about the point, quoting Tartini, Brahms, Mahler, Schoenberg and Stravinsky in support of the idea that at least some of the work of composition can be subconscious. One point that emerges is that many composers have felt that a work was 'there' waiting to be composed; the vision would come to them in a flash, and the hard work of composition was necessary in order to recapture, to work back towards, this vision, rather like a sculptor chipping at a block of stone until the finished shape he has imagined is revealed.[31] As Edward Schulz said of Beethoven, 'he never writes one note down till he has formed a clear design for the whole piece'.[32] Even more clear are Beethoven's own words on the subject:

I carry my thoughts about with me for a long time, sometimes a very long time, before I set them down. . . . At the same time my memory is so faithful to me that I am sure not to forget a theme which I have once conceived, even after years have passed. I make many changes, reject and reattempt until I am satisfied. Then the working out in breadth, heighth [sic] and depth begins in my head, and since I am conscious of what I want, the basic idea never leaves me. It rises, grows upwards, and I hear and see the picture as a whole take shape and stand forth before me as though cast in a single piece, so that all that is left is the work of writing it down. This goes quickly, according as I have the time, for sometimes I have several compositions in labor at once, though I am sure never to confuse one with another.[33]

Similar evidence is provided by Santeri Levas on behalf of Sibelius:

He once said that he wrote his music down when he first heard it in its final form in his mind. Between the first conception and committal to paper a long time— sometimes years—passed. A work thus came to maturity, at the same time acquiring its own style.[34]

Further evidence of this manner of working is given by Levas regarding Sibelius' eighth symphony:[35] the composer had a clear idea of this work in his mind, but yet could not capture the music on paper in a form which satisfied him entirely.[36]

Sibelius was certainly aware of the various aspects of unity, as is shown by his comment about the 'profound logic', and some of the processes evident in Beethoven's work can scarcely be other than consciously employed. Nevertheless, it seems highly unlikely that we shall ever know just how much of the process of composition was subconscious or instinctive, and how much the result of careful mental planning—and it is in any case true that the two types of working are not mutually exclusive, as Schoenberg's testimony, so often quoted, tells us. The mind may subconsciously arrive at a quite complex serial relationship between themes, as Schoenberg's did: Dorothy L. Sayers, in *The Mind of the Maker*,[37] comments that 'accidents' of construction can occur in a well-written work, and that in such pieces of writing quite important correspondences of ideas and material may be unnoticed by the author: they are included because of the subconscious working of the author's mind. On the other hand, it is quite possible that the sense of 'architectural planning' apparent in Beethoven's music may have resulted from his deafness: for a composer deprived of hearing may well have given greater than usual attention to structural procedures, just as Milton compensated for his blindness by the vividness of his visual descriptions. Thus it seems that the unification of a work of art may be arrived at by various means. As Meyer has pointed out, '*a relationship is a relationship* whether it was expressly devised by the composer, resulted from the orderliness of stylistic syntax, or in rare instances was the result of chance';[38] or, as Barrett-Ayres puts it, 'I maintain that it matters naught whether the composer realized fully what he was doing, or whether he unconsciously obeyed the intuitive urges of a musician and artist.'[39]

Professor Kerman has rightly pointed out that it is easier to discuss technical details than aesthetic results,[40] and this may well account for the extraordinary lengths to which some modern analysis goes in discussing features which are not even subconsciously audible. Naturally, aesthetic results and technical details are interconnected. But it seems to me that the proper business of musical analysis is not so much to ask the question 'What happens?' as to attempt to answer the question 'Why does it happen?'— to investigate, in other words, the working, subconscious or otherwise, of the musical mind, whether it be the composer's or the listener's, and this is the task I have attempted in the following pages.

CHAPTER II

The Thematic Approach

Of all the means used by composers to give unity to their work, none has received more attention than the thematic one, perhaps because it is easier to analyse a work showing that a few melodic fragments under lie the construction of all its themes than it is to identify other (and sometimes more important) elements which contribute to the 'symphonic unity', and perhaps also because the thematic manner of unifying a work is almost universally found after Beethoven.[1] The thematic approach—as I have called this way of looking at symphonic music—tells us nothing about the treatment of rhythm or tonality (which play a vital part in the construction of a symphony), very little about logical processes of thought and development (a *sine qua non* of symphonic music as I have defined it in this book), and nothing about harmony or instrumentation (which may well have some bearing on the thought processes at work in the music).[2] These other elements of composition will be dealt with later: in this chapter the thematic view will be considered by itself, in so far as it is at all possible to divorce it from the other compositional procedures I have mentioned.[3]

From many points of view, Sibelius' First Symphony is not a successful work, and an analysis based purely on the themes reveals rather few connections between them: such unity as the work possesses must be sought elsewhere. The slow introductory theme in the solo clarinet (which returns in slightly altered form to begin the last movement) contains some of the melodic formulae used, though by no means all of them: it must nevertheless be confessed that large stretches of the work are not 'unified' in this way, and that except for the first movement the work does not grow in a logical, symphonic manner. In this respect the Second Symphony shows a very considerable advance, though it has still not reached the closely argued and carefully integrated stage which can be seen in the later symphonies. Nevertheless, it is easier to trace the logical processes of thematic development in this work. The opening theme of the Second Symphony repeatedly outlines a rising figure which I shall call *x* (see Ex. 1).

Ex. 1

Above this figure an inversion of *x* works in counterpoint (see Ex. 2): the 'turn' which follows it (*y*) grows naturally from the second *x* of this example, which itself turns upwards from D to E at the end.

Ex. 2

As can be clearly seen from the accompanying figure in bar 3 of Ex. 2, *y* itself contains *x* or its inversion; and from bars 4 and 7 it will be evident that *y* is often used in two interlocked versions so that the resulting figure starts and ends on the same note. A new shape, which I shall call *w*, appears at the end of Ex. 2, and becomes the basis of a new theme (see Ex. 3): although the notes often vary, the general shape of this tune is that of an upward leap (often an arpeggio) followed by a short stepwise descent.

Ex. 3

It will be noticed that, like *y* in Ex. 2, *w* also contains *x*. The growth of this new shape is continued in retrograde motion at the same time as it is used in a shortened recto version (Ex. 4).

Ex. 4

(with additional D)   *w* (with additional G♯)

The cadential form of *y* used towards the end of Ex. 4 leads logically to the next idea—the pizzicato theme which begins by using *y* sequentially and proceeds by treating *x* in the same way. Following this is one of the most important subjects, which, like *y*, is introduced by being played in counterpoint against the music of Ex. 1: it is a further use of *w* (played backwards) and contains *x* as well (see Ex. 5), while the rushing string octaves which follow closely are interlocked versions of *y*, rather like a quicker form of the beginning of the pizzicato theme mentioned above.

Ex. 5

The final theme of the exposition (Ex. 6) expands an idea already alluded to several times, and marked *z* in the Examples (the same idea occurs on page 7 of the score,[4] bars 3 and 4): it might not be stretching the point too far to view this as a welding of two parts into one, both the upper and lower parts being in the shape *x*, and the upper parts also in the shape *y* (see Ex. 6).

Ex. 6

The exposition ends by returning to the music of Ex. 1—a reminder that, though the development section has not even begun, ten pages of full score have already developed from a simple figure of three notes. The themes of this symphony are often described as fragmentary; but behind each there is a compelling logic which is characteristic of Sibelius' symphonies from this point onwards. With the use of contrapuntal combinations, sequences, inversions and diminutions, the development section rationalizes these fragments by building them up to a continuous (and, it need hardly be added, thoroughly unified) melody,[5] after which the recapitulation returns to the feeling of the exposition: the final inversions of Ex. 1 serve yet again to remind the listener of the simple thematic basic of the whole movement. Nevertheless, as a later chapter will show, this is by no means the whole story.

A detailed analysis of the rest of this work would take many more pages than Sibelius himself wrote in his score, and to treat all the symphonies in a similar way would be tedious in the extreme. A close thematic analysis of the Fourth Symphony is, in any case, readily available elsewhere.[6] Sibelius may well have copied the process of evolving themes from simple motifs, as well as that of using them as a means of unifying a symphonic work, from the music of Beethoven, where such an approach is clearly discernible.

An interesting use of this process is seen in Sibelius' Fifth Symphony: the material of the work does not develop in quite the same way as that of the Second Symphony, for it is all announced in the opening bars rather than evolving gradually (see Ex. 7): it should be borne in mind, however, that this opening phrase was added only when Sibelius revised the work.

Ex. 7

The process of separating out these tightly packed segments begins almost immediately: *c* and *b* are first heard together, the *b* by itself in thirds on the woodwind until, at the change of key on page 6, a slowly rising scale (*c*, though it is somewhat chromatic) is the background for many statements of *a*. At Letter D this long rising version of *c* is balanced by a falling scale with *b* above it; then *b* is used alone at two different speeds (Ex. 8), as well as in recto and inversion simultaneously.

Ex. 8

This theme, which ends the exposition, shows Sibelius working in two different ways at the same time: by using various contrapuntal combinations and diminutions, he is not only developing the material announced at the opening, but also dismembering the music of Ex. 7 in order to treat the various motifs separately. The first few pages of the development section (pages 21–4) also deal with this theme alone: and it is only with the quickening pace as the movement shifts into the 'scherzo' tempo that subjects again begin to occur in combination. The new subjects of the 'scherzo' section combine the thematic elements in a different way (see Exx. 9 and 10) and the movement ends with all the material reassembled.[7]

Ex. 9

Ex. 10

Thematically, the second movement presents a simpler picture: *d* is used as the basis of a set of variations; other themes occur (notably *b*), though they are much less in evidence. The Finale first clearly recalls *a* (a theme not much heard in the preceding movement); then, having used *b* and *c* in its first subject (the latter with the long note which introduces it in Ex. 10), for its second and final subject it reassembles the elements of Ex. 7 in yet another way, using *b* in both recto and inverted form[8] (see Ex. 11).

Ex. 11

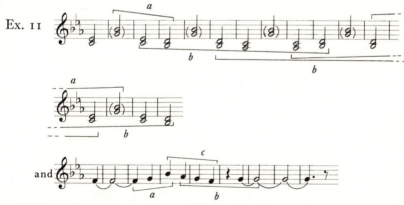

and

The motif which is missing here, *d*, is played prominently by the brass in the coda (pages 135f). Although there is also a certain amount of real growth of material in the first movement, this manner of working—a development of material that consists of dismembering the elements in order to fit them together again in a variety of different ways—constitutes a new approach to thematic unity.

The gradual evolution of themes from a melodic germ heard at the opening returns in the Sixth Symphony, though the result is quite unlike that of the Second. The process starts, as is only to be expected, in the first bar of the work (see Ex. 12), though the motifs are not yet announced in that clearly defined state which marks their later appearance.

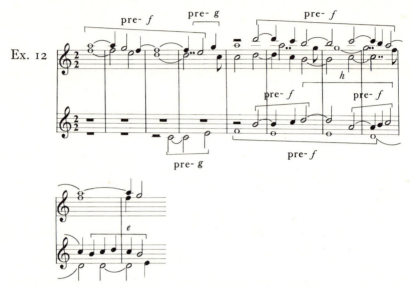

Ex. 12

From this vague opening several melodic outlines emerge: the scalic figure which I have marked 'pre-f' develops into the first clear statement of the most important thematic device after three lines of score. I shall refer to this motif as f (see Ex. 13).

Ex. 13

Attention is drawn to the importance of this theme in two ways; firstly by the scoring: not only does the entrance of f coincide with the first appearance of the woodwind, but, more particularly, the low notes of the oboe which announce the theme are in marked contrast with the high violin music which has preceded it. Secondly, the tonality emphasizes the importance of f since this is the point where D minor is first stated clearly. The motif is used in ascending or descending form and it frequently appears together in both forms—used either simultaneously in counterpoint or one following the other in a single part (see Ex. 14). Another idea which is closely related to f has already been foreshadowed at the end of Ex. 12; a type of vocal line in which upward and downward scalewise movement are balanced (see Exx. 15 and 16).

I shall call this arch-shaped feature *e*, even though it contains clear versions of motif *f*. A further development of *f* results from the omission of the fourth degree of the scale, as in the second and third bars of Ex. 16, though it might be possible to regard this phrase as being derived from the arpeggio figure *g* which was foreshadowed in the triadic skeleton of Exx. 12 and 15 and which assumes an important role in the symphony. One other melodic phrase which is frequently used deserves mention, and it likewise contains elements of *f*: the phrase is marked *h* in Exx. 12 and 16, where it appears in inversion and retrograde motion (see Exx. 16 and 17). The figure *h* of this Example is also associated with yet another unifying motif, which I shall call *j* (see Ex. 18): it is sometimes reduced to the two notes which outline a falling fifth.

All the material so far quoted from the Sixth Symphony may be found in only the first few pages of the score: to analyse their appearance in the rest of the work would be unnecessary, since the unifying motifs can easily be traced by the reader. The point I would wish to stress here is not so much that the work is an integrated whole because of its use of these features in its themes, but that the motifs themselves grow from those first few hazy bars of two-part counterpoint; and that the growth is a logical one, each motif being a clear development of some feature of a preceding one.

The construction of the Seventh Symphony will be dealt with elsewhere; but it is essential to say at this point that the thematic view outlined above is open to some abuse, as critics of this type of analysis have not been slow to point out. The reader may, for instance, care to identify the following themes from Sibelius' symphonies (Ex. 19):

Ex. 19

Critics of the thematic view would argue that, since these themes are very similar in shape and yet belong to different symphonies, the 'unity' of each of these symphonies is weakened:[9] we have merely succeeded in isolating one of Sibelius' favourite phrases—and one might do the same with the augmented fourth or the phrase.[10] Alan Walker has made the point that just because a motif occurs in work B as well as in work A, this does not in any way affect the unity of work A. Indeed, it is clearly sensible for a composer to choose as unifying motifs only those melodic elements which are most compatible with his own style—and such motifs are very likely to occur in more than one piece.

One can go further than this: in spite of their similarity, the themes quoted above are not, as one might perhaps expect, all interchangeable: the last two quotations would seem out of place in the Fifth Symphony, for example. Some could appear in another symphony without very greatly upsetting the flow of symphonic thought: but more important than the presence of each theme is the process of logic which has led up to it, and the relationship of each theme to the whole, as well as its position and the other formulae which surround it or which are embedded in it. A more important point is that the thematic view cannot give the whole answer to the questions posed at the beginning of this book (What is symphonic unity? Why cannot a movement (or theme) from one symphony be used in another without upsetting that unity?), as I hope very shortly to make clear.[11] The thematic analysis of the beginning of the Sixth Symphony, given above, is woefully inadequate to a true understanding of the nature of that work: the other features which contribute to the symphony's unity and those which are used as a means of unifying other symphonies, by Beethoven as well as by Sibelius, will be examined in the following chapters.

It is unnecessary to supplement this view of the music of Sibelius by comparing it with similar techniques in the music of Beethoven, since thematic investigation of Beethoven's work has been the sport of analysts for many years. A discussion of two facets is, however, essential at this point.

The composition of Beethoven's Fifth Symphony was interrupted by work on the Fourth, so that it is hardly surprising that the two works have motifs in common. He was interested at this time in the possibilities of the shape which I shall refer to as x. There are several things one could do with such a motif: firstly, one could use it as the skeleton of the work's various themes, which would then be developed in their own right. Secondly, one could write counterpoint against it and then develop the counterpoints. Thirdly, one could do either or both of these things, but using the notes in a different order, or in inversion or retrograde motion. All these methods of working are common to the Fourth (which is discussed elsewhere in this book) and the Fifth Symphonies. But one could work in other ways, too—and it is well to remember that a deaf composer may have compensated for his disability by his interest in the architecture of his major works. One could augment or diminish the note-values of x; and one could extend the intervals of a third to bigger ones—to fourths and fifths, for example. In the Fourth Symphony, Beethoven alters the note-values, while in the Fifth, he widens the intervals. Although Tovey maintains that 'no great music has ever been built from an initial figure of four notes', on the contrary, I would suggest that two of Beethoven's symphonies use these four notes as a unifying thematic device, and that, by their methods of treatment and character they form two sides of the same coin: I shall further suggest that the Sixth Symphony of Beethoven begins by using the same motif. A supreme master of variation technique who could build massive structures on the simplest material—as Beethoven could—would not be daunted by the prospect of having to derive much music from so few notes.

Beethoven starts the Fifth Symphony with a rhythm and a melodic shape only: even the tonality is uncertain for a while, a point to which I shall return in a later chapter. Both the rhythm and the melody are hammered out most powerfully, since both are of great importance in the construction of the work. It is clear that Tovey has missed the point:[12] the novel power of the delivery of this opening is Beethoven's way of drawing attention to the importance of the motif and the rhythm. Indeed, the alteration of the D in bar 4 so that it lasts for an extra bar (it had originally been only one minim in length) makes it quite clear that this note completes the sense—that the 'motto theme' of the work extends this far. In some form or another x permeates a great deal of the music of the symphony; and it is a relatively simple task to trace its use, either directly or as the underlying shape of the various themes. It would indeed be tedious to point out all the derivations—they are very many: for the present purpose, the relationship between these derivations of x and symphonic growth is of much more vital importance.

Immediately he has announced the opening motif, Beethoven begins to expand its leaps (although the original intervals are also used alongisde the expanded versions) until the second subject is introduced with a horn call in which the leaps are each a fifth (see Ex. 20), the use of the opening rhythm on the first note serving to make it clear to the listener that the two themes have a common source. I shall call this expanded version of the 'motto shape' y.

Ex. 20

The close relationship between x and y, which is made evident here by the gradual expansion of the intervals and by the repetition of the opening rhythm in the first bar of Ex. 20, is also demonstrated in other ways later in the work (at bars 228–31 and 388–401 of the first movement and bars

30–8 of the third movement, for example), and, like *x*, *y* itself becomes the basis of later themes.

The motto *x* is equated with other themes as the work progresses. One of the first of these, which becomes very important, is a four-note scale which uses exactly the notes of *x* (at bars 14–18 of the opening movement) but in a different order: the F and E flat are reversed, but as before the presence of the opening rhythm helps the ear to identify the common source. The relationship is alluded to in other ways, especially in the recapitulation and coda of the first movement. The oboe counter melody which accompanies the reappearance of the first subject (bars 254f) twice uses the four-note scale, and then, at the pause, a brief cadenza incorporates the scales with *x* as an underlying shape[13] (see Ex. 21):

Ex. 21

and at bars 406–15 the two motifs are combined in counterpoint, the opening rhythm again being used to point to the common source. Finally, there is in this movement a clear fusion of the two into a single line in an inversion and augmentation of the material just discussed (see Ex. 22).

Ex. 22

The relationship thus formed is maintained in later movements, though usually it is with *y* rather than *x*. At bar 71 of the third movement, the connection with *x* is suggested by the presence of its opening rhythm only, though the four-note scale is used soon afterwards in the outline of *y* (bars 85–90), and the same relationship is very evident many times in the Finale, with the scale both ascending and descending (for example, at bars 6–12, 22–5 and 44–8): the presence of the opening rhythm again helps the ear to make the comparison. Some further relationships with the shape of *x* and with its rhythm alone are shown at bars 122–30 and 362–78.

Lastly, a close relationship exists between *x* and a chromatic scale which develops into the shape shown in Ex. 29, a shape which plays an important role in governing the tonality of the work. The connection is first mooted in the bass at bars 82f of the first movement, where it is only the rhythm of the new theme that shows its relationship with *x*, and these two motifs are similarly used in the second movement at bars 87–92. Even if a link between the two at the opening of the Scherzo appears questionable (see Ex. 23), a later passage makes such a link much clearer.

Ex. 23

One thematic tag stands apart from this relationship with *x*—the falling semitone. The triadic figures are shown to relate to *x* at bars 25–8 of the first movement, and in other places, notably in the Finale where its shape is worked into a triadic theme (bars 26–32). The importance to the work of the opening four-note rhythm now becomes quite clear: it is an aid to the ear in relating the various themes to the basic shape *x*: the process of relating themes in this way was so new to Beethoven's audience that such an aid was essential. The power of the opening of the work (and indeed of the symphony as a whole, since it uses this characteristic rhythm widely) thus serves a 'background' as well as a 'foreground' purpose: without such clear attention being drawn to *x* and its rhythm at the very start, the relationships would not be nearly so easily perceived by the audience.

By the time Beethoven came to write his Ninth Symphony, such thematic procedures were no longer new, and a characteristic rhythm is not there essential to the understanding of thematic unity and development. The problem of unification and symphonic growth is, in any case, quite differently approached: it consists of an expansion onto a vast canvas of an idea already implicit in the 'Pastoral' Symphony—that of the growth of the main tune of the Finale from motifs presented throughout the other movements. The logical further step is taken in the 'Choral' of fusing several ideas—an arch shape, the shape ⸻ with its various inversions and retrogrades, and a falling fifth—into the two main subjects in the Finale, and then combining these two subjects contrapuntally into a single complex. It is because of the logical growth of these elements throughout the symphony that the two tunes of the last movement sound so right when they are heard.[14] The relationship between the themes and the Finale is best shown in diagrammatic form (other facets of the symphony are dealt with in Chapters IV and VII): in Exx. 24 and 25, the Roman numerals refer to the number of the movement, and the Arabic numerals to the bar. Two further points emerge from these examples: firstly, the motif of Ex. 25 occurs in the D major tune of the Finale itself (see Ex. 25, *26*), and secondly, the eventual fusion of the motifs in counterpoint is foreshadowed at two other important appearances of D major in earlier movements; in the Trio section of the second movement (Ex. 24, *9* and Ex. 25, *13*) and in the third movement (Ex. 24, *13* and Ex. 25, *16*), thus establishing the relationship between the Finale's main theme and the tonal goal of the symphony.

The sense of musical satisfaction provided by this scheme is, of course, an ideal accompaniment to the feelings expressed by Schiller's *Ode to Joy*, which is used as the text of the Finale. (Though not conceived on nearly such a vast scale, Sibelius' Fifth Symphony provides another example of a work whose main Finale theme is the culmination of several devices and motifs heard earlier, as I have already mentioned). In the 'Choral' Symphony, the introduction of voices itself heightens the satisfaction: the humanistic idea of 'the brotherhood of man' which is the basis of Schiller's poem needs human participation for its expression.[15] The appearance of voices in an otherwise purely instrumental work—so like the sudden appearance of human figures in an otherwise empty landscape—provides this.

Ex. 24

Ex. 24.6  II 22

7  II 93

8  II 354

9  II 414

10 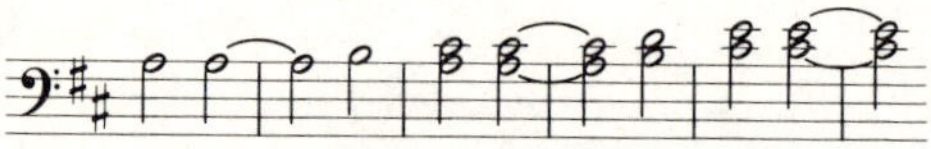 II 458

11  III 10

12  III 19

13  III 25

14  III 114

15  III 127

16  IV 59

Ex. 24.17  IV 72

18  I 1

19 I 20

20 I 116

21 I 480

22 II 9

23 II 412

24 III 26

25 III 120

26 III 153

27 IV 8

Ex. 25

Ex. 25.  IV 67

26  IV 100

27  IV 249

28 IV 261

CHAPTER III

The Expansion of Classical Tonality (1)

Beethoven's First Symphony

Symphonic form consists largely of a balance of tonalities.[1] In the classical symphony the main key, announced at the outset, is contradicted by another tonal area (usually the dominant for major keys, and the relative major for minor keys). Then, in a central area, other keys are introduced, and they lead back to a passage in which the music of the opening tonic section is repeated in its original key, and the music of the contrasting tonal area is transposed to the tonic (major, where the tonic key is minor). A leaning towards the subdominant (i.e. the flat side of the tonic) is usual in this recapitulation section, and such a leaning counters the effect of the dominant (i.e. the sharp side of the tonic) in the exposition.[2] The recapitulation section thus gives a sense of resolution to the conflict set up between the tonic and the contrasting key at the beginning. This conflict and resolution constitute a vital force in the construction of symphonies by tonal composers, even if key-relationships other than those commonly found in classical symphonies are used.

Beethoven's First Symphony is much on the scale of the symphonies by Haydn and Mozart; but it contains the germs of a bigger style of composition. Obviously, in order to fill up a larger musical canvas successfully all the materials must be treated in a bigger way.[3] This is especially true of tonality, since the symphony's perspective is largely tonal; and Beethoven's First Symphony shows signs of a desire to treat it in a new way. The conventional classical symphony used the simple device of repeating the tonic chord in order to establish the key at the opening: Beethoven, in his First Symphony, establishes the key in a much less direct fashion—and this is really the important point about the first chord of the piece. All commentators have said how remarkable it is (though it is by no means the first work to start with a dissonance)[4] but not many have asked why Beethoven did it. More remarkable than the discord (the dominant seventh in any case had come to achieve almost consonant status by this time) is the fact that the piece starts in the 'wrong' key. But neither was this an entirely new phenomenon: both Haydn and C. P. E. Bach had already done it.[5] In Beethoven's First Symphony, the tonality of C is not really established until the very end of the Introduction: the definition of key is achieved by balancing cadences on the flat side of the tonic with others on the sharp side: in bar 1 there is an F cadence (one flat away from the tonic); in bar 2 an interrupted cadence in C, and in bar 3 a G cadence (one sharp away from the tonic) so that *on balance* the tonal centre is C and the following passage—an extended C major cadence—confirms this. This balance of keys on the sharp and flat sides of the tonic is used on a larger scale in later symphonic writing. The first chord of the First Symphony, then, should not be seen in isolation—it is merely part of a chain of modulations which defines the tonality over a larger space than had previously been usual. The process of working on a larger scale tonally is, of course, extended to the rest of the symphony. Such treatment of the tonality does not make the work bigger than those of Haydn and Mozart, but it does herald the advent of an ability to handle a larger symphony.

One of Beethoven's problems in this symphony, therefore, was that of finding a new way to define tonality. In attempting this he weakened the tonic key: this in itself provided further grounds for argument about the identity of the tonic; the consequent availability of more material for discussion led to the possibility of constructing works on a larger scale, where the keys employed in the argument could range wider than in the simple conventional schemes such as tonic and dominant or minor and relative major. Classical key schemes are concerned with the establishment of the tonic:[6] in smaller scale pieces the dominant serves a dual purpose very simply by providing a contrasting tonal area, and yet at the same time one which can imply resolution onto the tonic. Such a limited tonal scheme needs some form of expansion if it is to be the basis of larger works, and this provides one of the main musical problems which Beethoven attempted to solve in his First Symphony. His approach is to strengthen the dominant at the expense of the tonic: there is a tendency in most movements to drift towards the dominant, and this is especially marked in the second movement so that, being in F, it veers continually back towards the tonic of the work as a whole (the second movement has fugal passages in it so that this tendency is inherent in the treatment of the material, and this may well be the reason for using fugal procedures).[7] Indeed, so strong is the dominant in this movement that Beethoven does not even bother to retune the timpani to the new key (F) but leaves them on G and C. The third movement moves to the dominant even before the tonic has been firmly stated: in fact, C major is only really established at the end of the Menuetto, and this results from Beethoven's expansion of the normal classical method of treating tonality by strengthening the dominant. The settled tonality of the Trio gives a welcome point of repose in the centre of the movement. Tovey noticed the 'dominant tendency' even though he did not point out its full significance:

I am delighted to find myself anticipated by Mr Vaclav Talich in the view that the opening [of the Introduction] is mysterious and groping, and that the first grand note of triumph is sounded when the dominant is reached.

Not only do I see the weakening of the tonic as a move towards a larger scale of writing, but I also see it as the germ from which the so-called 'progressive tonality' (as a few commentators have described it) of some of the later symphonies grew.

Beethoven's dynamic markings in the first four bars of the symphony are not, of course, fortuitous. The crescendo through bar 3 up to the dominant chord in the following bar draws clear attention to the 'dominant tendency' which I have already discussed. The *fp* markings on the dominant sevenths which start both the first two bars can be seen as emphasizing the chord at two levels; firstly, and more obviously, it draws attention to a chord which, although it had largely lost its power of dissonance, still generated the expectancy of resolution; secondly, and less obviously, the chords are emphasized because of their inherent 'dominant' nature. Dominant sevenths occur frequently in other works—this is so obvious that it scarcely needs to be said—but the chord is certainly peculiarly characteristic of this symphony. An excellent illustration of this is at the extension of the first subject of the first movement in the recapitulation, where the dominant seventh progression of bar 18 is extended in a long sequence from bar 188 to bar 198: sequences involving circles of fifths and many dominant sevenths (by no means a new feature) are also quite characteristic of the work. The realization of the importance of this chord to Beethoven's First Symphony explains certain other features, for example the long dominant pedal (with many sevenths) at bar 54 of the second movement, and the prolonged dominant seventh of the Trio.

These examples may help to explain why the dominant seventh is one of the features of this work. It is, as the Trio shows, most useful in establishing tonality firmly, so long as it has the dominant note as its root; but because of its tendency to call for resolution onto a chord whose root is a fifth lower, it can clearly weaken the tonality if placed on a degree of the scale other than the dominant. There is a dichotomy here in that the same chord can, according to its context, either strengthen or weaken the tonality: it is thus peculiarly useful to Beethoven's purpose of exploring tonality on a larger scale, and yet maintaining some degree of unity of style. (Chapter V will show Sibelius using a similar device with the same purpose in mind.) The Introduction provides a microcosm of the way in which this works: a dominant seventh over C moves the music away from the tonic; bar 2 helps to redress the balance, while the longer dominant seventh (over D) in bar 3 moves to the dominant; the rest of the Introduction is little more than an extended dominant seventh over the note G, which firmly establishes the tonic. The use of the dominant seventh chord as a unifying device calls to mind Johann Mattheson's statement that 'One can make use of many ordinary and well-known devices. Cadences, for example, are quite common . . . and may be found in every piece. When, however, they are used at the beginning of a piece, they become something *special*, since they normally belong at the end.'[8]

Later in the symphony, the tendency to move towards the dominant and the dominant seventh's tendency to resolve onto a tonic chord are brought many times into conflict (see Ex. 26):[9]

Ex.26

The opening phrase of the first subject (*x*), with its strong leading-note sound, makes an ideal foil to the dominant seventh chord. The final six bars of the second movement show the dominant tendency at work very clearly; though since the materials used by Beethoven are in any case part of the common currency of composers of his time, the importance of these bars has seldom been realized.

A development of this idea calls for mention: the 'second subject' of the first movement is prepared by movement towards the conventional dominant cadence, but Beethoven, after reaching the note G via its F sharp leading-note (bar 44), for several bars uses F naturals instead of F sharps, and does not again sound the leading-note of the dominant until the second subject actually begins (bar 53). It is a nice parallel that, at the recapitulation, the same conflict of F sharp and F natural is used to lead, not this time to the dominant, but back to the tonic (bars 204f).

The importance of the dominant has been paramount in this symphony: so, to make the point absolutely clear, Beethoven makes a feature of this note at the end of each movement. It is the point towards which the brass move in the coda of the first movement (bars 288–9); the dominant is repeated in the strings in the last six bars of the second movement: a feature is made of the note in unison at the end of the Menuetto (bar 76 and the bars leading up to it), and the coda of the Finale (which seems to have little relevance to the rest of the movement until one realizes this point—Grove says it contains 'nothing of importance') has a new theme in the oboes and horns which continually approaches the dominant note from C, yet always stops short until, at bar 293, the orchestra eventually reaches a high G in unison (the melodic outline of the opening tune of the movement is also used at this point). Two features of the work help to make these codas the more impressive: the usual emphasis on the dominant just before the recapitulation in both the first movement and the Finale is modified in this work, so that it shall be the more striking at the end. In the first movement the preparation for the recapitulation is not on the dominant at all, but on the dominant of the tonic's relative minor (bars 160f); and the dominant preparation in the Finale (bars 148–63) has the continual struggle between F sharp and F natural which is a characteristic of the symphony though here treated in a way which does not foreshadow the conflict's resolution: this ultimate resolution takes place only when the clear end of the coda is reached.

Beethoven's Second Symphony

Beethoven's Second Symphony in D forms a counterpart to the First, though surpassing it in size and power of utterance.[10] There are several unifying thematic elements, one of the most striking being an arpeggio (major or minor, ascending or descending) which can be used either in simple form or as a skeletonic basis of other structures. Nevertheless, as I have mentioned above, this technique is basic to all composers of Beethoven's time. There is, in the Second Symphony, a tonal device which parallels that of the First, and which is much more thoroughly developed: it has implications for the structure of the Ninth Symphony also, and will be seen to carry the 'progressive tonality' a stage further. Whereas the tendency in the First Symphony was towards the sharp side of the tonic, the tendency here is towards flat side keys, notably the tonic minor and its relative (D minor and F major), and B flat. Beethoven does, indeed, seem to have been looking for alternatives to the dominant in the early years of the 19th century.

The work has quite a long slow Introduction: one would expect that such an Introduction might follow the usual precedent of Haydn's late symphonies by being in the tonic minor, but in reality this is not so; and Beethoven has very good reasons for choosing a major key signature, even if there are long excursions into the minor and into B flat. From this, of course, derives the tonal scheme which unifies the whole work: a D minor Introduction would have had to stand outside such a scheme. The opening *coup d'archet* (which, as Tovey rightly says, is rather like Haydn's openings) gives no clue as to whether the key is D major or minor: it is only the following F sharp which defines it as major—and F sharp is the only note which can do this absolutely clearly, a fact which is of importance in the later stages of the work.[11] Repeated F sharps in the horns do indeed soon appear (bars 8 and 9, where they become the dominant of B minor), though very soon the music moves into the flat side area for a long passage which ends with a unison descending arpeggio in D minor (bar 23): this constitutes the first clear statement of the main unifying thematic device. A long dominant pedal then prepares for the Allegro con brio.

In the first subject group the tendency towards the subdominant and more remote flat side keys is very clear; and it is countered in the second subject by a dominant tendency (bars 79f) and by a phrase which begins in F sharp minor (bars 85f), a key perhaps suggested by the F sharps which define the tonality at the opening. There is, in spite of this sharp side tendency, a somewhat halting and uncertain excursion into the minor regions for a short while after bar 100, and a prolonged dominant cadence during which chords of D minor (and other chords which contain an F natural, many of them with sforzando markings) are frequent. The flat side tendency is very strong in the development section: indeed, it is clearly shown to be much stronger than the sharp side tendency of the second subject, since that theme, when it reappears in the development, is introduced on the flat side (in G major, at bar 182), after a long dominant seventh preparation of the sort normally reserved to introduce the recapitulation. Nevertheless, after a few more bars of flat side music, F sharp is again used (bar 199) in an attempt to restore the tonal equilibrium. A further long dominant seventh would only be an anti-climax after the misleading one which ushered in the second subject during the development section, so the recapitulation proper begins (at bar 216) with only the shortest of preparations.

The strong flat side feeling of the exposition is, of course, no less strong when the second subject group is recapitulated in the tonic key; and because of this tendency, a large and powerful coda is necessary in order that the tonic key can be firmly established. It begins at bar 304, and goes immediately to the subdominant, only to move away again to sharper keys: a further tendency towards the subdominant (bars 323f) is countered by a striking chromatic passage which recalls one in *The Creation* ('The Heavens are telling'): the bass, which rises stepwise and chromatically through a major ninth, establishes the key of D major beyond doubt. This rising bass has several precursors—one is the somewhat shorter descending chromatic bass in the development (bars 158f), but much more important is the slow rising chromatic bass (at bars 187f) which had returned the music to the sharp side after the misleading subdominant 'recapitulation' at the point where the second subject had appeared prematurely.

When one bears in mind the fact that the usual key for the second movement at this time was the subdominant, and that this key is on the flat side of the tonic; and also that any move to its dominant (the most 'obvious' modulation of all) would involve a return to D, one wonders why Beethoven did not choose the expected G major for the slow movement. As with the Introduction, there are good reasons for ignoring the precept, and they are connected with his new view of tonality.[12] He chose A major instead, and, although there are many excursions to flat side keys, D major (its subdominant) is almost entirely absent: the coda twice moves towards D in preparation for the return of that key in the Scherzo, but it is not clearly established. One very dissonant harmonic passage in the development section (dissonant on its appearances elsewhere, but much more so here) appears to be the result of choosing A instead of the more normal G for this movement: from bar 138 to bar 150 an ornamented pedal G sounds while chords seeking to move towards A (but eventually moving beyond it) grind against the pedal.

The clear establishment of A major (with scarcely any reference to D) in the second movement—one of Beethoven's biggest slow movements— now assumes a greater significance. In comparison with the slow movement, the Scherzo[13] sounds as if it might be in the subdominant key; moreover, Beethoven has kept the movement to very small proportions so that, because it follows such a large second movement, D major is not yet firmly established as the tonal centre of the symphony *as a whole*. Too big a movement at this point would leave less room for argument about the key in the Finale. The Scherzo begins with the same harmonic basis as the Allegro con brio of the first movement, and with the same arpeggio shape: flat side keys are prominent after the first double bar in a passage which unexpectedly reappears after the repetition of the opening, thus further strengthening the flat side bias. The first half of the Trio is again in D, but the second half (after the double bar) makes a very great feature of the F sharp which has already been referred to several times. This note, with its powerful repetition, is the one which can most effectively strengthen the major feeling in face of the B flat, F major and D minor tendency of the Scherzo.

The strong F sharp occurs again in the Finale: in fact it is the note with which the movement begins. The immense power of the first subject is necessary in order to strengthen the D major tonality which has not, as yet, been firmly established as the central key of the work. It is only towards the end of the exposition (bars 68f) that flat side keys appear, though the tendency persists almost throughout the development section, until a strong unison passage of F sharp tonality is followed by an ornamented F sharp pedal (the opening figure of the movement transposed by a semitone, at bars 165f) which ultimately restores the tonal balance and ushers in the recapitulation.

There is here an interesting parallel with the development section of the first movement: the unison passage in F sharp minor at bar 157 of the Finale is preceded by a rising chromatic scale in the violins which leads the music away from the flat side keys. This same rising chromatic scale had appeared at other moments of tonal uncertainty (for instance in the

Scherzo at bars 37 and 63 and in the slow movement at bars 138f), the most notable being at a similar place in the development section of the first movement. In the opening movement, the passage approaches F sharp minor (reached at bar 199), and the bass part of this F sharp section (bars 198–206) is strikingly similar to the outline of the unison passage at bar 157 of the Finale: both are, of course, based on the arpeggio which is a unifying thematic device of the symphony.

The tendency of one of the themes in the Finale's first subject group to rise from the tonic to the subdominant[14] (even though the harmony does not suggest modulation to that key) is developed in the recapitulation in such a way that the tonality does move to the flat side (bars 222f). As in the first movement, a strong and large coda is necessary to eradicate such a tendency towards the flat side: though the coda itself uses the flat side tonalities (bars 300–20), after a stop on the dominant chord we are reminded of the F sharp whose purpose is to bolster up the tonic major (bars 336–40). Nevertheless, a sequential development of the music which follows the F sharp leads to a series of cadences in G, the subdominant yet again. The uncertainty of the tonal direction here is rectified by a sudden loud dominant seventh chord on B flat (or, rather, the German Sixth on D) which resolves straight back onto a second inversion chord of D major. This attempt to re-establish the tonic is not absolutely convincing, as the powerfully repeated C naturals (which tend again towards the subdominant and the flat side) show in bar 386. The F sharp reappears to counter the flat side tendency, but instead of being harmonized and played softly in the strings, it now appears as a loud unison on all the instruments (except, of course, the timpani, which cannot play the note). The following passage, unlike the one after the previous F sharp interruption, does not move towards the subdominant, but remains firmly in D major. It is only in the coda, therefore, that the struggle inherent in Beethoven's tonal scheme is resolved.

The beginnings of two tendencies can be seen here—the throwing of greater weight onto the Finale than had previously been usual (this is perhaps the reason for choosing sonata form for the movement—for although Tovey calls it a 'sonata rondo', it is quite clearly plain sonata form without a repeat of the exposition), and a tendency to write movements which, even if they can be played alone with success, do not complete the sense of the argument when heard in context: the first movement of Beethoven's Second Symphony may well stand alone, but if it were to be followed by only the second movement, or even by the second and third movements, the overall tonal scheme would not be satisfactory. A sense of incompleteness is felt—subconsciously—at the end of the second and third movements, so that one is made aware that more music is to follow.

Beethoven's Third Symphony

It is not easy for us today to appreciate just how original the 'Eroica' Symphony was at the time of its appearance: we have heard the 'Choral', and the symphonies of Brahms, Bruckner and Mahler many times; but before the 'Eroica' only the two early symphonies of Beethoven and those of his predecessors were there for comparison. (Even if this is a truism, it is at least one which is worth repeating.) Such a vast undertaking as the 'Eroica' must have all its elements conceived on a scale in proportion to its vastness. The Second Symphony had already shown the way ahead in its exploitation of key areas further away from the tonic than had previously been common, and by emphasizing the pull of those areas against the tonic. Such a design must of necessity be writ large.[15] A parallel struggle between various types of thematic material—a device now taken to lengths never dreamed of before, and used previously in only a very small way[16]— is also employed, and a third element, that of rhythm, plays a conspicuous part in delineating the stages of the struggle.

Although this chapter is primarily concerned with tonality, it is as well to remember that this is only one element of composition in a symphony, and it would therefore not be amiss to take a brief look at other elements. Thematically, the struggle is between material based on an arpeggio and material based on a scale: there is also another basic shape round which many other themes are built (see Ex. 27).

Ex. 27

It is scarcely necessary to pursue this further, once these features have been isolated: the 'Eroica' has never lacked analysts, and anyone may trace the thematic material through for himself. There is here a more obvious unity in the material used than in any previous work, and also than in many later ones. The novelty of other features in the symphony may account for this fact: when so much else was revolutionary, it may well be that Beethoven decided to make the thematic logic as plain as possible in order that the audience should not be entirely at a loss. For the same reason, the basic melodic material is of the most easily memorable kind: the 'military directness' of the opening theme (which becomes a horn flourish) has thus a purely musical, as well as a programmatic, purpose.

The two detached tonic chords which begin the work constitute an upbeat before the start of the macrorhythm;[17] and upbeats of various types permeate the entire work, helping to unify it. The type of upbeat varies with the music: in the most dynamic sections they are syncopated, or they lead up to a strong beat which turns out to be a rest; when the music is more relaxed they are simpler. Even the slow movement has a form of upbeat, though it is sometimes written *on* the beat as an ornament—the double bass part at the opening, for example, which is thus made to serve a musical purpose as well as a programmatic one (it imitates the roll of muffled drums in a funeral march). The Scherzo begins with six bars of what might be termed 'upbeat' before the oboe melody appears, and the Finale has an even larger one (using Ex. 27 as its skeleton) before the theme of the Variations is introduced.

Even more important is the way in which these and other rhythmic devices behave in relation to the tonality of the work; and here not only the rhythm but also the thematic material plays a part, since the tonality of the work is largely derived from a struggle between two chromatic motifs (*x* and *y* in Ex. 28).

Ex.28

This fusion of rhythm, tonality and thematic material is not only novel but very remarkable: Brahms clearly admired it, since he copied it in his First Symphony. The opening bars of the work form an admirable example for illustration, besides reminding us that Beethoven normally demonstrates his musical material and suggests how he will handle it at the very beginning of every symphony. Two introductory chords establish a firm basic pulse and a firm tonality: the two do not necessarily go hand in hand, of course, though they tend to do so in this work.[18] Beethoven's sketches for the opening of the 'Eroica' all contain strong upbeats—many show dominant seventh chords on a B flat bass (instead of the tonic chord) which likewise establish the key of E flat clearly; and while they sometimes appear on beats other than the first, they nevertheless establish the basic pulse. Beethoven's final choice was also his simplest and most terse (Grove's *Beethoven and his Nine Symphonies* prints some of the sketches for this opening).[19] The first theme, which promises to be in conventional E flat tonality, is dragged away from that key by the first appearance of *x*, and at this point the regularity of rhythm in the accompaniment is mildly upset by the intrusion of a syncopated pedal G (another form of upbeat, in fact) in the first violins: as E flat is regained, so the regularity of rhythm returns. Beethoven makes it very clear that this is a reversal of the 'normal' way of thinking by writing an opening which, up to this point, has no surprises, rhythmic or otherwise. When the opening theme returns, the ascending chromatic figure *y* replaces the descending one, and a shift is made towards the dominant. Although at this stage music is merely written on the dominant harmony without implying complete modulation, the dominant key does play a very much larger part in the exposition than is normal in symphonic music, even when one takes all Beethoven's works into account. It is strongly felt well before the large second subject group is reached—even before the 'tutti' repeat of the opening material at bar 37— and this marked tendency away from the tonic (caused by the pressure of the chromatic figure) is accompanied by a similar noticeable tendency away from the regular rhythm, with sforzando chords on various beats of the bar disguising the underlying pulse.

The three features in this passage—the three-note falling chromatic scale *x*, its inversion *y*, and the repeated notes—are all worked into the thematic material of the symphony, as well as forming important tonal and rhythmic ingredients; and again, anyone can trace them through the work. A characteristic cadence results from the opposition of *x* and *y*, and it is much used, especially in the first movement (see Ex. 28).

The presence of the figures *x* and *y* is felt in the chromatic movement of the tonality in the development section: the shifting key centres result in the use of many sforzando chords on weak beats and other rhythmic devices which tend to unsettle the basic pulse. As the tonality approaches its most remote point, E minor, the violence reaches its height with a long series of detached dissonances and an elongated dissonant upbeat (the dominant ninth being particularly strong).[20] The new key, at bar 284, has been well prepared over the preceding thirty bars, more carefully indeed than any other key in the work except the dominant, since E flat has only appeared very briefly in the development section, and even there (bar 220) it had been made to sound like a dominant rather than a tonic, so little has Beethoven used E flat up to this point. Since it is the most distant key reached in this movement, E minor deserves considerable emphasis, so that the ultimate result of the tonal struggle may be more clearly perceived than if the music had merely modulated back to the flat regions. The arrival of a new theme in E minor provides the necessary emphasis,[21] and the more settled tonality is immediately paralleled by a more relaxed rhythm and smoother lines, though the fact that this key is so far away from E flat is not ignored by the violins, who play the same syncopated repeated-note figure as they had used at the beginning: the relevance of this new theme to the opening is made clearer still by the appearance (in the bass, bars 286 and 290) of *x* in precisely the same three notes as had started the weakening of the E flat tonality at the opening of the work (also in the bass, bars 6f, though E flat is written there for D sharp, of course). These two passages, closely linked by rhythmic and melodic devices, thus form the two opposing ends of the tonal struggle brought about by a chromatic bass which occurs in both of them: the fact that the themes are different (even if they ultimately derive from the same material) emphasizes the opposition of the tonal areas. (The new E minor theme of the development section—bars 284f—will be referred to as z in the rest of this discussion.)

Beethoven now prepares the listener carefully for the return of the opening material and the beginning of the recapitulation. The tonality moves towards E flat minor, and the new theme (z) appears in that key, a very flat one so as to balance the sharpness of E minor: because z has been given such importance, and because E flat minor—though a very flat key —is no more than the tonic minor, the ear is prepared for the re-establishment of E flat. It is more than just a lucky accident that the bass (E flat-D-D flat-C of bars 323 and 324) can accommodate x with its original notes just as well in this key as it had done a semitone higher in E minor: this is, of course, because Beethoven has used four notes descending by step chromatically, and it will be demonstrated later that this was not fortuitous. The way is now clear for the long dominant preparation for the recapitulation (a thematic as well as tonal preparation): the minor flavour already present leads to a tonal diversion from the dominant seventh onto C flat (bars 362f)—that is, the dominant chord of E minor written enharmonically; yet the suggestion implied here that the recapitulation might be in that key (so strong has its new subject z made it) is rejected: C flat, indeed, can *only* sound like the neapolitan home dominant, and not like the real dominant. The 'correctness' of the dominant seventh of E flat when it returns is corroborated by the relaxing of the rhythm and the dissonances, except that dominant ninths are suggested softly in the violin parts. These dominant ninths form a most impressive touch, since they provide a quiet parallel to the tremendously dramatic ones which had ushered in E minor at the height of the development section: the fact that E minor and E flat are at opposing ends of the tonal spectrum in this movement is most neatly suggested by quite different uses of this same progression. The dominant chords at the end of the development section are held far longer than the music leads the first horn to believe, and he enters with the first subject in the tonic four bars before the rest of the orchestra, and over the dominant chord (another form of anacreusis): the sense of expectancy generated by the tonal scheme and the reappearance of the tonic here could scarcely have a more eloquent testimony than this.

When the opening subject first appears in the recapitulation, the figure x reappears with it; but this time its power is greater than previously, and the music is immediately dragged away from E flat to the sharp side, F major. It is the power of z, to which allusions (either actual, or tonally or harmonically implied) have been made ever since its appearance in the development section, that produces this effect, since x now consists of four

—rather than the original three—descending notes (they come from the bass of z), and it is the additional semitone D flat-C which is responsible for moving the music away from the tonic. The power of z in destroying the E flat tonality results in the F major statement of the first subject (bars 408f) being given a relaxed rhythmical treatment: it is balanced by a D flat statement before moving back again to the tonic; and from here to the end of the movement the tonic key is much more in evidence than it has been up to this point.

It is well known that in the 'Eroica' Symphony, Beethoven expanded the development and the coda so that all four sections of the movement should have equal weight; and that the coda is in reality a second development section. In fact, the coda obscures the beat much less than does the development, since the music here adheres more closely to E flat. The figures x and y are still present, as is the theme z, but they do not succeed in upsetting the E flat tonality, and rhythmic figures which at first had appeared at points of tonal uncertainty (for example, the one in the first violins at bar 65) are now altered so as to emphasize the E flat tonality (as at bar 631). The use at this point of the syncopated pedal for the last time in the movement (bar 647) is an indication that E flat is not yet entirely established; nevertheless, further appearances of y (in bars 665–9) only lead back to the tonic. The prolonging of the dominant seventh chords at the end of the movement for four bars after the expected point of resolution forms a nice parallel to the extension of the quiet dominant chord which prepared the recapitulation; and the final E flat chords echo those of the opening of the movement. It is only with these two tonic chords that the rhythmic disguising of the beat is eventually resolved, since the previous dominant chords do not conform to the underlying pulse. (They have the added advantage of reminding the ear of such passages as bars 25f.) The E flat chords, therefore, not only set up the basic pulse at the beginning of the movement, but also signal its eventual return. One other reference to previous material will now be quite evident: the dominant preparation for the re-establishment of the tonic key in the coda after the appearance of z (bars 603f) parallels the similar passage in the development in that it is interrupted; here, as there, a flavour of E flat minor is evident, and yet the digression on this occasion (bar 623) is made from the dominant seventh to C minor, not C flat major. In the coda, C flat becomes its enharmonic equivalent, B natural, and acts as a leading-note: the reason for this is clear. The tonal power of z is here much less, and is not now sufficient to draw the music back towards E minor: C minor—so much closer to the tonic than C flat major—is all that can be managed before the dominant preparation is resumed.

As Grove has pointed out, the 'Eroica' is the first symphony Beethoven wrote after telling Krumpholz in 1802 that he intended to take a new road, since he was not satisfied with the works he had written up to that time. After a close analysis of the first movement of the 'Eroica' Symphony (of which there has only been room to give the barest outline here) there can be little doubt of what the 'new road' entailed, for symphonic music at least. It entailed the use of all the elements of composition—harmony, rhythm, melody, tonality and even orchestration and dynamics—to create a large-scale unified discussion of some problem inherent in the musical material chosen.

Although x and y appear in the 'Marcia funebre', they do not greatly affect the tonality. The most powerful appearance of x is at the two interruptions to the return of the March after the Maggiore Trio. The first of these, which begins at bar 158, is a loud passage with x as its bass, and a rhythm from the 'trio' section used in the brass; the second interruption, a quiet one, at bar 209, uses the figure in the violin parts. Upbeats are completely removed at bar 155, whereas at the end of the movement (from bar 238) the music is again reduced to fragments in the violins and consists of 'upbeats' only, until the last two bars.[22] The use of upbeats in this particular cadence ensures that it is unified more closely with the rest of the material than had usually been the case before the 'Eroica' was written: it will be remembered that the first movement had a cadence which was likewise carefully woven into the argument of the rest of the movement. A link with the first movement is also found in the treatment of dominant pedals: the dominant ninth at bar 168 (with its resolution) is a parallel to those in the first movement; and both of the A flat major passages are introduced by means of 'interrupted cadences' after a long dominant seventh chord—a feature of the first movement. In addition, the two A flat sections use rhythmic ideas like those of the first movement: the dramatic power of the first—showing the 'incorrectness' of the key—gives way to the uneasy quiet syncopation of the second interruption which serves to make the same point.[22]

Although x and y both occur in the first two movements (x started the entire argument, and y was set up to counter it), y is more frequently found in the Scherzo and Trio and in the Finale. The appearance of x in the first movement had caused wide modulation and attendant violence of harmony and rhythm; in the second movement, its appearances are accompanied by a feeling of disquiet, if not of outright terror. The Scherzo and Trio, however, find in the their use of y a force that restores the tonic in music of a triumphant nature. The Scherzo—a larger third movement than any symphony had previously been provided with, even if it is the shortest movement in the 'Eroica'—sets the problem of thinking on a large scale in a fast tempo and maintaining the listener's interest. Beethoven here shows the utmost rhythmic ingenuity in his use of off-beats, hemiolas and the like, which interest the ear by obscuring the macrorhythm, and in his employment of quickly rotating chords (which have the effect of forming long 'upbeats'): these features sustain the tremendous pace and size of the movement by providing the ear with interesting music. Furthermore, tension is provided by the pianissimo opening which, because of its enormous length, erupts with the greater power when the fortissimos are eventually reached at bar 93. But Beethoven's use of tonality is crucial here, and has many points of contact with the third movement of his First Symphony. As in the first movement of the 'Eroica', there is a strong tendency to write music on the dominant harmony; so much so that it is not until the first tutti at bar 93 that E flat is clearly stated at all. The whispered dynamics of the music thus far testify to the weakness of the tonic. The strong descending unison arpeggios at bars 115 and 123 herald the establishment of E flat, and the Trio forms a point of tonal repose in that the tonic is strongly felt until the very end, when a few appearances of y lead back to the repeat of the Scherzo. The final establishment of the tonic is greeted with unison descending arpeggios, but the second of these is this time much more powerful because of the rhythmic drive of the short 'alla breve' (bars 381f).[24] A brief coda twice makes the point that y is merely an inversion of x by repeating the progression D flat-D natural-E flat: as the figure had directed the tonality away from E flat early in the work, so here it focuses attention onto the keynote.

One would expect the main function of the Finale to be the establishment of the tonic beyond doubt. In a sense this is what happens, since Beethoven has chosen to write what is basically a set of variations on a theme in E flat—one he had already used elsewhere. It is interesting to speculate as to why he decided to use pre-existing material for this movement. One possible solution is that he had already resolved the tonal problems inherent in his material—that the creative force had, as it were, worked itself out to its logical conclusion by the end of the Scherzo—and that there was no more to be said on the matter. E flat is, after all, decisively regained by the end of the Scherzo, and needs no further argument to justify its presence. Nevertheless, in order to balance the enormous power of the excursions into distant tonal regions in the earlier movements, Beethoven needs to prolong this establishment of the tonic in spatial terms even though the argument as such is already resolved. In order to maintain interest in such a prolonged statement of E flat, Beethoven very sensibly decided to write a set of variations: the theme chosen so clearly fits in with the thematic material of earlier movements that one can readily imagine the composer trying to find a completely original theme, but being eventually forced to accept that nothing would work better than the tune from *Prometheus*.[25] This theme (bar 12) has clear reference to an arpeggio, a version of y, the motif shown in Ex. 27, and strong dominant implications, including repeated dominant notes: every one of these features is a characteristic of the 'Eroica' Symphony, and helps the feeling of unity it possesses. The opening flourish of the Finale gives a momentary sense of disquiet (very like that which is created at the corresponding point in the 'Choral') because of its tonality;[26] but, in spite of strong dominant tendencies, the variations are firmly anchored to E flat for the first hundred or so bars. Indeed, so strong has E flat become in the first few variations that the modulation which begins at bar 107 sounds awkward, even though the music only moves to the dominant of the relative minor. This is not the only modulation to sound somewhat forced in this movement—but, perversely, this is not entirely loss, since the whole object here is to maintain the tonic in the firmest possible manner, and the 'unnatural' sound of distant keys can be made to serve this purpose: the abruptness also serves to force the attention away from the strictness of variation form. (Since the dominant is so strongly stressed in the theme itself, it is avoided in the other modulations away from E flat.) It is one of the few appearances of x (in the bass, bars 171–5) in the second half of the symphony that moves the music to B minor, in another rather surprising modulation. After a strong return to E flat and three slow variations,[27] a coda begins at bar 431 with the opening flourish, this time written around the tonic instead of the dominant chord. The remainder of the symphony reinforces E flat, with scales and arpeggios in that key, and a rhythm which is firmly tied to the underlying pulse: the two tonic chords which close the work balance the two which had started it.

We can see in the last movement of the 'Eroica' the beginnings of a difficulty which was later to afflict many composers; that of providing a Finale which satisfactorily rounds off the symphonic argument and gives an answer to all the problems raised in the earlier movements. The Finale of the 'Eroica' so nearly does all that is required of it, yet it is idle to suggest that it provides quite such a satisfactory solution as any of Beethoven's subsequent Finales, since it is almost redundant. As mentioned above, the unprecedented scale of the first three movements raises enormous problems for the composer: the Finale must be of a size that will balance these earlier movements, as well as provide a type of music which will constitute the culmination of the heroic first movement and Scherzo with their interactions of rhythmic ingenuity and wide-ranging tonality, and its 'Marcia funebre' with the sense of resignation that the Maggiore Trios give, the grinding counterpoint of the fugue and eventual disintegration of all the elements. No less a genius than Beethoven could even have approached the writing of a Finale which would satisfactorily bring such ideas to consummation: it may well be that the sense of disquiet which the Finale produces for many listeners is the direct result of applying programmatic elements to a type of work which purports to be absolute, at a time when Beethoven's command of composition was not yet mature enough to solve the problem. It is a stroke of great genius that he managed to follow his gigantic conception of the opening movement with a slow movement of similar intensity, and a miracle that he was able to follow that movement with a Scherzo to balance them. But, fine as the Finale is, the burning heroism of the earlier movements is not found there, and the handling of rhythm on the large scale does not measure up to that of the first three movements: in variation form (unless it is treated with very considerable freedom, as in the Finale of the 'Choral' Symphony) there is little scope for such a treatment of large scale rhythm. Indeed, the first three movements set up a type of symphonic forward motion[28] which it would have taken superhuman power to outdo in the Finale. Beethoven does, indeed, displace rhythmically each large section of variations: but in spite of this, it is in the lack of a forward motion comparable to that of the earlier parts of the work that this last movement just fails.

Much more, of course, can be said of the 'Eroica', and it can be analysed in other ways; but before leaving the work, several features which point the way forward for Beethoven are worth noticing. The growing power of the third movement—and indeed also of the Finale—is an obvious one; the new tendency to use all the elements of composition in order to create a symphonic discussion is likewise obvious; the programmatic tendency, too, is noticeable here, though not an entirely new element in music. Moreover, the feeling is created at the end of the second and third movements that the work has not come to a satisfactory conclusion, though for different reasons. By the end of the second movement the problems inherent in the musical material are not solved, and though they are solved by the end of the third movement, the time is not yet right for a conclusion: there is a noticeable imbalance in the proportions of the work, and therefore the feeling is created that more music must follow. Less obvious among the new features is the diminution of themes (for instance in the last movement, bars 329–33, and also bar 405, as compared with the repeated notes of the theme) which points towards the techniques Beethoven exploited in his Fourth Symphony.[29]

Symphonic form as it is understood in this book virtually began with the 'Eroica': it would be very surprising indeed if such an early attempt at a work of this magnitude and complexity were to be entirely satisfactory. The Finale, for all its merits, represents a glorious, heroic failure.

Beethoven's Fifth Symphony

Since a discussion of the thematic material of Beethoven's Fifth Symphony appears in Chapter II, only the tonal scheme need be considered here, with passing reference to those melodic elements which affect the tonality. The idea of 'progressive tonality' is taken a stage further than in the works

previously discussed: every movement has a tendency to move towards
C major, and the importance of this key is seen in the triumphant nature
of the music written in it.[30] The struggle which is necessary to reach the
brightness of C major from the more sombre minor regions (and from the
perhaps more 'relaxed' A flat—the effect of the music in that key in the
second movement is one of calm) coincides with the presence of a rising
figure (*a*) which is partly chromatic (see Ex. 29):

Ex. 29

a

This figure derives from the chromatic bass of the second subject in the
first movement (bars 82–90) and the violin parts which follow it (bars 91–4).

The opening of the work must have been tonally ambiguous to the first
audience: by now listeners have become so used to relating the first few
bars to C minor (as Beethoven himself does later in the movement) that the
possibility of these six bars suggesting the key of E flat never occurs to us.[31]
Yet to the original hearers this must have been the effect—and it is one
deliberately calculated by the composer: its purpose is to suggest the tonal
—as well as the thematic—relationship between the first and second
subjects of the piece. When the opening shape (bars 1–6) recurs at the
start of the second subject, it is with the intervals expanded so as to ensure
that the phrase is clearly related to E flat (bars 59–62): hence the G and D
are replaced by B flats.[32] C minor is not to be regarded as the most
important key in the work; hence the setting up of an ambiguity. The
compelling logic behind this apparently simple device seems to have
escaped most analysts. Apart from this ambiguity, the exposition is
astonishing in its terse classical logic and contrasts strongly with that of the
'Eroica' just discussed: the first subject does not move away from the tonic,
and a single detached chord is sufficient to modulate to E flat for the second
subject. Here only the first appearance of the chromatic bass from which *a*
develops moves the tonality momentarily away from E flat:[33] this chromatic
rise reflects the bass of the modulating passage in bars 52–8.

. The figure *a* is evident in several places in the development section
though on only one occasion does it again have this power of obscuring the
tonality: that is in the chordal passage (bars 195–240) which has puzzled
so many commentators. Nevertheless, it would be unlike Beethoven not to
make his developments clear; and here, no less than elsewhere, the thought
processes are perfectly logical. At bar 195 the music has reached C major
for the first time, and the composer reinforces that key in the most powerful
way (though at this stage it can only act as the dominant of F minor): he
introduces the opening idea in the expanded form which had ushered in
the second subject (though of course in exact transposition it would begin

on G, and not on C: the effect of this would be to anticipate the recapitulation of the second subject, and thus to lessen the effect of that part of the recapitulation). The final C, however, which the ear expects to hear as the last note of the phrase in bar 198, appears only in an inner voice in a chord of a different tone-colour and much lower in the orchestra than one had been led to expect: the chords which follow are derived, quite simply, from those which occur in the corresponding place in the exposition—though Beethoven removes the 'tune' and also the rhythm from the original second subject, leaving only the accompaniment, with its melodic shape (*a* is found here, as there) and the wandering tonal scheme. This obscuring of the C major tonality, due to the use of *a*, is also attested by the uneasy feeling which the antiphonal orchestration gives. This forms a splendid parallel to the uneasiness of the orchestration of the first subject—the thematic material of bars 7–13, for example, is divided between the various string instruments, and witnesses to the ambiguity of the tonality at the opening.[34] (The first subject is slightly less unsettled in the recapitulation, due to the 'binding' effect of the additional oboe counterpoint; and the same is true of the end of the coda, bars 482f, where other woodwind instruments are also added: in these places, C minor has become stronger.) The purpose of *a* in obstructing C major's becoming established is clear. It is also clear that, for the relationship between this chordal passage and the accompaniment of the second subject to be appreciated by the listener, more than one hearing of the exposition is necessary. The repeat, so essential here, in no way makes the tonality of the opening any less ambiguous, since the opening bars, when played the second time, will follow a cadence in E flat. As is quite normal, the second subject is recapitulated in the tonic major, and here again the establishment of C major is, at least momentarily, obstructed by *a*: the 'antiphonal' scoring of the subject at this point reflects that used in the development section. A large coda—almost exactly the same size as each of the other three sections—is of course essential to re-establish the minor key.

The key of A flat would be normal for the slow movement of a classical symphony in C minor: nevertheless, the importance of the tendency to modulate to C major is shown by the fact that Beethoven does not retune the timpani, but leaves them on G and C. The appearances of C major—with the brass and drums prominent, sounding a note of triumph—are each time preceded by a melodic line which uses the phrase *a* from Ex. 29. On the first two occasions the notes are C-D flat-E flat-F-G flat (becoming F sharp)- G natural: the reinterpretation of G flat as F sharp occurs at a point where *a* approaches the G flat several times, yet cannot get beyond it until the note is treated enharmonically and the tonality becomes C major. (The modulation is made by the same means as the one which eventually established D major in the coda of the Finale in the Second

Symphony.) The presence of *a* in this movement has to be overcome so that C major can emerge (a process that happens three times), and the triumphant arrival of C is twice destroyed by *a*, just as in the opening movement *a* had frustrated the establishment of the tonic major. In the second movement the progression provides no more than a mere glimpse of triumph, since the music returns to A flat with inversions of *a* in the strings (bars 41f). It is worth noting that this short but triumphant interlude itself uses the theme *a* in a diatonic major form. Before the third arrival of C major (bars 133–46) the woodwind make great use of this diatonic major version (though in A flat) until the second clarinet gives the theme its chromatic inflection again (at bars 144–6): this is the signal for the most powerful C major passage yet, the tonic of that key being prolonged so as to give it greater emphasis; and it is not *a* that forces the music back into A flat, but a series of rising arpeggios.

An important point arises here: it is an extraordinary feature of the first movement of the Fifth Symphony that, whereas there are many descending arpeggios, there is only one very brief reference to rising ones. (This occurs just after bar 185, and significantly enough leads up to the cadence in C major. One of the most striking of the early glimpses of hope in the symphony, indeed, concerns the inverting of the opening four notes of the work, in the coda of the first movement, so that the beginnings of a rising arpeggio are heard.) In the second movement, ascending arpeggios begin to be used, and become more frequent after the third C major interlude, for the rising arpeggios gradually lengthen and become more prominent until the end of the movement: even the drooping outline of the main theme is turned upwards to fit in with this scheme. Nevertheless, in the second movement these arpeggios always stop when *a* appears, to be resumed as C major is reached.

With the added hope which attends the more frequent and more powerful appearances of C major comes an increase in the use of rising arpeggios. This hope, however, seems far away at the opening of the Scherzo, where the rising arpeggio is in C minor and the scoring and dynamics create an impression of gloom. Perhaps it is too like 'paper analysis' to see in the second and third bars of the Scherzo a rearrangement of *a* (as shown in Ex. 23); but *a* is clearly present later (for instance in the bass at bars 66–70). Modulations to the flat-side keys take the music far from C minor by bar 44—the point where repeat marks might be expected; but Beethoven writes out the repeat, since it is a tone lower than the opening, and (being in B flat minor) sounds even more gloomy. The wide range of keys used here contrasts markedly with the first two movements. The appearance of C major is reserved for the Trio, and the upward arpeggios are almost entirely confined to the bass of a cadence formula which is several times repeated, and which later becomes the main theme of the Finale. As in the first two movements it is a version of *a* that forces the music away from C major (bars 228–36). The Scherzo is now repeated, but with significant changes: it is rescored in a whisper—only soft instruments are used, and the strings are marked pizzicato, except for the arpeggiated chords which occur mostly in the violas. The modulations to remote keys do not reappear, and the music remains in C minor: Tovey's description of this movement as 'that dream of terror' is indeed an apt one.

Instead of ending quietly in C minor, Beethoven's most original stroke of all in this work intervenes: the passage which links the Scherzo and the Finale moves first to an A flat harmony (recalling the key of the slow movement),[35] then it moves back to the dominant of C. The passage, in which many commentators have said 'nothing happens' does in fact have one feature of tremendous importance—the note C sounds throughout it with a single-mindedness of purpose, dragging the music towards C major, even when that note itself conflicts with the harmonies in the rest of the orchestra. The A flat and C minor of the earlier parts of the symphony are gathered up in this long pedal and turned into C major.

The great outburst of C major at the beginning of the Finale is the more powerful for following such a whispered 'dream of terror': for even though the timpani have been playing a pedal C for many bars, the crescendo which leads into the Finale is reserved for the last four bars of the Scherzo: the reinforcement of the symphony orchestra for the first time with trombones, contrafagotto and piccolo makes the Finale the more impressive when seen in historical context. Now that C major is at last reached—and the brass and drums, with much tonic and dominant music suggest a triumphal march—*a* almost entirely disappears from the scene.

The Finale is a large one: so important has C major become in the overall psychology of the work that few excursions away from it are made. A major is heard at the beginning of the development section (bars 90f), and this serves to balance the large amount of music in flat keys which has preceded it in the first three movements; yet in order that the arrival of the recapitulation shall have no less effect than that of the exposition, it is essential that some form of contrast be introduced into the development. Here—as in other places noted in this book—Beethoven plays on the expectations of the audience. The long dominant seventh which is the normal preparation for the recapitulation starts correctly enough (bar 132) and at bar 150, over a dominant chord, even the shape of the expected tune appears—the triad which forms the opening of the first subject: this subject does not materialize, however, as a quiet reference to the Scherzo interrupts, and when the dominant pedal reappears, it is joined by a pedal C in the timpani which, as before, pulls the music back into C major so that the recapitulation may begin.

It is well known that Beethoven's intention was to repeat the first

Scherzo and the Trio before going on to the pizzicato version of the Scherzo which forms the end of the third movement. There may be some programmatic reason for repeating the Scherzo in the Finale—if there is, we do not know what it can be; but it seems likely that in realizing the need for some such preparation for the Finale's recapitulation as had appeared just before the opening of the movement, Beethoven decided to repeat the long linking pedal; and that this in turn suggested the reference to the Scherzo itself. This made it desirable to have fewer repetitions of the Scherzo in the third movement proper; and even the dissimilarity of the two versions of the Scherzo in that movement becomes a positive advantage, since it removes any feeling of tautology. The introduction of C minor which results from the reminiscence of the Scherzo at the end of the Finale's development also provides very necessary tonal variety.[36]

The recapitulation and coda reinforce C major in the strongest possible terms, and make much use of the 'triumphant' rising arpeggios which are a feature of the main theme of the Finale. The continual reduction of dynamics and quickening of pace only to build up in a further crescendo —*reculer pour mieux sauter*—has become a time-honoured method of ending large-scale pieces. Basil Lam makes a good point when he says:

Although it surpasses immeasurably all its successors, Beethoven's Fifth Symphony was the first of a new kind of symphony, which, because it expressed in musical terms the optimistic humanist philosophy, became almost the norm in the nineteenth century. In the works written on this general programme, emphasis is shifted from the first movement to the Finale, where all contradictions of mood ('masculine' first subject, 'feminine' second subject etc.) are resolved in a triumphant conclusion in the major key. This dangerously attractive scheme lends itself to rhetorical affirmations of shattering banality to which the fitting response can only be 'we might believe you if you didn't shout so much'. Beethoven's coda excludes such hollow apotheoses by refraining from any kind of thematic inflation.[37]

This is by no means the only original, or even the most original, feature of the work:[38] the terrified whisper in which the Scherzo is repeated, and its reappearance in the Finale; the joining of two movements not only by means of a musical link but by the quotation of themes already heard; the tight cross-referencing of themes and classical construction; the expanded orchestra; the novel one-in-a-bar first movement with its driving rhythm; and above all the tonal scheme in which every movement strives towards that glimpse of triumph which, in the Finale, becomes a glorious blaze of C major—all these contribute in the Fifth to one of the most epoch-making works of all time (the more so when one reflects that Haydn was still alive when it was written); surely a judgment which has been dulled by the popularity the work has attained. This popularity has, in some ways, hindered an understanding of its nature: we know it so well that we hear it only with the hindsight of one who is aware of the end of the story. To appreciate its originality fully, and to understand its logic, it is necessary to put oneself in the position of the original audience, hearing the work for the first time. Beethoven said that he always worked to a picture; and one feels instinctively that there must be some kind of programme behind this work, yet the only clue we have is Beethoven's remark (apropos of the opening), 'Thus Fate knocks at the door'.[39] Whether or not there is a programme is of little moment: what is important is that the piece is unified by purely musical means.

Although Beethoven's Finales from the Second Symphony onwards have been gaining in importance, so that in the Fifth the short first movement throws a great deal of weight onto the last movement, yet none of the Finales so far could stand as an opening movement. None of them has the close logic of symphonic argument which is a *sine qua non* of a first movement, since they serve a different purpose—one of summary rather than of intense argument.

Beethoven's Seventh Symphony

One of the most important characteristics of the Seventh Symphony is aptly summed up by Robert Simpson:[40]

It seems to me that Beethoven in this symphony strongly anticipates the so-called 'progressive tonality' of Nielsen; in the first movement F and C are notable foreigners to the tonic A, in the Allegretto they are more easily related to the prevailing A minor, and in the Scherzo F major is strong enough to take over, the first change of key being to A, which is now itself so much a foreigner that it can behave only as the dominant of D, into which key the Trio inevitably falls. After all this, only the greatest vehemence can restore A—hence the tremendous insistent energy of the Finale.

Beethoven, according to his normal procedure, announces his intentions at the outset. The Introduction begins in the tonic major for the same reasons as does that of the Second Symphony: to have written the Introduction in A minor would have meant that the tonal scheme would be much less clearly announced. The tonic minor is reserved for the second movement instead; and, since the normal subdominant (D major) cannot be used at this point, it is reserved for the Trio of the third movement. The tonal design is laid out clearly in the Introduction: the opening A major is twice moved towards flatter keys by a chromatically descending bass, one of the unifying thematic features of the work (see Ex. 30).

Ex. 30

As the modulations reach C major (bar 23) there appears a new subject whose purpose is the same as that of the E minor tune of the development section in the 'Eroica'—to draw attention to the new key.[41] Rising versions of x now take the music into F major, where the new tune is repeated, also in order to draw attention to that key. Once x has introduced these two new keys, it takes little further part in the tonal argument, though it appears as a melodic element in many themes.

The normal key for the second subject, E major, is interrupted after only a few bars by a passage in C major: somewhat later (at bar 162) F major is heard in a neapolitan chord. The keys of C and, to a lesser extent, F are widely used in the development section, and in the recapitulation F is again much used, replacing the C major tendency of the exposition. The coda, which begins in A flat, uses all three tonics, C, F and A, without modulation: this is the nearest that C and F come to being seen in relationship with each other in this movement. It is not Beethoven's purpose to explore the relationship between these two close keys, but only the relationship of each individually with A major. Thus in the Introduction the 'new theme' in C major is followed by a long series of modulations before F major is reached (even though this means returning again to the chord of C major which forms its dominant). So, throughout the movement, C and F are not shown as being in close relationship with each other: the nearest Beethoven gets to this is to play the relative minors of both keys side by side in bars 309–14. As I have mentioned above, the coda does place all three keys together (bars 395–400), but only in a context in which they sound distant. After this point, all the repetitions (in a long crescendo) of a bass derived from x cannot weaken the hold of A major, which is firmly maintained until the end of the movement. The very striking passage in which A major (with an inverted dominant pedal) continually sounds over a bass which consists of x serves to show how much more powerful A major is in the coda than in the previous parts of the movement where C and F had often appeared to alter the 'normal' tonal processes; but another feature also points to the strengthening of the tonic. The new canonic figure introduced near the beginning of the development section (bar 185) serves the purpose of drawing attention to the importance of C major at this point: it manages to do this precisely because it is new, even though the rhythm used has been common throughout the movement. The new bass which accompanies the first subject at the beginning of the recapitulation (bar 278) derives from the same material, and is used at this point in order to draw attention to the tonic key.[42]

Besides providing the tonic minor section that one might have expected of an Introduction, the second movement, by being in A minor, provides a great deal of music in the minor key to counterbalance the very large amount of major music in the first movement. The pull towards A major for the two 'trio' sections, after an opening theme which frequently modulates to C major, is another expression of the relationship between two of the 'pivotal' keys, C and A, the former being the relative of A's tonic minor. There is, of course, much more to the movement than this: in its use of a set of variations built up by adding layers of counterpoint (or layers of harmonic figures), it parallels the gradually thickening counterpoint of the opening bars of the symphony. Moreover, the theme on which the variations are based consists partly of an inverted pedal, a dominant pedal moving from a chord of A minor to one of C (and eventually returning to A minor): the fact that dominant pedals are one of the great unifying features of the work explains the nature of this rather 'tuneless' tune. A link with the Introduction of the first movement is again clear in that inverted dominant pedals start as early as the third bar of the symphony, accompanying the 'new theme' when it appears in both C and F, and is gradually altered rhythmically until it becomes the prominent inverted dominant pedal which begins the first movement proper, its development section, and also its coda. The use of this dominant pedal in the second movement as a bass in some of the variations leads to the use of second-inversion chords (as at bar 150, for example), just as it had done many times in the first movement; and it leads to the unusual first chord of the second movement (repeated at the end), in which the bass note of the chord (E) is the beginning of the dominant pedal which from bar 3 onwards is placed in the top part. The pedal is altered to become a tonic one in the two A major sections. In this way, and because it maintains its rhythmic independence in preserving the duple rhythm of the A minor section against the introduction of triplets, attention is drawn to the A as a tonic. It can thus be more firmly established as an important key: the pedal serves a further purpose by maintaining in the mind the presence of A as the tonic, whether major (as in the two 'trios') or minor (as in the surrounding music). Nevertheless, on moving away from A, it eventually reaches C natural, where its repetitions emphasize the importance of the C major tonality. Repeated As on the trumpets (at bars 174f and 224f) also draw attention to this importance.

One other feature links A minor with A major in the audience's mind: the phrase E-F sharp-G sharp-A twice leads from the former key into the latter; and Beethoven makes use of the somewhat 'major' quality of the phrase (the sixth can sometimes help to define a key as major or minor as well as the more important third) to create in the listener the feeling that A major will follow. He strengthens the feeling by placing the F sharp of the phrase (on its last appearance at the very end of the movement) on the strong beat: the uneasy tonality at the end is due not only to this but also to the fact that the final chord has its fifth in the bass. Further implications of this chord are discussed in Chapter VII.

It is not, in any case, A major that next appears, since in the third movement there is an exploitation of the relationship between the other
important key centres, F major and A; and the movement is written in F.[43]
That this is a most unusual key for a symphony in A is obvious from the
fact that the music immediately moves away from F—and the first four
notes of the tune (F-A-F-A) are themselves an indication of the direction
to be taken. The strong A major cadence is followed, after the double bar,
by a passage in C major which is now shown in relationship with F, since
it acts as the dominant of that key (bars 116–26): the continual octave
repetitions of F-A at the end of the Scherzo are another clear indication of
the pull of A major, and the final A remains as an inverted dominant pedal
which sounds throughout the D major Trio: the magnificent effect of this
long A, especially when played by the trumpets, is necessary so that the
listener shall be aware throughout that the pull of that note has not been
relaxed.[44] It has been said that the final (and very short) appearance of the
Trio is an indication of Beethoven's humour: he leads the audience to
think that the whole Trio and Scherzo will be played yet again, but then he
curtails the movement with a few abrupt chords. This is indeed true; but
Beethoven also has a more significant purpose. The four-bar version of the
Trio which he uses in the coda serves to remind the listener of the pull of
the inverted pedal A: without this reminder, F major would be too strongly
felt as the tonic here. The rising version of x in the last five bars can now
return the tonality to F major with such brevity and in such a way that it
leaves the audience with the feeling that more music is essential for the
successful resolution of the tonal forces set up.

The move from F (at the end of the third movement) to E major (at the
beginning of the Finale), though E is a dominant, is one which the
listener by now accepts as perfectly logical. Beethoven has prepared the ear
for it very carefully: it was with this progression that the first long F major
passage had modulated back to the tonic (first movement, bars 52f), and
the semitone descent gives rise to similar progressions elsewhere (e.g. first
movement, bars 115–16, 325–6, and 386–95; and the modulations between
the Trio and Scherzo: it also occurs later at bars 210–20 of the Finale, as
well as providing an important melodic element throughout the work).

As in the first movement, E forms a prominent dominant pedal in the
Finale: so strong is A major now felt to be—a reflection of the insistence of
A pedals in the previous two movements—that the alternative tonalities of
C and F can make little headway against it. C natural, appearing in the
bass at bar 104, causes some violence in the music for several bars; and its
reappearance at the start of the development section (bar 124) ushers in a
short F major statement of the main tune, the C acting as a dominant
pedal. Naturally, since A major is now so strong, a certain amount of tonal
confusion follows this, and in bars 129–31 the orchestra clearly rejects F

natural for E (it uses a rising sixth from the main theme of the movement—an interval which plays a large part in the thematic material of the work, and which derives ultimately from an inversion of the opening three notes of the Introduction to the first movement). The E acts as the dominant of A—though the presence of the C natural makes the tonality minor instead of major. This leads, naturally enough, to a statement of the main subject in the alternative key of C major, and the preparation for the recapitulation appears only after this key has again proved to be the dominant of F (bar 194). As in the 'Eroica', the dominant preparation is interrupted: F natural again appears, but now it is not strong enough to act in its own right, and can behave only as the dominant of B flat until the recapitulation interrupts in the tonic. Here the presence of F natural is felt in a long passage in D minor (bars 255f), and C natural appears in the bass (as it had done in the exposition) with such force that, after bar 319, repeated cadences attempt to establish F major (C being the root of its dominant seventh chord) until A major again intervenes. Nevertheless, F is clearly not yet entirely overriden, as the dissonant passage containing many Fs just after bar 333 shows.

Clearly a coda is now essential in order to establish the complete ascendancy of A major: Beethoven does not re-establish the tonic immediately, but writes a modulatory passage over a bass derived from x, the motif that had started the whole argument. This bass spends many bars (beginning at bar 368) looking, as it were, for the correct tonality: A is tried as the dominant of D (the function it held in the Trio of the third movement), then G is tried as the dominant of C minor, then F as the dominant of B flat minor, and finally E as the dominant of first A minor (as in the second movement) and lastly A major. Two appearances of loud G naturals cannot move the music to C or take over from the dominant pedal in A major, the tonic key which is now established with great force. The final chords of the movement balance those which had opened it, and the final downward scale mirrors the slower rising ones heard at the opening of the work.

In spite of what many commentators have said about the Finale of the Fifth Symphony, the last movement of the Seventh is Beethoven's first to contain the same weight of argument (as opposed to mere summary or resolution) as one might expect of a first movement: here is the tendency that led Beethoven to extend the same type of tonal scheme a stage further in his Ninth Symphony. Important as an understanding of this tonality is, there are other features of the Seventh which should not escape attention: whereas the first movement uses upward scales and falling arpeggios, the Scherzo inverts these tendencies. Scales and arpeggios do, indeed, help to unify the work, but they are in any case part of the style of any composer of the period. Perhaps more striking is Beethoven's use of rhythm: a single

rhythm—different for each movement—permeates each of the four movements, and led Wagner to describe the work as 'the apotheosis of the dance'.
Striking it may be, but the work is not unified because each individual
movement is itself unified by a different rhythmic device: the discussion of
the relationships between C, F and A, and the presence of x, provide a
feeling of unity here. The use of a scheme involving three keys which are
not closely related in contemporary theory gives the work a feeling of size
and newness, and also of great power, in spite of the fact that only a
relatively small orchestra is needed to perform it.

CHAPTER IV

The Expansion of Classical Tonality (2)

Beethoven's Ninth Symphony

The tonal schemes which Beethoven uses in his 'Pastoral' and Eighth Symphonies are discussed in Chapters VI and VIII: a comparison of the use of tonality in those works with the procedures discussed in Chapter III makes it clear that Beethoven was beginning to explore relationships between keys other than the tonic and dominant, the tonalities most frequently used in sonata form before his time.[1] This exploration is taken a stage further in the Ninth Symphony.

The weakening of the dominant key has been a feature of the works leading up to the 'Choral' Symphony:[2] the 'normal' key has been used briefly for the second subject area in these works, but large tracts of that subject area have veered off into other tonalities. As the Ninth is in a minor key, the relative major (F) would be the classical choice for the key of the second subject: Beethoven, however, replaces it with B flat. Thus, whereas classical symphonies in the major use a key which is one degree sharper than the tonic for the second subject, and minor key symphonies use the brighter quality of the relative major, Beethoven has chosen to use a key area which is one degree flatter than the tonic for the second subject of his 'Choral' Symphony. This balances the 'sharp' feeling of the long opening dominant chord (though it is only recognized as a dominant by hindsight, and its 'sharpness' is muted by the omission of C sharp).[3]

D minor and B flat are thus prominent in the exposition of the first movement; and the relationship between them is often shown to be very close. (See Ex. 31).

Ex. 31

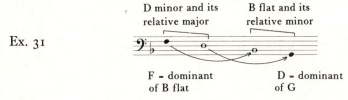

I shall refer to the notes shown in this example as 'pivotal notes' and to the keys based on them as 'pivotal keys'. D minor and B flat, coupled with their respective relative major and minor keys, are prominently used, and an additional advantage is gained by using F as a pivotal tonality: not only is it the relative major of D minor, but it is also the dominant of the other important key area, B flat.[4] D itself, when it becomes major, is also used as the dominant of G minor (the relative of B flat). The resulting series of keys a third apart gives rise to the use of thematic material which also consists of thirds, and, in the third movement, to a tonal scheme which extends that shown in Ex. 31 with yet more roots a third apart.

There is, of course, a danger in using such a scheme if one wishes to avoid creating the classical tonic-dominant feeling: B flat, however prominent, must not be handled in such a way that D minor (one degree sharper) sounds like its dominant (for even though it is only the relative of the dominant of B flat, the danger is a very real one). For this reason, Beethoven cannot repeat the exposition: clearly, if the second subject (in B flat) were to be followed by a repeat of the opening of the work, the effect would be one of tonic followed by dominant, rather than of a return to the tonic.

The second subject area of the movement is treated in a new way, for B flat is not merely set up in opposition to the 'normal' key for that area, but does in fact replace it. One further reason for this might well be the drawback, in classical minor-key sonata schemes, that the second subject does not move to the sharp side during the exposition, but merely changes to the relative major. Beethoven's new approach avoids this difficulty, but the contrasting keys are closer to each other than in some of his previous symphonies. The closeness of these keys has been shown in Ex. 31: Beethoven demonstrates their compatibility (and their inherent conflicts) in many ways, as I hope to make clear. The new function of tonality in this work is also evident in the range of keys used in the first movement: Beethoven's biggest opening movement prior to this was in the 'Eroica', where the tension generated by a chromatic phrase took the music through many distant keys. In the first movement of the Ninth Symphony, however, the exploration of new tonal relationships results in the use of a narrower range of keys.

When the Ninth Symphony begins, we are clearly in a new world of sound: eleven years separate it from the Eighth, but in spite of this the opening—a bare fifth appearing from nowhere, almost as if the sound had been going on unheard before it reached our ears—helps to define the scale of the work by its very nature: the changes of chord, moving slowly and often on weak pulses, help greatly to create the feeling that something on an altogether vaster scale than normal is about to follow. A tendency towards B flat is evident even in the early bars of the work, for immediately D minor has itself been clearly stated for the first time, G minor and B flat are suggested (bars 23f). The tendency is strengthened when the first subject is repeated, and the initial string tremolando open fifths occur on

D and A, for at the very point where D minor had first appeared in the opening statement, B flat is used in the repeat of the theme. A modulation back into D minor (bars 56f) is built around the notes D-B flat-E-C-sharp-F-D (see Ex. 32): moreover, the phrase turns around three of the pivotal notes (as is shown by the arrows in the example), and by twice shifting it upwards by a step, Beethoven introduces the missing pivotal note, G.

Ex. 32

The progression, while not recurring in the recapitulation, is of importance later in the work. The compatibility of D minor and B flat—or maybe even the struggle between them—is shown in the repeated B flat-A figuration over D minor harmonies after bar 63: the falling semitone which is prominent here becomes an important means of modulation, as well as a thematic element, later in the work, and the attention drawn to it at this early point does much to prepare the listener for its use later on. I shall call this figure x in the following discussion.

The dominance of B flat now leads logically enough to a change of key signature as the second subject area begins.[5] Beethoven demonstrates the compatibility of B flat and D minor by writing an accompanying string figure which could well belong to either key (bars 80f),[6] and one or two other equally ambiguous passages, such as bars 120f. The appearance (at bars 108ff) of B major—another key a third away from the tonic—is a foretaste of a tonal area that becomes more important later in the work: the return to B flat is made by using x, with the notes B natural and B flat. B flat is firmly stated at the end of the exposition, before x, now using B flat and A, moves the music back into the key and style of the opening. The quiet low A on the trumpets and drums (bar 160) which immediately follows this return serves as a demonstration to the audience that the key just quitted (B flat) was neither the tonic nor the dominant—for the audience of the day would expect the trumpets to play only the tonic and dominant at this very low pitch. The sounding of a low trumpet note a semitone below B flat enormously helps the ear to identify the chord in bar 160 as the dominant. For the same reasons, it is also quite clear that the tonality just quitted cannot have been the classically correct relative major. By such a simple device does Beethoven draw his hearers' attention to the novelty of the key of his second subject.

The arrival, at this point, of the symphony's opening music naturally enough leads the audience to suspect that the exposition is about to be repeated. It is some bars before Beethoven makes it quite clear that this is not his intention, and that in fact the development is now under way.[7] As I have already suggested, to repeat the D minor of the opening would be tantamount to providing the dominant-tonic feeling which Beethoven was trying to avoid; and so he develops the opening material in a new tonal direction, in which the first step is to provide a major third in the bass of the tremolando open fifth D-A. (Nevertheless, the detached trumpet and drum D's remind the ear of the dominant-tonic progression in the *harmony*.) Although F sharps have appeared previously, this is the first time they have been used to suggest a clear D major. D major is, as it were, the tonal goal of the whole work, even though the audience cannot yet know this: here it acts as the dominant of G minor, and thus fulfils two functions. Firstly, it shows yet another area of compatibility between D and B flat (or rather, B flat's relative minor) and, secondly, it keeps the tonality within the orbit of B flat so that there shall be no 'dominant' feeling. (There is a parallel here with Beethoven's interpretation of C major as the dominant of F minor in the opening movement of his Fifth Symphony.)

Why then did Beethoven return to the opening of the music at all in bar 162? It was his normal practice, when the repeat of the exposition was omitted, to start the development with the material of the opening of the work, not perhaps so much to mislead the audience (though this is some-times the effect) as to make the proportions clear—that is, to act as a mile-post which indicates clearly to the listener what point the work has reached. During the exposition B flat has become the main secondary tonality: I shall refer to this key as a 'substitute dominant' (even though the relative major rather than the dominant would have been expected for the second subject in a classical scheme). In descending from the tonic, B flat is a semitone short of the dominant: by recalling the music of the opening (which we now know to have been on the dominant chord) and by using the trumpets, as mentioned above, to mark the difference between the substitute dominant and the real dominant, Beethoven demonstrates that the short-fall is expressed by the motif *x* (B flat-A). This function itself draws attention to another way in which *x* is important. A normal approach to the dominant would be by way of its own dominant chord, so that the leading-note-tonic in Λ (G sharp-A) would be prominent. Such a pro-gression would savour too much of the dominant-tonic schemes which Beethoven was at pains to avoid in this movement; and *x* inverts it, approaching the dominant from a semitone above instead of a semitone below. Naturally, these functions continue in the remainder of the work.

A large G minor section at the opening of the development is followed by a fugue which starts in C minor (and, naturally enough, veers towards G minor since the dominant is the key of the normal answer in fugue) with the later entries in B flat. In this section Beethoven clearly points to the compatibility of the tonic key with B flat, since the trumpets and drums (bars 236ff) sound D against the B flat entry of the subject.[8] The develop-ment makes much wider use of tonic-dominant relationships: D major-

G minor-C minor (up to bar 218) provide a very slow-moving circle of fifths, while a fast-moving one of D-G-C-F-B flat is found in bars 228-32. In spite of these relationships, the effect of the movement as a whole is not one of tonic and dominant. The leaning towards keys on the flat side of D minor has so far been very strong; and Beethoven now counteracts this with a long passage in A minor, its dominant: he is, however, very careful that the key shall not at any point be *felt* as a dominant. It is not introduced after D minor, nor when modulation away from that key occurs does it act as a dominant: moreover, the modality of the harmony (especially in bars 266-71) and the lack of an A pedal (which might sound like a dominant pedal) encourages the listener to regard it as something other than the dominant key—and this, as I have suggested, was very much to Beethoven's purpose in this symphony.

A dominant pedal would be the normal preparation for the recapitulation; but there are good reasons for avoiding one in this movement. Firstly, the normal type of dominant seventh could only be less impressive than the astonishingly powerful open fifth on the dominant which Beethoven has already used at the beginning of the exposition; and secondly, the repeat of that opening at the beginning of the development renders it unavailable for the recapitulation, since a third hearing could again only lessen its effect, especially at a point in the symphony where a sense of excitement is needed to accompany the return of the tonic and of the opening material. Beethoven has found an ideal solution by using the 'wrong' dominant pedal for a while: in bars 287-94 he uses a decorated C pedal while chords of F and C above it suggest that the pedal might be preparing for the reappearance, not of D minor, but of its relative major, F, the key which a classical treatment of tonality would have adopted for the second subject. The insistence of the F chords at this point in the movement suggests that they may themselves be the dominant (for, as Tovey has pointed out, such insistence tends to create this impression, at least under certain conditions) :[9] the C pedal would thus be the 'dominant of the dominant' in B flat (though this tendency is admittedly less strong), providing a counterpart to the double pedal on the dominant and dominant of the dominant in D at the opening of the work as a whole. The feeling is created that F might either be the key of the recapitulation (since it was avoided for the second subject earlier), or that it might be leading up to B flat: Beethoven is thus exploiting still further the close relationships between his pivotal keys. The appearance of C sharps settles the matter, leading neither to F nor B flat, but D; and not to D minor, but D major.

The first subject is considerably altered when it reappears at bar 301: the open fifth is now played very loudly on brass and wind, and the F sharp in the bass defines the triad as major. The opening of the development is immediately called to mind, since the same chord occurs in the corresponding position there. In the recapitulation, however, the D major chord acts first of all in its own right, and not merely as a dominant of G minor: the revised orchestration and dynamics are an indication of the growth in power of the tonic major. It is essential to reach D minor for the remainder of the first subject, and Beethoven modulates there via his other pivotal key area, B flat (in bars 313f). The B flat chord, technically a German Sixth, is approached as the bass part (in bars 312f) falls from F sharp to F natural and then B flat: this shape, of course, is another expression of the B flat-A-D shape implied at the close of the exposition, at the point where Beethoven had related his secondary key area to the tonic (bars 158ff). The recapitulation of the first subject then proceeds in D minor, but with the addition of a new bass line with a G minor tendency, which is actually the second part of the opening subject of the exposition: thus two elements are dovetailed in the recapitulation.[10] The advantage of this to Beethoven is that two of the pivotal key areas are yet more closely linked than previously.

The second subject, as one might expect, reappears in the tonic: nevertheless, so that the tonic *major* shall not become too strong, some of the material which appeared in B flat major in the exposition is reworked in D minor for the recapitulation. Naturally, other tonal alterations are necessary in order that the music shall still conform to Beethoven's key scheme: in particular, the progression from G minor to B flat which begins at bar 92 in the exposition is altered in the recapitulation (bars 359ff) so that the phrase begins in B flat and moves to D minor, in both places using two of the pivotal keys. This transposition of one section which revolves around pivotal keys so that it uses a different selection forms an interesting forerunner of the device used by Sibelius in the Finale of his Second Symphony, discussed below. Beethoven's transposition of bars 120ff (in which B flat's minor and major are suggested) so that D minor and D major are heard at bar 387 is an even more striking instance of the same method of working (see Ex. 33). The G flat (bar 120) is not only the enharmonic equivalent of the F sharp which does much to establish D major in the Finale, but by being a semitone above the root of the harmony also expresses the interval x. The other three important pitches of this passage in the exposition (see Ex. 33, lower stave) are all pivotal notes. In the recapitulation x is expressed by the B flat-A, and the pivotal pitches of the two passages occur at different points, as indicated by the arrows. The use of B natural as a way of helping to establish the tonic major will be evident later in the work.[11]

The large coda is in many ways a mirror of the development section: the two begin similarly, and both are largely concerned with the tonal areas of D and B flat. The struggle for dominance between the two is evident in bars 463–9, where the chords alternate between the two keys, only to be

Ex. 33

Exposition (bar 120)

foresight of D major ?

Harmony:

[as dominant
of B♭(minor?)]

Recapitulation (bar 387)

implies D major

[as dominant
of D minor]

followed by a D major version of the fugue subject from the development section. From three points of view this is useful for Beethoven's purpose. Firstly, it provides another glimpse of the D major which is the ultimate tonal goal of the symphony. Secondly, it provides a sharp-side key area to balance the large amount of flat side music so far heard in the coda, in a more effective way than the dominant could. Thirdly, the subject is used here without the continual leaning towards the dominant and without the circle of fifths which had been part of the development section's fugue: the conflict between the two types of tonal working evident at that point in the movement is here resolved, the horn tune remaining in D major. The contrast of methods of tonal treatment is a vital element in the remainder of the symphony.

When D minor reappears at bar 477, it is with a long passage of octaves in the strings: the weight given to this in the orchestration shows how important the figuration here is. Naturally there are octave breakbacks in this consistently descending line, but when one has taken these into account, the string parts provide a series of seventeen descending thirds—a thematic development of Beethoven's tonal scheme which assumes even greater importance later in the work. More string octaves occur from bar 513 onwards, and here the thematic ideas are again closely allied to the tonality: the chromatic figure continually moves between strong pulses on D and B flat against a solid D minor in the rest of the orchestra, and later (after bar 531) it repeatedly approaches a cadence on D which is frustrated because the C sharp leading-note falls to C natural (*x*, in fact), instead of rising: there is an apparent refusal here to accept D major (the wind have prominent F sharps) as the established tonality; and D is eventually reached by the strings only as the tonality becomes minor. In spite of the fact that the octaves continually fail to cadence on D and are diverted to the seventh (C natural), they never, in descending chromatically, manage to reach the other main pivotal note (B flat) either.[12] The awesome power of this passage is in large measure due to the conflict between the *tonic-dominant* type of tonality (which the expected resolution of the C sharps up to D would imply) and Beethoven's novel tonal scheme, whose motif *x* for a time frustrates the final resolution of the leading note.

The octaves which end the movement—reminiscent of the falling fifths which had opened it—do not define the key as either major or minor, though in this context the listener understands it to be minor. Satisfactory and powerful as this ending might seem, anyone who has followed the tonal scheme of the work closely must feel that the tensions have not yet been resolved, and that this movement cannot by itself complete the sense of the argument.

The second movement does not so much carry the argument forward as question the whole basis of it: this is in fact the first Scherzo to take such a vital part in the debate which constitutes symphonic form.[13] There is here a considerable use of tonic and dominant relationships of the type largely avoided in the first movement: indeed, the Scherzo starts with a fugue[14] which, of course, involves continuous leanings towards the dominant (even if B flat is often prominent in the melodic lines): this helps to explain the choice of such an unusual form for a Scherzo. Many other tonic-dominant relationships are found, of course, and Beethoven does much to draw his audience's attention to them by his use of the trumpets, for they were still normally confined to the notes of the harmonic series. The movement from D minor to G (bar 77) and C (bar 143) constitutes part of a circle of fifths, an idea which, while it is occasionally found in the first movement, is not in keeping with the tonal scheme postulated there; and it is copied (with a much faster rate of chord change) at bars 110–17 and 225–50. The Trio, too, which forms a tonal point of repose, has a tendency to move towards the dominant, even though there is also a brief move towards F.[15] To set against these clear indications of a 'classical' way of considering tonality, there are as many instances in which Beethoven uses his new tonal scheme: melodic material based on thirds begins to play a prominent part after bar 127. In addition, the bass descends through an even longer series of thirds than that found in the coda of the first movement: beginning at bar 143, eighteen such intervals follow each other (with octave breakbacks), taking the tonality to distant areas.[16] By inverting the falling semitone (x) which has played such a large part in the modulations of the first movement, Beethoven reaches B major—a key a third away from D which becomes of great importance later in the symphony. B is not strong enough yet to act in its own right, since the tonality of the movement as a whole is not D major but D minor; so it is taken as a dominant, and the Scherzo starts up again in E minor—a third above the previous firm cadence (in C major at bar 143). If because of the confused tonality of the previous bars most of the orchestra has 'mistaken' these keys for B flat and D minor, the timpani have not: loud repetitions of F (a note clearly defined for the listener since it is the only note of the triad which the timpani play in the opening bars of the movement—and timpani do not retune in the course of a movement in Beethoven's works) call the music back to that tonal area. This is, of course, one of the pivotal keys, as D minor at the opening and G (though it is major and not minor) at bar 77 were: D, G and B flat follow again several times before the Scherzo ends; and Beethoven, when recapitulating the opening modulation from D to G major, alters it to conform to his scheme (D-B flat in bar 296). Immediately after this point, the shift from B flat to A reminds us of the use of x for modulation in the first movement, and in addition it mirrors the pull of the timpani at bar 195, where E minor had moved up to F. Clearly there is a struggle here; not the struggle—as in the Seventh Symphony—between the pulls of two different tonal areas, but between two different methods of treating tonality, the classical dominant-tonic one and Beethoven's new one based on thirds. Again the listener who has followed the tonal scheme attentively will be aware that the argument cannot end after this Scherzo any more than it could have done after the first movement.

If the Scherzo raises some doubts about the viability of Beethoven's new tonal scheme, the third movement raises others. The fact that the movement is in B flat need not surprise us: this is the 'classical' key for the slow movement of a D minor symphony, and thus in this instance, Beethoven's new tonal scheme and the classical manner of working are compatible. Moreover, the symphony continually veers towards D major, and the last movement is in that key: it need not surprise us, then, that G major (the normal key for a slow movement in a D major symphony) is also prominent in this movement, and that G is one of the key areas shown in Ex. 31. The lyricism of the movement results in part from this compatibility of the classical tonic-dominant tonalities with Beethoven's new scheme. Beethoven's manner of working in this movement follows the rules of his own logic: the opening two bars (which begin with the B flat-A figure x so important elsewhere for modulation) at first suggest various keys, of which F and D minor are the most likely. Subsequent instrumental entries during these two bars, however, gradually define the underlying chord as the dominant of B flat, further exploring the relationships between the pivotal keys. This gradual definition of key parallels that of the opening of the first movement, even though the means employed are different. At bar 23 a chord of D major is reached, and is taken as the tonic of a new section.[17] The theme already heard and the D major one which begins here together serve as the basis for a set of variations: in view of the overall tonal workings of the symphony, it is worth remarking that both themes have much underlying tonic-dominant harmony (though inversions are liberally employed). After a varied repeat of the opening B flat tune, a D major chord is again reached, though this time it is taken as a dominant (as it sometimes was in the first movement) and the second section is then repeated in G major, a D pedal being a continual reminder of the importance of that note—perhaps an indication that dominant relationships are growing in power. The modulation from D back to B flat which had occurred at the end of the second section is now repeated a third lower in order to modulate from G to E flat. The E flat section, in its turn (bars 83ff), begins with a dominant pedal B flat which serves to remind us of the tonic of the movement. In the middle of this variation there is a further shift downwards by a third, to C flat major: this modulation takes the tonality to the enharmonic equivalent of B major, and also demonstrates an important connection between that key and B flat.

The route by which Beethoven has travelled from B flat to C flat major is a logical outcome of his new approach to tonality. Though the classical tonic-dominant relationship when extended to form a circle of fifths will eventually return to the key from which it began, Beethoven's new third-based scheme (unless it happens to use only minor thirds or only major thirds and not a combination of both types) used in a similar circular fashion leads from B flat down to C flat. Moreover, C flat-B flat, the interval by which this scheme falls short of a complete return to the point of departure, is neatly expressed by the modulatory figure x. The fact that Beethoven has gradually descended from B flat through (mostly) flatter keys results in C flat being heard not as the sharp key of its enharmonic equivalent B but as a very flat key. B major, as mentioned above, attains great importance later in the work, for its sharpness serves to balance the many flat-side tonalities in the symphony, as well as to draw particular attention to the major sixth in the scale of D—an important stage in the eventual establishment of the tonic *major* in the Finale. The importance of C flat in the third movement is shown by a very unexpected cadenza for the fourth horn when this key is reached; for though this famous horn passage had begun at the point where Beethoven begins to move down his 'circle of thirds', it is with the reaching of C flat that the most obviously cadenza-like passage occurs. The 'relaxed' nature of flatward tendencies (for such is the effect of movement to flatter keys) serves Beethoven's purpose well. Moreover, to have made the key of C flat sound like a sharp key (B major) would have come dangerously close to setting up D major as a firm tonic—a process which must occur only in the Finale.

The falling semitone x (this time G flat-F at bar 98) is used to modulate back to B flat, and a further variation of the opening theme in that key leads into a long coda which begins at bar 121. Here, in a fanfare, first B flat and then F is taken as the dominant, a process which is then repeated: the chords E flat, B flat and F provide the beginnings of a circle of fifths instead of the earlier circle of thirds. The new direction of the argument in this movement is nicely paralleled by the reservation of the trumpets for this point. The second of the two fanfares (bar 131) is followed by yet another shift of tonality to a key a third lower, and a passage which starts in D flat modulates back to B flat for a tranquil ending in which the timpani, in unusual fashion, play a two-part chord consisting of the pivotal notes B flat and F, clearly making use of the tonic-dominant relationship.

What difficulties, then, does this quietly flowing music raise? The scheme follows the logic of Beethoven's system fully, and if the key relationships heard in the first two movements have been absorbed, there ought to be no surprise here. By avoiding dominant-tonic relationships between the keys employed and substituting modulations to keys a third apart, and yet at the same time using much dominant-tonic harmony, Beethoven is keeping open the debate between the classical approach to tonality and the one he has devised in this work. There is, however, another important issue: that is, the growing prominence of D major. This key, as opposed to D minor, is a long way from B flat in terms of classical tonality. Although the symphony is working towards D major, it is still too early for this key to become firmly established. Therefore, Beethoven moves through most of the pivotal keys, but since none of them is reached in the conventional manner, the ear is somewhat reluctant to accept them as properly established. Instead, he shows that he is primarily concerned here with the relationship between the keys: he does this by keeping his modulatory processes to a minimum, often using only a single chord to slide from one key to another, rather than by extending the use of dominant-tonic progressions to approach fresh tonal areas gradually through intervening non-pivotal keys. The attention drawn to the pivotal relationship of the tonal areas is the more evident when one considers that this is balanced by the large amount of dominant-tonic harmony in each of the tunes on which Beethoven bases the movement: in a sense the music consists of sections of dominant-tonic harmony played at various pitches *not* in a tonic-dominant relationship. Indeed, it may well be that one of the reasons for choosing this form of variations on alternate themes (so beloved of Haydn) was to draw clear attention to the tonal relationship between the various statements. In a similar manner, the use of fugue at various points in the work may result from a tendency which counterbalances that of these variations—the tendency to use strong *tonic-dominant* tonal (as opposed to merely harmonic) relationships.

The Ninth Symphony has so far, among other things, postulated a new type of tonality to replace the classical dominant and tonic; shown how some keys a third apart can be compatible; questioned the viability of this hypothesis in a dynamic movement which shows the two types of tonal construction struggling against each other; and used strong tonic-dominant harmonies in tonal planes governed by thirds. Beethoven now needs to resolve all these conflicts in the Finale, which must be on a vast scale not only to balance the foregoing movements, but in order also to settle the tonal argument convincingly, so big are the issues involved and so far from a solution have the first three movements brought us.[18]

The B flat tonic at the end of the third movement is replaced by a violent pedal A on the timpani at the start of the Finale. Thus the 'substitute dominant' gives way to the classical dominant in an expression of the falling semitone x. Although this statement of x is hidden between the two movements, B flat remains over in the woodwind so as to start the Finale with a violent discord. This B flat also moves downwards onto A. The opening discord which results has puzzled many people, including Berlioz, yet anyone who has followed the argument so far cannot fail to appreciate its purpose. The chord consists of D minor and B flat major triads played together over a pedal A in the timpani, and its force can be attributed to two factors. Firstly, because it follows the lyrical slow movement it has the added power of contrast, which it would lack if Beethoven had followed the normal order of movements. Secondly, although the dissonance is really only the same as the $^6_5$ chord featured in the development of the first movement of the 'Eroica', there is a greater feeling of surprise in the Finale of the 'Choral' because here it is unprepared.

The conflict between the substitute dominant and the classical dominant is not resolved at this point, of course, but the growing power of the latter (already in evidence towards the end of the third movement) is apparent from the manner in which B flat is violently dragged down to the timpani's A before moving onto D. Indeed, the trumpet parts at the opening of the Finale reinforce the impression that tonic-dominant progressions are increasing in power, for Beethoven has made a virtue of necessity—the trumpets, confined to the notes of the harmonic scale, here sound only A and D.

Beethoven had for some time been contemplating setting Schiller's *Ode to Joy*: even when he had decided to make this setting the Finale of his Ninth Symphony, he was very uncertain as to how to introduce the human voice, and there are reports of him striding up and down his room trying to solve this problem. Clearly, the introduction of the voice in an instrumental work must sound logical, or there will be a feeling of incongruity. His solution is to introduce a vocal style—recitativo secco—into the instrumental music first, and then to add voice and text to the music thus created. However logical this may be from the composer's point of view, it is equally important that the listener should accept the introduction of the voice as being perfectly natural. The programmatic background—the brotherhood of man—provides one reason for the introduction of the voice: the addition of a text removes any uncertainty as to the music's programmatic meaning. The rejection of the themes of earlier movements in favour of the instrumental version of the D major tune of the Finale, and the subsequent rejection by the baritone (by implication at least) of all the previous music including this instrumental version, form another logical preparation for something novel, in this instance the introduction of the choral Ode.[19]

Why does Beethoven reject the themes? And why does he introduce them at all in the Finale, since the audience can scarcely need to be reminded of them? The answer is at least partly tonal. We have already seen that there are conflicting elements in the tonality of the earlier movements, and the rejection of the themes is an indication that the tonal problems are about to be resolved. The three different styles evinced by the openings of those movements, too—the arpeggio figure over an open fifth, the fugal Scherzo, and the melody fully harmonized—are likewise rejected. The reason for introducing these themes briefly into the Finale is not to review the material so much as to make it clear than when the baritone sings 'O Freunde, nicht diese Töne!' he is referring not only to the music which has immediately preceded his solo, but to the whole instrumental part of the symphony.

D major is the tonal goal that has been in view throughout the work, and it has been the key that has caused at least some of the conflicts of earlier movements: indeed, the stronger it has become, the more it has tended to override Beethoven's new tonal scheme. It is with the main tune of the Finale that this key is eventually firmly established: it is not perhaps surprising that on both its first appearance and its first vocal appearance it is introduced by a few bars of pure dominant harmony. The major quality of the tune is the more obvious since the third is a very prominent feature: this F sharp is strengthened so as to counteract the F natural tendencies which have gone hand in hand with the D minor and B flat tonalities of earlier parts of the work. The tune is given out in the simplest possible form, partly because it is the basis for a set of variations, and partly because its simplicity (especially after the more complex rejected music) is of a folk-like directness which not only aptly expresses the idea of the 'brotherhood of man' but which can be easily appreciated by all men.

The tune starts on the third and moves around this note by step, rising to the third above it and descending to the third below in the two opening phrases. The first two leaps are likewise those of a third (F sharp to D). The overall range of this portion of the tune (bars 92–102) has thus been a fifth—the tonic to the dominant of D. This fifth is expressed in another way when Beethoven introduces the biggest leap in the tune (if one disregards the leap back to F sharp from A, which is a 'dead' interval) at bar 103. This leap downwards from E to A expresses the range of a fifth already heard, but at the *dominant* pitch: moreover, the leap itself uses the same notes as at the opening of the symphony, though in a different octave. The prominence of F sharp is assured by other means than simply that of making the tune revolve around it: twice the tune makes its biggest leap— a major sixth (the 'dead' interval mentioned above) perhaps recalling Ex. 32—in order to return to this note from bottom A, a crescendo being marked up to the F sharp.[20] The tune thus represents a culmination of tonal elements in the symphony and is therefore a focal point: the fact that it is announced in unison helps the ear to concentrate its attention on these features.

Three instrumental variations on this splendid tune, all firmly in D major, follow its initial statement. The first of these (bars 116ff) avoids the obvious tonic-dominant harmony, which gradually attains prominence during Variation II (bars 140ff), until in Variation III (bars 164ff) the tonic and dominant harmonies are uppermost. At bar 203 there is a shift to what sounds like the beginning of a second subject in the dominant key, but this is not allowed to become established, perhaps because it conflicts with Beethoven's alternative scheme, and this conflict is not yet played out. The result is a passage of wandering tonality which leads to a restatement of the Finale's opening fanfare. The fact that the dominant is immediately replaced by B minor is a further omen of the importance that the note B is to attain in establishing the tonic major.[21]

When Beethoven repeats the opening fanfare at bars 208ff he intensifies the initial dissonance in order to restore some of the impact lost through repetition. But there is much more to it than this. Whereas at the opening of the Finale, the chords of B flat and D minor are sounded together over a dominant pedal, here the dominant chord has assumed greater importance and is sounded simultaneously with the chord of B flat: thus the dominant of classical tonality and the substitute dominant of Beethoven's new scheme are brought into violent collision, with the result that B flat is again dragged down to A before this chord, like its predecessor, leads to D minor. The baritone, using Beethoven's own text, now rejects all that has gone before and introduces the choral setting of Schiller's *Ode to Joy*.

It is not until bar 330 that the music again moves away from the tonic: the variation in Turkish style—rather like a military procession drawing near—is in B flat. By producing a piece with a special character for this variation, Beethoven not only illustrates the text 'Wie ein Held zum Siegen' (like a hero to conquest flying)—for his contemporaries in Eastern Europe were conscious of a continuing military threat from the Turks—but also draws special attention to the key in which it is written. As in the third movement, Beethoven keeps his modulatory processes to a minimum, merely the new dominant chord on F being used to link D and B flat. It is significant that this modulation to the substitute dominant occurs at a point where the music has been moving strongly towards A, the classical dominant: Beethoven leads the ear to expect that he is moving in one tonal plane, only to frustrate that expectation by sheering off into the other. The importance of B flat is also made clear by the transposition of the Finale's main theme to this key with the effect that the most prominent note of the tune, previously F sharp but now D, becomes the tonic of the symphony as a whole. Moreover, the tune in this transposition is based around three of the important pivotal notes shown in Ex. 31 (D, F and B flat). Of the four centres shown in that Example, G is missing from this tune (it occurs, of course, as a passing-note at times, though it is not prominent): in the fugue which follows, therefore, it is to G that the music modulates once lip-service has been paid to B flat and F for the first two entries (bar 441).

So far in the movement, until the B flat variation, there have been a fair number of dominant and tonic relationships which have grown in power; but at this point there is an attempt to set against them the new way of working. B flat is on the flat side of the tonic, and shortly after the beginning of the fugue there is a modulation to G flat (bar 477), a third further on and still flatter. There is a brief suggestion, too, of E flat minor, yet another third below. Beethoven now begins to treat G flat enharmonically, and F sharp becomes more powerful until it is repeated in a series of octaves and tried out first as the dominant of B major (bar 529), then as the dominant of B minor (bar 535), until finally it is shown not to be a dominant at all, but the major third of D (bar 541). This point is of vital importance: firstly, it is because the Finale's main theme has made such a feature of F sharp that Beethoven is able to use it in this way. Secondly, whereas previously, by going round his 'circle of thirds', Beethoven has always ended a semitone short of recovering the tonic (hence the necessity for x), here, by interpreting the G flat enharmonically and referring it to the main tune, he is able to recover the tonic immediately. Indeed, the brief references to B major and minor which precede this recovery of D major help to counteract the minor key tendency which a B flat in the scale gives, and which the flat keys of the fugue have given. Hence Beethoven's new scheme has now become a complete circle, and there is therefore very little reason for *x* to be used after this point. If *x* is used at all, it tends to be expanded to a tone, B natural-A, conforming to the D major tonality. In fact, it is in the maelstrom of the fugue (bars 431ff) that the power of B flat and the flat keys generally is overcome in favour of the major keys and dominant-tonic schemes.

Now that B flat has largely given way to B natural the G of Ex. 31 will become the tonic of a major rather than a minor key (even if it now remains in the scheme merely because D is its dominant); and it is in this key that the second big theme of the movement is introduced at bar 595. Like the D major tune, this one gives considerable weight to the pivotal notes D, B (natural now, of course) and G. As in the B flat variation, Beethoven soon introduces the missing pivotal note, F natural (bars 612f); but before this happens the music becomes very modal in order to accommodate the pivotal chords of B major, G and D (bars 606–10): the use of modality is one of the ways in which Beethoven succeeds in solving the tonal problems which he has set in this work. The completion of the set of four pivotal notes—given out strongly in unison (bars 612f)—results in a last F major section and one in G minor, both very modal in sound.

A triple fugue in D major,[22] the following variation, has something of the function of a development section: the two main themes of the movement are combined in counterpoint, and the rhythm reminds the listener of the 'Turkish' B flat variation. As befits a fugue, there are continual tendencies towards the dominant, so that various features of the work are here brought together and resolved: this contrapuntal fusion of thematic elements is foreshadowed at earlier appearances of D major in the work. By being so tightly knit, this fugue throws a weight of argument into the scale such as can counterbalance the weight given by the turbulence of the B flat fugue. By now it has become evident that throughout the symphony, fugue has been making regular appearances. This has been useful for Beethoven's purpose, since there is a built-in dominant-tonic tendency in the form as it had normally been used up to that time.

This tremendous piece of counterpoint is followed by quite the opposite, for the firm thickly scored D major gives place to a wandering chromatic line, completely unharmonised (bars 730ff) and scored very softly. This passage (shown in Ex. 34) begins by illustrating the text 'Ihr stürzt nieder, Millionen? Ahnest du den Schöpfer, Welt?' ('O ye millions, why kneel before Him? World, dost seek thy Maker?'), the rests in the vocal line suggesting the breathless adoration of, and somewhat uncertain approach to, the Creator.

Ex. 34

3rd higher

Ex. 34
(cont.)

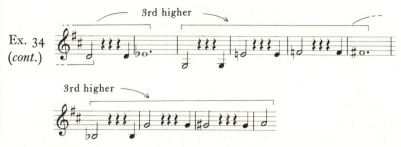

The passage also acts as a recapitulation of an earlier one in the exposition of the first movement (see Ex. 32): it had not returned during the recapitulation of that movement, though there are possible references to the shape at bars 313ff of the second movement, and bar 98 of the third movement. Though the mention of these two references might be construed as 'paper analysis', the passage at bars 730ff of the Finale is a clearly audible recapitulation of this theme. In effect, Beethoven takes only the long notes of its first four bars (as shown in Ex. 32), and leaves the initial D until after the C sharp. Then (with the exception of the occasional note) Beethoven twice repeats this shape, a third higher each time, providing a reversal of the descending thirds of the tonal scheme he has so often used earlier in the work. The line shown in Ex. 34 is largely compounded of thirds (with octave breakbacks) and it is used to rise from the depths to the heights in order to express the line 'Such ihn überm Sternenzelt!' ('Seek Him above the starry sphere.') The passage negates Beethoven's earlier scheme of thirds: though the keys of D and B flat are much used, there is only a directionless wandering between them and it appears that the 'circle of thirds' is now broken.

There are three more elements which are still to be brought within the scope of the Finale's music before Beethoven can end satisfactorily with all the tensions resolved. The melodic lines using many descending thirds which derive from the new tonal scheme are introduced: at bars 806f and 827f the thirds are made to conform rigidly to D major, while at bars 895 and 899 they are also made to fit in with the surrounding dominant harmony.[23] B major is at last prominently woven into the music at bars 836f, the soloists, by their lyrical virtuosity, drawing considerable attention to that key. This passage recalls the horn cadenza in the third movement which had reached its height at the enharmonic equivalent of this key, C flat. The Puritanical objection to virtuosity evinced by some critics is here irrelevant, since Beethoven has used it structurally, to focus the listener's attention on his musical logic, as well as to give greater expression. Basil Lam[24] has suggested that the vocal cadenzas are the outcome of the horn cadenza in the Adagio, though without mentioning that the keys are in fact enharmonically equivalent. Beethoven had taken enormous care in the third movement that C flat should be heard as a very flat key, by continually descending through flatter areas and by using tonalities each a third lower than its precursor. Here, towards the end of the Finale, he ensures that B major is heard as a very sharp key by approaching it from the opposite direction. Beginning in D (bar 827) he modulates towards the dominant, but takes *its* dominant chord (E major) as a tonic, and then moves quite naturally to E major's own dominant. He has thus used tonic-dominant progressions in place of the new 'circle of thirds' scheme heard in the slow movement to reach the same point.

Beethoven regains D major by moving first to B minor and then lowering the bass to A, the extended form of x which had already been used in bars 530–40. To make the point quite clear, Beethoven continually repeats the figure (in its new, major, form) until bar 851. B major may well have taken over the pivotal nature of B flat now that the ultimate goal of D major is firmly attained, but F natural still appears, and the modal harmony after bar 880 includes chords of B major (with a seventh) and F major within a small space: nevertheless, the orchestral coda makes a great feature of F sharp (as well as using many thirds melodically) to compensate for this, and after a blaze of D major, the work ends with a unison falling fifth—the same one as had ended both the first two movements, and a tonic version of the interval with which the entire work had started.[25]

The importance of the falling fifth in the thematic construction of the symphony is discussed in Chapter II above. But it is not without interest that a tonal scheme such as that found in the Ninth Symphony, in which key centres a third apart are placed against conventional tonality, should be thoroughly permeated by a thematic device which, even if it is compatible with both types of tonal construction, yet clearly states the dominant and tonic. Dominant-tonic relationships, of course, form the basis of classical tonality; and it is significant that Beethoven demonstrates at the outset of the work that the musical discussion is to be concerned with different ways of handling tonality. The aggresively dominant opening of the work suggests that Beethoven intends to follow classical models, and thus the ear accustomed to classical symphonies expects the first modulation in a minor key work to take the music up by a third to the relative major, F. But Beethoven frustrates the expectation by treating that note as a dominant and using it to modulate to B flat, a third *below* the tonic. Thus the struggle between the two schemes is set up, the difference between them often being expressed by x. As the work progresses, the classical scheme gains in power as a direct parallel to the introduction of the idea of 'the brotherhood of man' in the setting of the *Ode to Joy*. Here the prominence of F sharp leads to the substitution of B natural for B flat; and whereas in the earlier part of the symphony the tonal scheme based on thirds had been set against dominant-tonic melodic tendencies in such a way that a classical sense of balance—not unlike that found between verticals and horizontals in architecture—had been created, so in the Finale the balance is maintained, since the emerging dominant-tonic tonality goes hand in hand with a wide use of thirds in the melodic material. That Beethoven considered the understanding (even if sub-conscious) of the tonal scheme important is shown, perhaps rather surprisingly, by his careful use of trumpets and drums. Since his listeners were well aware that trumpets, in their contemporary form, were limited to the notes of the harmonic series, and that the timpani were normally tuned to the tonic and dominant, it follows that the notes they play act as a standard against which the surrounding tonality can be heard in perspective. It is a great pity that this point has so often been misunderstood, and that Beethoven's scoring has been changed in order to make use of chromatic trumpets.

The use of the chorus (and perhaps even the use of the other new instruments which appear in the Turkish music) throw an unprecedented weight onto the Finale: Beethoven is said to have had second thoughts about the success of this choral ending, and there are reports that he intended to replace it with a purely instrumental movement. However logical the thematic and tonal progressions might be throughout the work, the introduction of the voices into the last movement alone is bound to sound less logical than would the use of voices in every movement. The overwhelming desire to express his humanistic feelings in a clearly communicable manner, coupled with the long-standing desire to set Schiller's Ode, has led him to take a step which cannot easily be justified by the music of the first three movements. Whether or not we agree with Beethoven that the choral Finale is somewhat less than satisfactory,[26] the Ninth Symphony remains one of the greatest creations of the human mind.

The vast canvas of the 'Choral' has found its imitator in Bruckner, and its 'all-inclusiveness' in Mahler; and the ideas of the 'brotherhood of man', of the gradual attaining of a goal of some kind, and of vocal participation, in very many Romantic symphonies. But the new kind of tonality which Beethoven was evolving in his symphonies from the 'Pastoral' onwards —the use of keys a major or minor third apart, as opposed to a fourth or a fifth, and the resulting modal harmony—found an echo in many non-German composers, and especially in the Nationalists. This wide-ranging influence is indeed a tribute to Beethoven's greatness; and the depth of thought that has gone into the evolving of his new kind of tonal structure, as well as the evolving of the thematic material and the other elements, can only be palely reflected in cold print. Beethoven's achievement becomes the more astonishing when one reflects that he was working at several pieces of a similar scale at the same time that he was writing this symphony. The amazing distance travelled by him in just over twenty years will be evident to any listener who, after hearing the 'Choral', pauses to cast his mind back to the style and the scale of the First Symphony. Something of the struggle which Beethoven encountered in achieving his results is reflected in the conversation which Rochlitz recorded from the year 1822: 'I find I no longer settle down to write so easily. I sit and think and think and what I have to say is all there, but it will not get down to paper. I dread beginning works of such magnitude. Once I have begun, then all goes well . . .'[27]

Interlude

The works of several composers might well be taken to illustrate the developments in symphonic style between the mature works of Beethoven and those of Sibelius. For the present purpose Bruckner serves ideally, for he had an intuitive grasp of the principles underlying Beethoven's manner of symphonic writing and was deeply affected by them: in trying to progress further in the same direction he produced massive works of immense power and beauty, and of considerable originality, yet without the extraordinary constructive ability which makes his mentor's symphonies such a succession of masterpieces. There are many fine works among the Bruckner symphonies, yet perfection of form and logic of argument are very much rarer in his music than in the other works discussed in this book.

Bruckner's social naïveté is legendary, but it is too easy to write down his failures in the symphonic field to simplicity of mind.[1] An analysis of his works carried out with care and devotion demonstrates quite patently that his musical understanding of symphonic matters was deeper than that of the great majority of his contemporaries. The reasons for the failure of some of his movements may well serve to emphasize the considerable intellectual qualities of the construction in Beethoven's and Sibelius' works, at the same time as providing a link between those two men. A careful look at one of the Bruckner symphonies may also help to redress the view that he was a rather simple composer.

It often happens in Beethoven's symphonies that the first note heard outside the basic key plays a large part in the tonal construction of the whole piece: this idea is copied by Bruckner at the beginning of his Fourth Symphony in E flat (*Romantische*).[2] The opening horn-call makes a feature of such a note (C flat), placing a tune above a string tremolando which, though a clear descendant of that in Beethoven's Choral Symphony, is yet quite different in effect. The romantic nature of the work is evident from the start: that most romantic of all instruments, the horn, with string accompaniment, produces a haunting sound which characterizes the opening of several other 'romantic' symphonies—Brahms' Second and Vaughan Williams' Fifth, for example. But it is not the *Waldweben*, the hunting-horn or the love of nature which concern us here: the influence of the opening horn motif on the remainder of the work is of paramount importance for the present purpose (see Ex. 35).

Ex. 35

The C flat which appears so unexpectedly has several effects on the work. Firstly, the interval of a minor sixth which this note creates above the tonic becomes a feature of many subsequent themes.[3] The second subject (at Letter B, p. 8) is full of such intervals in both tune and accompaniment, and so is the second subject of the Finale (at Letter C, p. 110): the minor sixth shape is, indeed, worked into a very large number of passages. Since the minor sixth (or at least, the note C flat) stands outside the key, there is a tendency at times to oppose it with the major sixth above the tonic: one can see this process at work soon after the opening. In the second movement the dichotomy between the minor and major sixth above the new tonic (that is, between A flat and A natural) is suggested. It is not an idea that is strongly developed by Bruckner, however, and is one instance where the possibilities inherent in the musical material chosen are not fully explored.

The use of the flat sixth of the scale for thematic construction is closely bound up with its use as a tonal agent. Such use is plainly evident in the climax of the opening B flat horn-calls in the Scherzo, which appears in a sudden and unexpected G flat, and also in the main theme of the Finale (see Ex. 36).

Ex. 36

Such a treatment naturally gives rise to the employment of tonalities a minor sixth apart (the interval being used either ascending or descending): for example, the second subject of the opening movement enters after a series of F major chords, not in the expected B flat, but in D flat, a minor sixth higher. The repetition of the F major chords which ends the first subject group is essential to the understanding of this method of writing: Tovey has pointed out how in Beethoven's music repeated chords tend to take on a 'dominant' feeling, yet in his castigation of Bruckner's passage[4] he has not taken this view. The repeated chords are there to make the listener expect a B flat continuation, rather than one a minor sixth away, and to make clear to him the importance of this shift of a minor sixth. Such shifts are a feature of the rest of the work (they are, indeed, often found in other works by Bruckner), and need not be enumerated in detail.

The tendency of the C flat to fall back to B flat is evident in Ex. 35, even though an E flat intervenes: the string parts at the opening of the symphony illustrate the tendency even more clearly. At its simplest this semitonal fall foreshadows the use of the same figure in many portions of the work: it is prominent at the end of the second movement, for example, and continual flat 9–8 repetitions are often used above a dominant pedal during a crescendo, sometimes even with the original notes C flat and B flat (as at bars 245–52 of the first movement). The figure plays a large part both harmonically and melodically in the chorale just after Letter K in the first movement. In the larger view, however, the semitone fall provides the start of a descending chromatic scale, a feature hinted at in the string parts which accompany Ex. 35.

If, because it resolves downwards, C flat leads to a descending chromatic line, the C natural which opposes it tends to lead upwards. From bar 30 to bar 47 of the opening movement we hear the two opposing tendencies grinding against each other very clearly, the music gradually opening out in chromatic contrary motion. It is a stroke of symphonic genius that the tonic key (with C naturals prominently placed) is re-established with a tutti that itself makes great use of contrary motion (from Letter A, pages 5f) and that this gradual opening out into a vast striding E flat phrase and its inversion (rather like a mountain range mirrored in some great lake) provides the musical reason for the widespread use of inversions in the remainder of the work. The 'dominant of the dominant' cadence (bars 65–73) then reverses the outward contrary movement of chromatic parts, and a chord of F major is approached by moving inwards from G flat in the treble and E natural in the bass. The whole of this first subject, whose argument begins with a solitary C flat and gradually opens out into opposing chromatic lines culminating in a great contrary motion tutti, should be enough to counter the view of Bruckner as a simple-minded man (at least, musically); yet this is by no means the whole tale.

The three-note shape marked x in Ex. 35 is itself capable of development in various ways. Its most obvious one is the expansion which immediately follows its first appearance, though the figure is much used with the order of its notes altered, and in inversion (see Ex. 37):

Ex. 37a

First movement, bar 173f

Ex. 37b 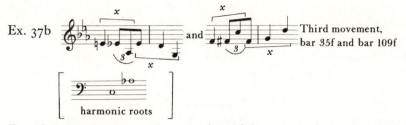 and Third movement, bar 35f and bar 109f

harmonic roots

Ex. 36 demonstrates another way in which *x* can be incorporated into the melodic material.

Such a figure is capable of frequent use in the cadential formula IV-V-I, which naturally appears many times. Such small-scale uses of the figure in a harmonic scheme are not so important as the less obvious large-scale uses: although these are many, one of the most striking occurs at the end of the first movement. From Letter S (page 47) the tonal scheme is as shown in Ex. 38:

Ex. 38

This represents a clear use of the figure *x* transposed so as to end on the tonic instead of the dominant. The subdominant nature of this ending and the transposition of the material neatly parallels that of the final phrase of Ex. 35: in that opening statement the subdominant leaning was disguised by a chromatic bass, but at the end of the movement the A flat harmony is not only plainer, but also coloured by the all-important note C flat with its attendant falling chromatic movement (as shown by the bracketed notes in Ex. 38). Moreover, the final regaining of the tonic is heralded—as it is also at the very end of the symphony—by the opening phrase of Ex. 35, played repeatedly and loudly on the horns.[5]

Yet another process has led to the E major tonality shown in Ex. 38, and this seems to derive from Beethoven's search for an alternative to the dominant. Bruckner uses the flat sixth for purposes similar to those for which it is used in the 'Choral' Symphony, though he applies it to a symphony in a major, rather than a minor, key. C flat at times virtually becomes a new tonic: this happens, for example, in the second movement at Letter N (bars 225–8) before the C flat is reinterpreted as a leading-note and the tonality slips back again to C. C flat (in the guise of B) also acts as a dominant, so that passages in E (sometimes notated as F flat) result: the passage shown in Ex. 38 thus has a further logical process underlying its use. The somewhat novel ending of the first movement is recalled at the close of the Finale, the final cadence being basically that shown in Ex. 39. Such a fresh use of cadences is firmly rooted in symphonic logic: the F flat

Ex. 39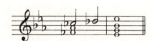

chord of Ex. 39 is itself introduced by the passage which I find the most impressive of the whole work. The coda of the Finale begins with the first three-note phrase shown in Ex. 36 repeated several times simultaneously with its inversion, leading the tonality again and again from E flat into C flat; a quiet chorale in A flat minor reconciles the E flat and C flat chords, and the trumpets recall the tonality to E flat, until—the most shattering moment of all for me—the E flat-G flat of the inversions of Ex. 36 become E flat-A flat (bars 513ff) and the tonality shifts magically into F flat (E major). E flat has become a leading-note (as had happened at the end of the first movement, bars 531 and 532), and the E flat-C flat-F flat harmonies yet another version of *x*. Even the trumpet cannot this time recall the tonic, and the harmony rises in a slow 'chorale' (with considerable use of 6-5 progression in the strings, and with the shape *x* in the bass) through wide-ranging keys suggested by the C flat or B natural, until the cadence figure shown in Ex. 39 is reached. The final long tonic harmony reconciles into one chord the various elements of the work: the horns repeat the opening notes of Ex. 35 to herald the re-establishment of the tonic (as they had done at the close of the first movement and at bar 79 of the Finale),[6] the trumpets play rising sixths, the violins make a feature of the original C flat-B flat-E flat notes of *x*, as well as the falling semitone. This is a magnificent piece of symphonic writing, quite in the tradition of Beethoven.[7]

Even the discussion of these elements does not, by any means, give an adequate impression of the stature of this work. The final 'chorale' of the coda is extraordinarily apt, we instinctively feel: is it just the use of the shape *x*, and the use of the sixth which give this impression? The truth is that one's subconscious mind recalls a much earlier chorale—though given in a much cooler scoring—in the slow movement (Letter B, bar 25): at that earlier point in the work the chorale had veered between the 'pivotal' keys (for the slow movement) of C flat and C, E flat and E. At that point the wandering of the tonality was not conclusively resolved, neither of the semitonal discussions being dominant over the other. It is now clear that Bruckner did not repeat this quite striking passage in the slow movement's recapitulation so that the mind should subconsciously record the omission. In the Finale, the coda's chorale recalls the earlier one quite vividly (the shape *x* is clear in the bass of both): Bruckner saves up his recapitulation of the second movement's chorale (though the quotation is by no means literal) for the end of the Finale, where the tonalities used, instead of being inconclusive, lead through a great many keys to the ultimate resolution shown in Ex. 39. (A reference to the Scherzo also occurs at the opening of the Finale.) Such references between separate movements were clear in Beethoven's 'Choral' Symphony, and the device was also used by Sibelius.

The elements of Bruckner's Fourth Symphony so far discussed all derive from the presence of a C flat in the horn solo at the opening: although much material derives from this one note, tonally the argument between E flat and such keys as are suggested by the 'substitute dominant' C flat is by no means so clear or so carefully worked out as one expects to find in the symphonies of Beethoven and Sibelius. For instance, C flat plays very little part in the Scherzo: Beethoven or Sibelius, having applied C flat as a 'substitute dominant' to E flat in the first movement and to C in the second, would surely have applied it to B flat in the Scherzo, especially as the C flat-B flat progression is prominent in Ex. 35 and in some of the melodic material elsewhere. Bruckner's treatment gives the impression that the appearance of keys governed by the 'substitute dominant' are tendencies to be felt at certain points in the work rather than part of a logical scheme of argument in the Beethoven or Sibelius sense. The nearest that Bruckner gets to providing this sort of tonal logic is by starting the Finale with a pedal B flat (linking the tonality with that of the Scherzo) and its minor sixth, and by referring back in the final coda to the inconclusive tonal wanderings of the chorale in the slow movement.

A feature of the work which has no connection with the 'substitute dominant' is the rhythmical one. The basis of much of the rhythm of the symphony is the figure ♩ ♩ ♪♪♩, which is applied in various inversions and diminutions (see Ex. 36, for instance). Bruckner finds these rhythms useful, often making them overlap in various stretti in order to build up excitement during a crescendo. He also parallels his procedure for treating melodic elements in inversion by 'inverting' the rhythm so that it becomes ♪♪♩ ♩ ♩, sometimes playing this version simultaneously with the original. The large number of augmentations and diminutions, and the tendency to use the rhythm at two speeds simultaneously corresponds to processes used by Beethoven and Sibelius, as I hope to show later; yet in Bruckner's *Romantische* the rhythmic treatment appears to stand apart from the remainder of the symphonic argument—it almost constitutes an 'optional extra'. One can sympathize with Bruckner, for the appearance of this rhythmic figure often points to a difficulty in construction on the enormous scale on which he was working: this vast scale presupposes an enlarged view of tonality, and generates a tendency to use a very slow rate of chord-change (this is clearly evident in the treatment of Exx. 38 and 39). Such long chords necessitate the use of triadic themes—or at least themes which are easily compatible with a single chord—and they lead to an impoverishment of the rhythm by virtue of the fact that the element of harmonic rhythm is well-nigh expelled. Within a static harmony, therefore, rhythms such as Bruckner uses in this symphony (and in others, for it is one of his favourite devices) provide an impetus which replaces that lost because of the generally very slow rate of chord-change. The new breadth of symphonic style has led, for the moment, to a reduction in the amount of integration: later Bruckner and others were able to handle the new style with more assurance, and more thorough integration of all the elements.

If the rhythmic treatment of the work is on a different plane from the motivic and tonal logic, it is clear too that not all the melodic elements are bound by the underlying idea. A really successful symphony—even one on this scale—could have been built from the elements already discussed: yet Bruckner occasionally goes beyond his argument and introduces irrelevancies. An example of this is to be found in the Finale. After a most impressive recovery of the tonic major following a long dominant pedal, and a gigantic unison theme in the tonic minor with prominent C flats, Bruckner introduces a second subject (Letter B, bar 93) which, while it contains thematic elements that are part of the symphony's stock, yet interrupts the logical flow of the argument—C minor and C major have very little to do with the case. The triteness of a considerable part of this group and its tendency to sequential repetition of small phrases both serve to hold up the forward motion of the music which Bruckner has so magnificently built up in the first ninety bars of the Finale.[8] This interruption would be less ruinous if it were not repeated; yet Bruckner brings the second subject back at Letter Q in the recapitulation (beginning on the dominant of C flat, it is true) at a point where the foregoing music has made us—and, I suspect, Bruckner too—expect a peroration. The composer leads his argument to a climax at bar 410, but then, instead of dispensing with the trammels of sonata form, feels that he ought to bring back the second subject in the conventional way. The logic of his thought will not here be forced into sonata form, and the result is far from satisfactory. It is only the return to a firmer intellectual underpinning in the coda which rescues Bruckner from this disastrous situation.

The work can illustrate several other principles which are of interest to the discussion of Beethoven and Sibelius. At Letter F (bars 165–8) of the first movement, Bruckner clearly intends to write a 'powerful' passage: the repeated chords of D flat, then G flat (or, rather, a German Sixth chord in B flat) which he uses in the brass at this point possibly suggest that G flat (used like a dominant seventh) will lead on to the important key of C flat. In addition, it is perhaps not too far-fetched to regard the tonal basis D flat-G flat-F as another version of x. Neither of these ideas is sufficiently strong to warrant the amount of weight thrust on them by Bruckner's brass fanfare. Indeed, because the underlying symphonic logic virtually ceases to function in these bars, the passage has a slightly embarrassing, 'powerless' and frustrated air: it is much less striking than passages like those at bars 51ff of the first movement or even the much quieter bars 513–20 of the Finale, where the underlying logic makes the music much more telling. In a work of this nature, power is governed less by weight of scoring than by the logical processes of thought and construction.

The momentary cessation of logical thought in passages like the one just discussed results partly from Bruckner's inability in his earlier symphonies to fill up the enormous canvasses which he gave himself: this is evident, too, in the frequent static repetitions of short phrases over the same harmony, and in the treatment of rhythm already described. It is evident, too, in Bruckner's inability, at first, to move far enough away from sonata form when his material is incompatible with it.[9] As Beethoven had written most of his works against the background of sonata form, so did Bruckner begin in this way. In a sense there are two sorts of logic to be followed in his symphonies; the logic connected with the development of his chosen material, and that of the sonata background. Bruckner will lead the ear to expect a perfectly normal continuation, only to frustrate this expectation with something else which is itself part of another logic. One is only aware of this logic in retrospect, for Bruckner follows some logic other than the one laid down by his material, only to change abruptly from the one type to the other. This is the real basis of Tovey's objection to the 'stiff archaic pause' of repeated F major chords just before the second subject of the first movement.[10] Beethoven was quite content to loosen the bands of sonata form in his later works when he considered it necessary, and Sibelius likewise modified it. The 'abnormal' continuations, for the logic to be absolute, should be evident as pre-ordained (i.e. logical), and not sound illogical even in retrospect; and here is the problem of forcing such material into a sonata form which conflicts with it. Bruckner was either not aware of this difficulty, or had not the confidence in his earlier symphonies to burst the bands of traditional first movement form; or else he felt that his style was so novel that some form of 'traditional' reference would be essential to his audience.

CHAPTER V

The Expansion of Classical Tonality (3)

Sibelius' Second Symphony

It was customary for many years to regard symphonic music in terms of sonata form, that tripartite structure which is said to consist of an exposition with two subjects in different keys, a development section which discusses the foregoing material, and a recapitulation in which the two subjects of the exposition are repeated, both in the tonic key. Although analysis along these lines is useful for some types of work, it can only be of limited value to a study of the music of Beethoven and his successors.[1] More recent analysts have realized that the part played by tonality has very much more importance than the skeleton form mentioned above, a fact to which the discussions in the previous chapters of this book testify; and that the notion of sonata form is a *post-facto* theoretical abstraction, so that many works do not fit the scheme. In order to understand the true nature of symphonic form, it is perhaps necessary to glance at the steps which led to the use of tonality as a vital force in its construction.

Modal music written before the Baroque period did not modulate: there might be cadences on various degrees of the mode, but there was not (except in very rare instances) a technique of modulating from a mode at one pitch to the same mode at another: modulation between *different* modes was, however, sometimes practised, and a few works were written in mixed modes. There were losses as well as advantages in adopting the tonal system in the years around 1600: the colour of the various modes (resulting from their different scale formations) was lost, but the new technique of modulation between keys was gained, and this fascinated many Baroque composers. Simple dance forms, as well as longer movements, began to make a feature of the polarity of keys on the dominant and tonic: the binary movements would frequently have a cadence in the dominant at the midpoint, but remain in the tonic for the second half, or begin after the midpoint in the dominant and balance the first half by returning to the tonic. The element of tonal balance and the solution of the dominant-tonic dichotomy by repeating in the tonic material that had first appeared in some other key became an important feature of tonal music. Tonal equilibrium on the large scale could be maintained by balancing keys on the sharp side of the tonic with correspondingly flat keys so that the key which is felt to be midway becomes, as it were, the tonal 'centre of gravity'. The implications of moves away from the tonic, or of notes outside it, were thoroughly investigated, an important feature being the resolution (or sometimes the lack of resolution) of the opposing elements. Such ideas were not confined to the first movement of a work, and they clearly take precedence over arguments about such details as where a second subject begins or where an exposition ends. Eventually, it was possible for Sibelius to use this power of tonality for the setting up of tension and its resolution, while at the same time making use of the colour which is an appealing characteristic of the modes.

The Second Symphony of Sibelius is a good example of a work which employs modal colour, though this feature does not affect the tonality of the work. (In this respect it differs from the Sixth Symphony, where a mode actually governs the total construction.) The Second Symphony is thus an excellent piece with which to begin this investigation of Sibelius' expansion of tonality in symphonic music. A discussion of the thematic material has already been given in Chapter II: in addition to the motifs isolated there, it should be remarked that repeated notes are an important feature of this symphony. It has been mentioned by every writer on the work that the Trio of the third movement begins with repeated notes, but it often escapes notice that repeated notes are prominent at the opening of the first and third movements, and in the accompaniment to the opening of the fourth. The most important notes to be treated in this way (though others occur less frequently) are D, F sharp (or G flat) and A sharp (or B flat), and these comprise a tonal 'axis' around which the music revolves.[2]

The choice of these three notes poses an interesting problem to a composer. Since each is a major third away from the one below, a continuous circle of modulations to keys a major third apart will eventually return the music to the tonic (it will be remembered that a rather similar process was evident in the third movement of Beethoven's 'Choral' Symphony): in each key centre, if the pivotal notes are clearly included in the music, they will still be present (though changed around as to function) in each modulation. Thus the root of one key becomes the third of another, and vice versa. The keys of D, F sharp (or G flat) and B flat do, indeed, act as rival tonal centres in the symphony.[3] In addition, the notes chosen are those which define a scale as major or minor. In D, for instance, when B flat is more prominent than F sharp, the music will tend towards D minor, and the F will be more likely to be natural: conversely when F sharp is more prominent than B flat, the music will tend to be major, and the B flat will be mutated to A or B natural. B flat is a force which it is difficult to reconcile with D major, as was evident in the 'Choral': much of Sibelius' Second Symphony is concerned with finding a solution to this problem, and for this reason there are various attempts in the work to combine all three notes into a single tonality. This cannot, of course, be a tonality of the 'classical' type, since only two of the three will fit such a scale (unless, that is, one regards one of the axial notes as a 'leading-note' of a minor key—thus the axial notes can belong to E flat minor, G minor or B minor: these keys certainly occur in the symphony, but the objection to them here is that the all important tonic note cannot be one of the axial notes). The importance of this point to the composer is that he is able to use a non-classical harmonic language in his search for a scale that will include all three axial notes (it is interesting that, although the whole-tone scale of Debussy's music would serve the purpose, this is not a solution favoured by Sibelius). A further important point is that this manner of working explores a different kind of tonal relationship from the tonic-dominant polarity of classical German symphonic music. Such a struggle between dominant and tonic as is found in such music can be of no value when harmonic language itself has gone beyond the classical stage, and has tended towards modality: the rather outmoded tonal struggle is therefore replaced by one of a new type. The use of a new type of tonality is thus inextricably bound up with the composer's choice of thematic material.[4] Sibelius himself said:

It is often thought that the essence of symphony lies in its form, but this is certainly not the case. The content is always the primary factor, while form is secondary, the music itself determining its outer form. If sonata form has anything that is lasting it must come from within. When I consider how musical forms are established I frequently think about the ice-ferns which, according to eternal laws, the frost makes into the most beautiful patterns.[5]

I hope that the truth of this observation will be evident in every chapter of this book.

One of the guides to the 'tonal axis' is presented clearly at the very beginning of the work: the long pedal D, consisting of repeated notes, clearly defines the tonic key, while the upper part begins as a series of repeated F sharps; on the first three pages of score, too, the only notes outside the D major scale are A sharps and B flats. One of the more prominent B flats occurs in the unaccompanied two-bar flute passage just before the move to the dominant (see Ex. 42). This phrase, which is played twice, never returns, yet its appearance is not, of course, accidental: its function is to draw attention to the B flat, a note which plays an important part later in the work. Thus the recapitulation of the theme itself is unnecessary since the tonal effect of its B flat remains almost throughout the symphony. The note occurs in passing where it is not expected: indeed, sometimes Sibelius combines all the axial notes into a single chord (see Ex. 40).

Ex. 40

The resolution of the A sharp upwards should be noted, for it is of importance later: the use of this augmented chord, which recurs at important
points in later movements, was no doubt suggested by a similar, but much
less developed, device which Sibelius had already used in his First Symphony. Far more important, though, is the fact that the axial notes F sharp,
B flat and D begin to take over from the traditional dominant-tonic
relationships of German symphonic music. On page 8,[6] for example, the
important new subject is announced in F sharp minor, with the note D
prominent (see Ex. 41).

Ex. 41

There is, indeed, a certain amount of struggle between the conventional
dominant of the second subject (as seen in Exx. 3 and 4) and the new
tonality governed by axial notes (as in Ex. 41). The struggle is evident in
the wandering tonality of the pizzicato passage which leads up to Ex. 41,
a passage which conforms much more closely to the axial tonality when it
reappears in the recapitulation (pages 31f) since on that occasion each
phrase begins with one of the three axial notes. This struggle between the
conventional dominant-tonic method of handling tonality and a new
method set up to replace it reminds one forcibly of the procedures in
Beethoven's 'Choral' Symphony, discussed above. The struggle is evident
in its simplest form in the unaccompanied passage for two flutes which
leads into the second subject area (see Ex. 42).

Ex. 42

This seemingly innocuous passage which, as I have remarked above, never
returns after its two consecutive appearances early in the symphony, is in
fact of great significance for the work as a whole. The axial note which has
so far appeared as A sharp is now enharmonically reinterpreted, and
Sibelius avoids using it as the leading-note of B minor, even though the
phrase begins on B and ends with the tonic chord of that key. Instead of
acting as the leading-note of B minor and moving upwards by a semitone,

it first moves down to A,[7] and then (in a modal cadence like those discussed at the beginning of Chapter VIII) up to B natural, so creating the feeling that the 'normal' leading-note treatment of A sharp is being replaced by a new and more modal treatment. Two bars later the same axial note is used to modulate to the dominant, so that although two alternative interpretations of the note are shown to be possible, only the one which accepts it as B flat is used for the present; and the influence of B flat is to grow very much stronger as the work progresses. The charge that such enharmonic changes cannot be perceived by the audience and are therefore unimportant is countered by the fact that Sibelius is careful to write A sharp in phrases which rise to B, but B flat where the music falls onto A: it seems clear that the composer himself regarded such changes as significant.

Though Sibelius' exposition ends, as a classical exposition would, in the dominant, the semitone fall F sharp-F natural is heard in the harmony. This progression, with the F sharp being immediately contradicted by the natural, is of considerable importance later: it governs the opening of the development section (page 11, bar 8), which is in F major and begins (using the phrase shown in Ex. 41) with a long F natural, unaccompanied on the oboe. It clearly derives from the B flat-A figure of Ex. 42, and it follows a motif (see Ex. 6) embodying the rising semitone that had resulted from the interpretation as A sharp of the one axial note foreign to the tonic key. This upward tendency is much weaker throughout the work than the downward one in which B flat falls to A. F major, the key with which the development section opens, could, of course, easily accommodate B flat, but it does not do so for long: this important axial note only returns much later, though with great power and using the phrase shown in Ex. 41, at page 19; repeated D's—another axial note—again appear in the bass: the missing note of the three is supplied soon afterwards (see Ex. 43).

Ex. 43

The attempt to combine three axial notes which defy combination in terms of classical tonality is here evident, as it was in chordal terms in Ex. 40. There is an additional point of some importance: the effect of the falling semitone, again making F sharp (actually written as G flat) into F natural, is that of turning the major third into a minor one, a useful device, since B flat can the more easily be accommodated when D is interpreted as a minor key. The music of Ex. 43 is repeated a major third lower on pages 21 and 22, so that the same three notes are given new functions while remaining in relationship with each other. It is at this point in the first movement that (augmented triads apart) the notes are brought into the closest relationship with each other: after this point the F sharp becomes a pedal note, so that pedals have now been heard on all three axial notes, D, B flat and F sharp; and the music returns to D, having completed the circle. The passage forms a microcosm of the tonal scheme of the symphony as a whole.

The influence of the new tonality and the resolution of some of the tension it had set up earlier in the movement are clearly evident in the recapitulation. The presence of B flat at several points (on pages 28–30) gives a minor flavour to the start of the recapitulation, and the pizzicato figure conforms to the axial tonality. The phrase shown in Ex. 41 also conforms by beginning on a long F sharp, and this time the pedal note underneath is also F sharp (there is, of course, an A sharp above the pedal, at the top of the string parts): by being in B minor at this point, the theme also resolves the tonal struggle in a more classical way, since B minor is a key much closer to the tonic than that in which it had appeared in the exposition. There is a resolution on two levels at work here: the two rival elements of the second subject in the exposition—the 'classical' dominant tendency and the 'axial' tonality—are resolved into a single tonal passage in the recapitulation. At Letter Q (on page 32) for example, the theme which had been announced in F sharp minor in the exposition is brought back in the tonic's relative (B minor)—a resolution in the classical sense: at the same time the important notes of the theme are made to fit into the 'axial' tonal scheme, F sharp and D being prominent. It need hardly be said that this is a stroke of great genius.

The F sharp-F natural progression referred to above is itself resolved, by implication, in the harmony at the end of the theme just discussed, where (on page 36, bars 3–6) a chord of F major eventually moves onto one of D major: this forms a neat resolution of a passage which had appeared in the dominant at the end of the exposition. Nevertheless, the F sharp-F natural progression which occurs in the harmony at the end of the exposition becomes a similar movement from B flat to A at the end of the movement as a whole. This minor flavour at the end of the first movement gives a clear indication to the listener that the symphonic argument is not yet complete: the power of B flat is, indeed, felt to grow stronger in the next two movements, so that D major is thrust almost completely out of sight.

The tonal structure of the first movement of Sibelius' Second Symphony is paralleled by the composer's treatment of his thematic material: this provides an interesting contrast with the classical manner of working, in which, usually, themes are first presented as a whole, then broken down into fragments for purposes of development, and finally reassembled. Sibelius here announces fragments—fragments which have melodic formulae and rhythmic devices in common, to be sure, but which are nevertheless presented as fragments—and these are built up into a long continuously melodic passage at the end of the development section before being recapitulated in a new way: the original fragments are still fragments, though several of them now appear in a new contrapuntal combination, making this section a shorter one than the exposition.[8] It is hardly surprising that, after such a process of development, the themes are themselves subjected to change in some details: as with characters in a tragedy, themes can hardly be expected to come through the turmoil of the development as though nothing had happened to them. Both the exposition and the whole opening movement of Sibelius' Second Symphony end with music which is similar to that at the beginning of the work: the usual description of this movement as being in 'arch' form is, therefore, not wholly satisfactory. The striking parallel with the tonal procedures will be immediately obvious: the classical exposition with its settled tonic and dominant was followed by a development in which many keys were used before the re-establishment of the tonic for the recapitulation section. In the first movement of his Second Symphony, in addition to reversing the normal thematic process, Sibelius reverses this tonal procedure also. In the exposition a tension is set up between the axial notes: in the development section a tonal language is used which can contain all three notes, and in the recapitulation the feeling of the opening returns, though with some transpositions of exposition material from one axial note to another and some new harmonic colouring which results from the steadily growing importance of B flat.

The idea of building fragments towards a unified whole in the development section before returning them to something nearer their original shape in the recapitulation can be applied also to rhythm and orchestration, which are fragmentary in the exposition and recapitulation, but built up into a more continuous form in the centre of the movement. For this reason the 'arch-shape' description, despite the reservations mentioned above, is perhaps more apt than it appears when the skeleton form of first and second subjects is all that is taken into consideration: the logic expressed in this movement makes it by far the most satisfying of the Second Symphony.

The slow movement is in D minor, the tonic minor of the symphony as a whole. G major would have been the normal 'classical' key to use here, but the key actually used has the advantage that it contains two of the symphony's three axial notes: whereas the key of the first movement had contained D and F sharp, with B flat standing somewhat outside the 'normal' scale of D, the key of the slow movement contains D and B flat. This is the result of the growing importance of B flat already noticed; and that note is introduced as early as the second bar of the movement. The effect of the note in making the key minor is also evident throughout this movement: indeed, the piece consists of a struggle of titanic proportions between the various axial notes. If the first movement was merely discussion, the second is total warfare. Much of the material here derives from the rival methods of handling A sharp or B flat: the rising and the falling semitones are common. Attempts to establish F sharp, and the major tonalities which must result from its establishment, are continually thwarted. F sharp does, indeed, appear as the tonic of the second section (page 45), the key being major so that A sharp (B flat) can also be included. Several phrases of the long tune of this section make their own attempt at a tonality which will include the three axial notes (see Ex. 44).

 Ex. 44

The solution is that the notes will fit into a minor key of which one of the pivotal notes is the leading-note (here it is B minor, heard briefly). The appearance of prominent D naturals in the strings denies the acceptance of the key of F sharp which has been suggested by a firm cadence (page 46, bars 2–4), and a violent passage follows. This passage is unsettled as to tonality and ends in an indecisive way (on page 47), but the triads of B flat (actually written as A sharp) and F sharp are clearly heard, with D natural present as the upper note of the swirling string figure. The opening D minor theme then reappears in F sharp minor, because the prominent D, when combined with a tonic F sharp, suggests that key, as does the momentary triumph of the B flat-A figure. The movement can now only be satisfactorily rounded off by a return to D. This is achieved by increasing yet again the importance of B flat, though it is some time before the influence of G flat or F sharp is overcome. In the bars around Letter I on page 54, for example, there is a clear struggle between G flat and F natural; and although the second subject had been in a major key (F sharp) because of the power of A sharp, the power of that same note reinterpreted as B flat insists that this subject be recapitulated in D minor rather than D major. It is with new harmony and very sombre orchestration that the theme reappears on page 58. Ex. 44, now transposed to its new pitch, still includes the pivotal notes, but, over a bass D, F sharp is used in the accompaniment and B flat in the tune: this changing of the function of each of the axial notes by transposing a passage by a major third was also, it will be remembered, a feature of the development section in the first movement. This passage, which inevitably has a G minor feeling, is much extended in comparison with its first appearance. The attempt to establish a firm D major cadence at the end of it (on page 63) is thwarted by the prominence of B flat in the strings, and a further violent section of uncertain tonality, which includes clear F sharp and D triads as well as a prominent B flat in the strings, leads to the coda. Motifs from the movement are heard in disconnected fashion in this passage, and D and B flat are present, but every attempt to find and accommodate G flat or F sharp is frustrated. All major key tendencies are rejected: the figure at bar 2 of page 67, for example, is an uncompromisingly minor version of a cadence figure which has several times earlier in the movement been used in a firm major tonality. The music surrounding it seeks unsuccessfully for the major third, F sharp. The movement ends (after briefly referring to the E flat which has appeared at several points) in a firm D minor, F sharp being utterly rejected in favour of F natural, and the music being of a most sombre minor type.

Sibelius carries the rejection of F sharp due to the power of B flat a stage further by writing the Scherzo in B flat: its opening repetitions of the tonic (followed by the B flat-A semitone already mentioned) emphasize the importance of this note, as do the three loud dotted minim B flats on page 70 (a feature which never returns). G flat and F sharp are also occasionally repeated (page 69, bar 7, and page 70, bar 12, for example), though no more so than many other notes. It is only with the well known Trio section (page 79) that F sharp (now interpreted as a G flat) again claims its importance: the flattening of the tonality beyond the B flat by a further step to G flat will be noticed. The tune, in G flat major, is linked with the tonality of the Scherzo and also with the axial notes by its nine repetitions of B flat, a note which is by now a very strong force in the tonal scheme of the work: the repetition of the major third of a chord, of course, also recalls the opening of the first movement. Moreover, as in the opening movement, the first accidental of the Trio is again the one axial note which has not been sounded: indeed, the augmented triad G flat-B flat-D natural is an enharmonic version of the one shown in Ex. 40. This very same chord is the one on which the first Trio ends: the chord serves to link it to a repetition of the Scherzo section in B flat (though B natural is heard in the brass at first in an attempt to upset the powerful hold of that note). Sibelius'

approach to F sharp via the flat side tonalities ensures that it is heard as a
flat key (G flat). This weakens any function which F sharp might have in
establishing D major. There is, however, a passing tendency to reinterpret
the note as F sharp, for the brass, taking it as a dominant, attempt to begin
the repeat of the Scherzo in B minor. B natural, as I have pointed out in
Chapter IV, plays a large part in the final establishment of D major,
replacing B flat; but it is too early in the work for this tendency to be felt
strongly here. The similarity of the processes used by Sibelius in this
symphony with those used by Beethoven in his Ninth Symphony is evident.

A second Trio is also in G flat, and a long crescendo links it to the Finale.
If D major is to reappear in the Finale, two interlinked tendencies must be
reversed at this point. The first is the tendency of the tonality to flatten.
The second is the continual interpretation of the third axial note as B flat
instead of A sharp by means of its appearance in the B flat-A figure, and
the consequent B flat or D minor feeling. The process of reversing these
tendencies begins (on page 95) with the rising phrases and the appearance
of many ascending semitones in each of the string figures: and these two
features play a prominent part in the link between the Scherzo and the
Finale.

The fourth movement opens in a blaze of D major, a key not heard since
the first movement: the repetition of notes is here given to the trombones,
and the growing importance of rising semitones is attested by the movement
of the decorated pedal in the bass. Several short motifs are given out, one
of which (in the horns) moves briefly back into the axial key of B flat; but
this is balanced by another in F sharp minor, during which B flat first falls
to A, and is then reinterpreted as A sharp, so that the tonality can move
back to D major (pages 102 and 103). With the triumph of the A sharp
interpretation of this axial note, an extended version of the opening tune is
heard in a more firm D major, reharmonized, though the augmented triad
of Ex. 40 appears, as well as a brief modulation to F sharp, just a single bar
before finally cadencing on D: B flat is at this point only sufficiently powerful to act in its enharmonic guise of A sharp (see Ex. 45).

 Ex. 45

A long second subject leads to F sharp minor, and a plaintive tune in the
woodwind is many times repeated above string scales which, while they
always have F sharp on the strong beat, continually rise to D and fall away
again, making a feature of the two axial notes which are most important

to the Finale. The repetitions end in a more triumphant F sharp major, showing the pull of the third axial note, A sharp. D is still present in effect, however, as the brass phrase which follows (page 111, bars 2 and 4) includes a D natural, and the subsequent string passage which soars through an octave and a half moves towards D major in a series of chords that start and end in F sharp major. The use of continual repetition of a phrase during the second subject reflects the repetition of single notes which has been such a feature of earlier parts of the symphony.

One of the functions of the development section in this Finale must, of course, be to return from F sharp to D major: the use of rising phrases, and especially of rising semitones, provides this, as at the end of the Scherzo. The pull of both F sharp and D is clearly evident just before the recapitulation (page 119) where A sharp is three times sounded against the dominant pedal (A) which has been set up so as to prepare for the recapitulation, a grinding dissonance with the upward resolution of A sharp onto B natural which fails to upset the power of F sharp and D in establishing the tonic major. (An inability of the strings to reach F sharp is noticeable on page 117.) The first subject returns with a new accompanying B natural-A figure, a reinterpretation of the falling semitone which is symptomatic of the gradual rejection of the B flat-A figure so important earlier in the work.[9] As one might by now expect, the second subject is in B flat, balancing the F sharp used at the corresponding point in the exposition: this soon moves to D minor, and the same string figure as before many times rises from D (on the strong beat) to B flat and falls back, while the woodwind phrases are many times repeated. The passage is extended by comparison with the exposition, so that when the cadence in the major is eventually reached (after many in D minor) the feeling of achievement and release is much greater: the revised scoring (which includes brass) also helps to create this feeling. The point about the axial notes could scarcely be made more clearly (see Ex. 46).

Ex. 46

The balancing effect of this scheme is plain: the gradual flattening of the tonality, in the second and third movements, under the influence of B flat is compensated for in the Finale by the 'sharpening effect' of the music shown in Ex. 46, especially when one considers the fact that these two passages appear after long stretches of music in the minor key. This simple device adds yet more power to the growing importance of F sharp and to the return of the tonic major at the end of the symphony. A final point about the progressions in Ex. 46 is that the power of B flat (in its enharmonic guise of A sharp) to draw the music into F sharp major in the exposition is overcome in the recapitulation, where D minor, a key resulting from the use of the repeated string scales which make a feature of D and B flat, is turned into D major because F sharp has now at last taken over the important function which A sharp (or B flat) had exercised earlier. A final reference to B flat is heard in the trombones on page 142, but the triumphant D major, with all clouds occasioned by the presence of minor tonalities and B flats dispelled, persists until the end. The final plagal cadence—used for a similar purpose to that at the end of the first movement of Sibelius' Third Symphony, which is discussed later in this chapter—makes a feature of B natural, the 'resolution' of the B flat which has been banished from the music along with the other feelings of minor tonality.

The knowledge of this tonal plan helps one to understand the seemingly endless repetitions of the Finale: the struggle between B flat and the key of D major results in a struggle between D minor and D major. Perhaps this knowledge is insufficient to save the movement from giving the impression of bombast which many commentators find in it. To be a great work, it should, of course, be viable as pure sound as well as intellectual construction: if it fails in one area, the other will not save it. Robert Layton[10] finds the Finale of the Second the weakest movement in all Sibelius' symphonies. Personally, I prefer it to the last three movements of the First Symphony (which are loosely constructed, and stand outside the processes of argument so ably demonstrated in that symphony's first movement), because the Finale of the Second does, in an impressive way, clearly resolve the tensions set up by the axial notes. This view opposes the one often expressed that because of its tunes the movement is acceptable (it has become something approaching a Finnish National Anthem, since it is thought to express so well that country's aspirations), but that it fails as a piece of musical architecture. Most would agree, though, that the first movement of this symphony is the finest and the most original of the work. The advance in symphonic technique shown in Sibelius' Second Symphony as compared with his First is comparable to the advance made by Beethoven between his Second Symphony and the 'Eroica'.

The Use of the Tritone: Sibelius' Third Symphony

The sound of the sharpened fourth seems to have haunted Sibelius almost throughout his life. In two works, the Third and Fourth Symphonies, the tritone is used not only for its innate quality of sound (as it is, for instance, in the slow movement of the Second Symphony), but for purposes of construction. It is a sign of growing maturity in a symphonic composer that

all the elements of a particular piece should be thoroughly integrated.
While the use of the tritone in the Fourth Symphony has provided a fertile
field of investigation for analysts, its importance to the Third has seldom
been discussed.[11]

Sibelius' Third Symphony has several thematic devices which contribute
to the feeling of unity (see Ex. 47). All are announced within the first few
bars of the work, except for Ex. 47c, which is found mainly in the Finale.

It is characteristic of great symphonies that the features which govern the
unfolding logic of their works are announced as early as possible, usually at
the outset. This is as true of Sibelius as it is of Beethoven. In Sibelius' Third
Symphony, the first notes outside the scale of C major are heard in bars 14
and 15 (see Ex. 48).[12]

Ex. 48

With kind permission of Robert Lienau Music Publishers, Berlin

G sharp, the first chromatic note heard, attains importance later in the
work, and is used as the tonic of the second movement; but the prominent
tritone C-F sharp (the latter note being marked 'rinforzando' for emphasis)
is a more important feature, which Sibelius also emphasizes by the manner
of its introduction: the music immediately prior to this would lead the
listener to expect a C natural on the first beat of the second bar of Ex. 48
(the progression does, indeed, occur in the bass at this point), and the
surprise which is occasioned by the appearance of F sharp instead draws
attention to that note. The far-reaching implications of this passage have
apparently escaped analysts because of the frequent occurrences of the
sharpened fourth elsewhere in Sibelius' work: such a love of the interval as
he clearly had is good reason for using it as the foundation of a symphonic
structure. Once the feature is noticed (and Sibelius has made the point so
clearly that it is difficult to see how it can fail to be noticed), the fact that
many other F sharps occur in the exposition of this C major movement will
also be evident. Although F naturals also appear, the description of the
tonality of the opening group as basically 'Lydian C major' or 'C with a
tendency to use F sharp' is a fair one. The progression C-D-E-F sharp, in
fact, is used to link the first and second subjects (page 7, bars 1–6).

The Third Symphony is the work in which Sibelius turned his back on
the large romantic and national form of the symphony, and in which he

created a work which has always been admired for its classical sense of proportion.[13] In particular, it represents a reaction against the enormous slowing-down of the pace of music evident in the second half of the 19th century, as for example in Bruckner's Fourth Symphony discussed above. The more classical style of Sibelius' Third Symphony (as compared with that of the first two) calls for a more classical treatment of tonality: indeed, the progression from C to F sharp at this point in the work (page 7, bars 1–6) forms a parallel to the modulation from tonic to dominant in the classical symphony, a change of tonality made in order that the second subject might provide an area of contrast with the opening by being in a key one degree sharper.[14] Sibelius honours this classical convention by writing a new key signature (of one sharp) for the second subject, though the music itself has to be one degree sharper still since the first group had already included many F sharps. Hence, Sibelius writes a second subject in B minor—a key one degree sharper than 'Lydian C major'. The second group nevertheless ends in the classically 'correct' key of G, since (pages 8–10) the C natural-F sharp tritone plays a considerable part (see Ex. 49).

Ex. 49

and other flat-side keys

The development begins with a question posed by the composer: Is the F a sharp or a natural, and is the C a sharp or a natural? This question is a corollary to the one which asks: Is the tritone to be resolved by moving the C up to C sharp or the F sharp down to F natural (see Ex. 50)?

Ex. 50

With kind permission of Robert Lienau Music publishers, Berlin

The tritone occurs several times harmonically, and soon afterwards its 'accidentals' are, as it were, reversed so that C sharp and F natural occur together: the C sharp has itself been suggested by the new tonality of G, since it is in the same tritonal relationship to it as F sharp had been to the tonic of the movement. The logical outcome of using the original tritone in close proximity to the interval C sharp (interpreted as D flat)-F is the key of D flat, a tonality which is reached on page 12 of the score. Ex. 49 makes clear the progressions involved: F sharp and C can, of course, form part of the dominant seventh chord of G major, and it is towards this key that the exposition eventually moves: it is, however, on pages 11–12 that F sharp/G flat and C occur along with C sharp/D flat and F natural, the tritone here being reinterpreted as belonging to the dominant seventh chord of D flat. The progressions are not, of course, presented in the bald terms of Ex. 49: they are merely tendencies heard at certain points in the music.[15]

In the recapitulation the second subject (written now, of course, with a C major signature) follows classical convention by being brought into line with the tonality of the first subject. In this instance, since the first subject is in 'C with an F sharp', the second subject is in E minor, and this has the added advantage that it recalls the first chromatic phrase from which the tritonal relationship derived, which could itself be interpreted as E minor (Ex. 48, second full bar quoted). This does not quite resolve the tonal ambiguity inherent in the C-F sharp relationship: that resolution takes place in the coda, starting on page 29 of the score. Here Sibelius poses the problem (in a passage similar to that shown in Ex. 50) in terms of 'Is the key to be one with an F sharp (G major or E minor) or is it to be F major (C being its dominant, and F an ideal resolution of the F sharp)?' The chorale-like passage at rehearsal number 16 narrows the choice to E minor or F (with a cadence in C), and the end of the movement dispenses entirely with F sharps. The three final cadences clinch the matter in a way which is brilliant in its simplicity: two plagal cadences in E minor (which can easily be also interpreted as secondary cadences in C, since they do not contain an F sharp) are followed by a final plagal cadence in C, the F natural-C of the progression resolving, for this movement at least, the tritone stated so clearly at the opening. The cadence has a further structural function: this final harmony of the movement is the same as the first harmony heard at the opening of the work.

One other effect of the tritone is apparent in this first movement: the C-F sharp interval is used (page 5) in conjunction with the tritone A-E flat which interlocks with it to form a diminished seventh chord—a chord used here to cadence directly onto C major. Though subsidiary in importance, the A-E flat interval is used at times in place of the primary 'parent' tritone: the reduction of the beginning of the development section to bare statements of A-E flat with a few wisps of G major is a case in point, and the passage provides relief from the 'parent' tritone while keeping the basic tonal argument in view. In the recapitulation the original diminished seventh chord appears as it did in the exposition, though it is followed immediately (page 21) by another chord which opposes it, and uses instead B and F with D and A flat, a diminished seventh chord which is used to resolve onto a chord of F major. The tritones of this new diminished seventh chord (F and B, D and A flat) during the remaining pages of the movement balance the effect of the opening set of tritones, establishing an F tendency which strongly counteracts that of F sharp. The final plagal cadence, with its prominent F major chord following a passage with quite strong subdominant leanings, is not the only outcome of this tendency, for the A flat-D tritone suggests in addition the tonalities which dominate the second movement.

The second movement is in G sharp minor: this might at first seem a rather extraordinary key to choose for the slow movement of a C major symphony, yet a moment's thought about the tonal processes in the opening movement shows that the choice is quite logical. Ex. 49 has shown two ways in which Sibelius uses his pivotal notes C and F sharp in the first movement to create tonal areas opposed to C; but F sharp has a further function in that it acts as the dominant of B. This is clearly evident at the start of the second subject (page 7), where the prominence of F sharp leads naturally to B minor. The note B maintains its importance from this point onwards: this is obvious on page 10 of the score. Such a prominence of B can be used for a further structural purpose: it can be reinterpreted as a leading-note, and thus prepare for the recapitulation: this function is evident on page 18. In order to achieve it, a tritone above B must be sounded so as to form part of the dominant seventh chord of C major, the resulting F natural cancelling the F sharp of the original augmented fourth. The F-B tritone is clearly introduced on page 14 and is used to start the move back towards C major. The same interval again replaces the 'parent' tritone in the recapitulation at the link between the first and second subjects (pages 22-3) so that the octave progression C-D-E-F sharp of the exposition is 'resolved' to one of F natural-G-A-B in the recapitulation. The prominence of B is emphasized by the timpani (which simultaneously show the pull of C against it by alternating between the two notes) as the second subject begins, and also by the woodwind which accompany it— two elements of structural significance which did not occur in the exposition. This prominence is clearly questioned by the strong B flats in the coda to the first movement (pages 29-30): since the F sharp which was used as a dominant has been resolved onto F natural, it follows that B natural should likewise move downwards by a semitone. This new resolution of F sharp onto F is in its turn the result of interpreting one of the notes of the 'parent' tritone as a dominant, though it is now C and not F sharp which is being so treated. The processes are shown in Ex. 51.

Ex. 51

(dotted lines show
dominant - tonic tendencies)

With the prominence of B in mind, the choice of the relative minor of B for the slow movement is perfectly logical. One way of continuing the debate for ascendancy between B and C is to make them respectively the minor and major third of a key: thus a G sharp tonic has an added attraction for Sibelius, who makes the point very succinctly by starting and ending the movement on an open fifth, neither B nor B sharp being present. The opening phrases of the tune stress B, but one or two excursions into G sharp major show the pull of B sharp,[16] and the cadences in divided 'cellos between rehearsal numbers 6 and 7 (pages 37–8) make a feature of alternating B sharp with B. The tritone's importance is felt again in the move to D major and its relative minor at the centre of the movement (during which one phrase moves into the work's tonic, C major), and in the return by way of A flat. This use of A flat major for a while shows the power of C in its contest against B, though the prominence of the latter note eventually ensures that the recapitulation is in G sharp minor. Although the movement ends in this key (with the third omitted as if to imply that the struggle between B and C has been inconclusive), Sibelius prepares the listener for the return of C major by writing a phrase (which he immediately repeats to end the slow movement) whose tritone B-E sharp is a most characteristic interval: this enharmonic reinterpretation of the B-F interval (also used in the first movement to reintroduce C major) is reminiscent of similar enharmonic treatments of 'axial' notes and tonalities in the Second Symphony. Sibelius was clearly building on the experience of his handling of keys in that earlier work by replacing the thirds evident in its tonal scheme by tritones in the Third Symphony. Nevertheless, the work is much more than a mere extension of the earlier idea to a different intervallic structure.

Tritones are used in a most convincing way to re-establish the main tonality of the slow movement after the digression to D major and its relative minor. Only three diminished seventh chords, of course, exist, since all others are merely inversions of this basic set; and each of the three contains interlocking tritones, though only two of these chords include intervals used for purposes of construction in this particular work. Nevertheless, on page 41 of the score Sibelius uses all three diminished seventh chords in succession, and each in turn resolves onto A flat, which is then reinterpreted as G sharp for the rest of the movement.

One of the first functions of the Finale must be to overcome the importance which G sharp has attained because of its position as the main tonic of the slow movement; or at least to incorporate or resolve this note into the tonality of the last movement. The opening octave G natural begins this process immediately, and the clear tritone F-B in the harmony of the phrase (echoing the B-E sharp of the end of the second movement) also helps to re-establish C major. Nevertheless, the tonality is still open to debate: with some uncertainty (evident in the continually changing tempo markings) the original C-F sharp and B-F natural tritones as well as several prominent A flats (the G sharp of the second movement) are announced.

The idea of using uncertain rhythm to accompany doubts about tonality, which was to be the basis of Sibelius' next symphony, may well have been suggested by this passage. On pages 47–8 a passage (marked 'tacet ad lib' in some editions of the score) in the first violins wanders between the various 'pivotal' notes and keys of the work; B, G sharp, D, F sharp and C: the continual references to the importance of G sharp and B in this passage are due to the weight achieved by those notes in the second movement, a point made clear by the device of quoting the theme of the slow movement in the flutes at the same place.[17] The C-A flat and C-G sharp intervals just after this make the same point (see page 48), as the quotation of the slow movement theme in the oboe again testifies.

So complex is the system of tonal stresses and counterstresses in this symphony that a reminder of them may well be of some assistance. Ex. 52 shows the relevant forces in diagrammatic form.

Ex. 52

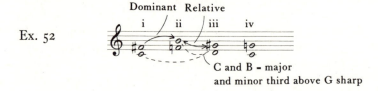

The F sharp of the 'parent' tritone (i) becomes the dominant of B (ii), a key also made important by virtue of its use of two sharps as compared with the 'C Lydian' of the first subject of the opening movement. The note B now gains great importance, not only as the leading-note of C (with the tritone above it, F, helping the resolution onto C in addition to cancelling the effect of F sharp) but as a tonal rival to it. This gives rise to the use of G sharp (iii) as the tonic of the second movement, and the use of a tritone from G sharp (D) in that movement logically follows the pattern of i and ii in the Example. The tritones ii and iii do, in fact, form a diminished seventh chord when played together: this colourful chord, so overworked in the 19th century and so often used purely for its emotive effect, assumes considerable importance in the structure of Sibelius' Third Symphony. The chord can, of course, be used to resolve onto F sharp, and the import-ance of this is not lost on Sibelius. The device of using a single chord to suggest modulation to two different tonal areas is, indeed, a further extension of the manner of working shown in Ex. 49.

The importance of G sharp is first felt in the Finale at the point where it leads to A minor (pages 48–9), and then just before rehearsal number 4 (page 51) where the C-A flat progression introduces F minor and hints at the most important tune of the movement. Statements of the 'parent' tritone interrupt the establishment of F minor, though this key arrives at the end of page 52 (the tritone iii of Ex. 52 being in the bass to recall the

scheme of the second movement and suggest the reason for the use of
F minor) with a full statement of the new theme in the horns. The previous
C-A flat leaps which have led up to this entry make the long tune sound a
logical outcome of the previous music, since it makes considerable use of
the same interval: one almost has the impression that the tune has been
going on unheard in the background before it reaches the ear.

At the beginning of the development section Sibelius again poses the
question: Is the F to be natural or sharp, and is the C to be natural or
sharp? (See Ex. 53.)

The result of this query is a highly chromatic passage in which various keys
(F sharp minor, C sharp minor and A minor) are tried out and rejected:
F sharp minor and A minor are, indeed, both introduced with tritones ii
and iii of Ex. 52. The problem is restated just before the C major recapitulation (a condensed version of the exposition). (See Ex. 54.)

Ex. 54

Exs. 53, 54 and 55
with kind permission
of Robert Lienau
Music Publishers,
Berlin

In the final subject (the chorale-like theme which is used from page 60 to
the end), the expected G and E minor cadences (which would involve
acceptance of F sharp rather than F natural) are almost always thwarted
by music which remains in C major. The occasional E minor cadences (as
on page 63, bar 12) are immediately contradicted by F naturals which
cancel the effect of the F sharp, and often by tritone iii of Ex. 52, the
diminished seventh chord frequently being used to modulate back into
C major (see Ex. 55). The appearance of the tritone D-A flat here serves a
similar purpose to that already described in dealing with the recapitulation of the first movement.

Ex. 55

A most prominent feature of the tune is the entrance of instruments on F sharp against the background of C major (and often after the appearance of tritone ii of Ex. 52): attention is clearly drawn to the F sharp by introductory runs and 'rinforzando' markings. The music nevertheless remains in C, and the resolution of the F sharp into pure C major is made clear by the brass in the last four bars of the Finale, where the notes G-E-C are given out fortissimo in octaves. G sharp is thus likewise resolved onto G natural (as is shown in Ex. 52), and the prominence of B, still evident in the string parts on the final two pages and in the first trombone just before the end, is overcome by resolution up to C. This idea of a resolution of tension between B and C was to play an important part in Sibelius' Seventh Symphony many years later.

The Use of the Tritone: Sibelius' Fourth Symphony and Tapiola

If one were not aware of the structure of the Fourth Symphony, one might perhaps be forgiven for thinking that the Third approaches the *ne plus ultra* of symphonic workings-out of the implications of the tritone. Gerald Abraham claims that 'in clearness and simplicity of outline, it [the first movement of the Third Symphony] is comparable with a Haydn or Mozart first movement . . . nevertheless, the organic unity of the movement is far in advance of anything in the classical masters; and even the general architecture is held together in a way that had classical precedents but had never before, I think, been so fully developed';[18] though perhaps something of an overstatement, this is not entirely without substance. In the Third Symphony, a melodious and happy work (C minor, for instance, seldom appears), the tritone acts as an element in the construction of the music: in the Fourth, a serious and tragic work written when the composer was in fear of his life while undergoing treatment for cancer of the throat, it acts as a destructive force. This point, I think, has not been sufficiently stressed by analysts, who have, quite rightly, shown how the augmented fourth appears in almost every theme of the piece. Indeed, the tritone is so frequently found in this work that it seems too obvious a device to use for purposes of unification: symphonic composers usually take great care that the listener shall be *subconsciously* aware of the unifying devices in their work, and few such writers have ever discussed them (they may, indeed, be only subconsciously aware of some of them themselves). The fact that not all the themes in Sibelius' Fourth Symphony contain a tritone; that whereas the melodic formula A-B-D-C (which I shall call *x* in this discussion) sometimes outlines an augmented fourth, it is at other times diatonic; the fact that each movement has some ideas which are not in any way found in the others; and the presence of a slow chromatic end to the Scherzo (a passage which seems to have baffled many commentators)— all these details make it seem that thematic analysis, as in the Third Symphony, will not yield the full explanation of the symphony's structure.

I have already said that good symphonists announce their intentions at the outset of each work. What, then, happens in the Fourth Symphony? We hear a clear tritone in the phrase C-D-F sharp, to be sure, and F sharp alternates with E over a pedal C for a while. Clearly, then, the tritone will be an important force. But what is the rhythm? We cannot tell when the next note will start (unless, score in hand, we watch the conductor very carefully), so irregularly do the sounds change. The rhythm only settles to a regular pulse when the C pedal ceases, thus removing the tritone. Here is the clue for which we are searching. The tritone is the interval which most easily destroys tonality:[19] the destruction of tonality in this work goes hand in hand with the destruction of rhythm, and also of what can best be described as 'melodic flow.'

In tracing the effects of the opening augmented fourth C-F sharp through the work as a whole, one notices first that this tritone sets up an opposition between the two key centres of C (or A minor) and F sharp: the rhythm is settled and regular when the music is clearly in one key or the other. In other places (that is, where the effect of the tritone is in force, drawing the tonality between one centre and the other) this regularity of the rhythm is disturbed: thus the brass chords on pages 3 and 4[20] are mainly off the beat, whereas the string figures in A minor on page 2 and in F sharp on page 5 are regularly on the strong pulses. In the development section (pages 6–10) the effect of the tritone is most clearly felt, the music here being completely atonal, and augmented fourths very numerous in the shape of x (among others). The complete destruction of tonality at this point is paralleled by the complete overthrow of the regularity of rhythm. There is much movement on weak semiquavers, but even these are not uniform, so that no regular pulsation (even on weak beats) shall be set up. Only with the return of tonality does the regular beat re-establish itself. In the last five bars of the movement, which Sibelius has so far led us to believe will end in A major, a C natural-D figure in the 'cellos and basses recalls the opening of the symphony, but breaks off before the expected F sharp; and the tritone versions of x again unsettle the tonality. There is a corresponding uncertainty about the rhythm, the phrases moving on weak quaver beats. The resolution of B flat onto the final A, repeated several times in these bars, is a feature which has considerable importance in the next movement.

The effect of the tritone as a destructive force is yet more clearly evident in the second movement, a Scherzo in F major. After only a few phrases of the main tune, a series of tritones upsets the 'flow' of the melody and, with a 'poco ritard.', the rhythm also falters, to pick up again as the tonality and the tune return. The C-G flat-F phrase which recurs three times in this passage (page 15, bars 22–6) has two notes—G flat and F—doubled by a solo oboe. The falling semitone recalls the repeated B flat-A motif at the end of the first movement; but, more important, it clearly makes the point that G flat is here the flat supertonic of F: the importance of this is realized only at the end of the movement. The next tritone to appear (a harmonic one this time, in the final chord of page 15) results in another rhythmic upset. The duple time section on page 16 is a feature which seems to have escaped notice by commentators: certainly it is difficult to account for until one realizes its connection with the tritone and tonality. It is a passage which becomes quite atonal, uses many augmented fourths, and is followed by long chords in the wind and brass which are without tonality or regular pulse. With a repeat of the same C-G flat-F shape mentioned above (the falling semitone being again picked out by the solo oboe), F major returns, and with it the main tune. As before, a chord containing F sharp (actually written as G flat) and C causes the rhythm to falter: the two notes act as part of the dominant seventh chord of D flat, and it is in this key that the Trio section (though Sibelius does not so call it) begins, 'tranquillo'. It is, like the Scherzo, a short section, and it ends in the key of G flat with a misleading return of the main Scherzo tune in that same key. After seven bars the tonality slides into the 'correct' key of F major (with a valedictory G flat kick from the 'cellos), a semitone progression which has not only been carefully prepared, but which also emphasizes the point that G flat (F sharp) is the flat supertonic of F major, the key of this movement.

The rest of the movement, as far as the shake on F and E at Letter K (on page 22, a passage which some commentators regard as the real Trio), is normal, leaving one to suspect that the ending is imminent, F being firmly established and thus, by implication, F sharp (G flat) being accepted as the flat supertonic. Then—just as Brahms had done (for completely different reasons) in the second movement of his *Ein Deutsches Requiem*—Sibelius plays on the audience's anticipation of this ending and writes an unexpected passage. He introduces one of the most extraordinary sections of music in the work by way of a coda, again using the tritone C-F sharp as a catalyst. First of all the F is reinterpreted as E sharp in order to introduce F sharp minor: the upsetting of the tonality is again paralleled by the upsetting of the rhythm, which now becomes 'doppio piu lento' and most unlike a Scherzo. Since the tonality and rhythm falter, the 'melodic flow' of the music does so too: material from the Scherzo proper is used, but it appears in a much more dissonant and chromatic context here. A further effect of the tritone is that the phrases alternate between F sharp major and C major, and that a double pedal on F and B natural is used at the end. The music returns to F only in the last two bars: the note is not harmonized, and is played softly, so that if the final F is interpreted by the listener as a tonic at all, it is certainly not felt to be one that is very firmly established. There is, in fact, a tendency for the note to sound as though it were an E sharp (that is, the leading-note of F sharp), so insistent has the coda been in proving the superior power of the F sharp over the F natural. The destructive force of the tritone is here at its height: the Scherzo's rhythm, melody and tonality disintegrate completely in face of it.

In a sense, the slow movement (the piece which Sibelius requested should be played at his funeral) seeks to re-establish the 'lost music' of the Scherzo: in other words, this movement works in the opposite direction, from atonality and unequal rhythm towards tonality and regular rhythm. It is in C sharp minor, though the opening chord of A minor recalls the tonic of the symphony as a whole, and the C natural is one note of the pivotal tritone. This note is gradually reinterpreted as B sharp in this movement, as a wonderful, wide-ranging C sharp minor tune develops from the few fragments presented at the beginning of the movement. Here the opening music is mildly atonal: it is triadic in nature, though the triads are unrelated: in parallel fashion, the rhythm is mildly irregular. Tonality and regularity of pulse are restored as the wide-ranging tune is built up: at the end x (with the outline of a tritone) returns to close the movement in a similar way to that in which the first movement had ended, the rhythm again becoming slightly less firmly governed by the regular beats.

The Finale begins in A (or, to be more precise, it begins with a phrase which is in both shape and key reminiscent of one near the end of the third movement, before moving more firmly to A), and the tritone is at first contradicted by being placed alongside a perfect fourth (see Ex. 56).

Ex. 56

This results in a very long stretch of A major in which the rhythm is correspondingly strong and the material tuneful: a few bright notes on the glockenspiel[21] help to underline the stability of the tonic major at this point in the movement. Excursions to E flat (a tritone away) do not upset the flow of the music (even when they appear in some instruments while others continue in A), but the introduction of C major does. This key is heard first soon after the beginning of the development (page 47, bar 12), after a passage in which sections of music in the opposing keys of A and E flat have been getting closer together until their respective tonic chords are themselves opposed in a single bar. A compromise between the two is effected by using the key half-way between them in terms of relative position on the stave and in terms of key signature, C major, which also corresponds to the symphony's own tonic of A minor. A different compromise between A major and E flat is next resorted to (page 48) in a series of grinding chords which can accommodate both these keys (the tritone A-D sharp is present in the viola part on page 48, bars 2–8): the lack of tonal direction which results from this causes a similar change in the rhythm and the melodic lines, slow chromatic suspensions being introduced. This tonal uneasiness between two keys which had at first co-existed well again leads to the appearance of C major, though for a much longer and more powerful passage than previously (pages 50–4). Against the chord of C, F sharp is heard, but it resolves upwards to G, and the glockenspiel helps to emphasize C as a tonal centre: indeed, throughout the Finale its three-note phrase appears with the purpose of emphasizing some important key or other. Again the tonality wanders until a partial recapitulation is reached on page 58. The keys of A and E flat are used again, though E flat claims more of the material and appears at an earlier stage than in the exposition. It is now quickly shown that the two keys cannot exist together, the strings playing in E flat and the wind in A (page 62), the resulting bi-tonality being much more astringent in effect than the less dissonant passage at a similar point in the exposition. Again the C major compromise is reached, the note F sharp being also in evidence (page 63, bottom line).

Here a long coda begins, in which the C-F sharp tritone ushers in the final disintegration of the music of the Finale: on pages 64–5 tonality disappears completely, while scraps of various of the foregoing themes are played loudly in a haphazard way and in an irregular rhythm. There is a brief attempt to establish A major (page 66) and the glockenspiel adds its three-note phrase in an attempt to bolster up this key; but the rest of the movement uses scraps of various themes played in longer notes (that is, the music seems to be slower) than in the Finale proper, in an uncertain tonality, and in a gradual decrescendo. The falling G flat-F of the Scherzo makes several appearances in a harmonized form, and the final bars of the work, in tragic fashion, reach a sombre A minor passage which, since it is undeniably tonal, is also absolutely regular as to rhythm; yet all trace of melody has vanished.

It will be clear from this that I cannot agree with commentators who think that this symphony ends on a note of hope. The tritone has destroyed the music of the work, and left it bereft of melody at the end. This must surely be a reflection of Sibelius' view of the musical trends in Europe at the time this symphony was written (1910–11), soon after the composition of Schoenberg's *Erwartung* and *Five Pieces for Orchestra*, Opus 16[22]—he himself admitted that the piece was a reaction against 'modern trends'. 'Nothing, absolutely nothing of the circus about it', he said. He had never been a great admirer of Schoenberg's music: he said, 'I was one of the first to get hold of Arnold Schoenberg's works for himself. I bought them on Busoni's

advice to learn something. But I learned nothing.'[23] The Fourth Symphony
is usually said to be a reaction against the overblown romanticism of
composers like Richard Strauss—Sibelius once remarked that, whereas
these composers gave the public cocktails, he himself offered them nothing
but pure cold water.[24] Nevertheless, such an intention cannot square with
the actual construction of the work. The symphony may be autobiogra-
phical and connected with his suffering from cancer, or it may be a
reflection of the political situation facing Finland at the time.[25] It is, after
all, characteristic of great works of art that they can be appreciated on
many levels. But one's thoughts on the work return to the musical meaning
of the events that have taken place. This seems clear enough: as an undeniably tonal composer, Sibelius wrote a symphony in which atonality,
in this instance the effect of the tritone, is shown to destroy the very
foundation of music as he understood it—not only the key and formal
structure of the work, but also the melody and the rhythm. This, from his
point of view, was an absolutely exact prophecy of the musical trends in
succeeding years.[26]

Other tonal features of the work which derive from the use of the tritone
also deserve mention before leaving Sibelius' Fourth Symphony. These
features derive, in the main, from the composer's choice of an augmented
fourth which does not include the tonic note of the symphony: C and F
sharp, when used in a work in A minor, have an effect somewhat similar
to that of the axial notes of Sibelius' Second Symphony, discussed above—
the C defines the scale of A as minor, whereas the F sharp tends to suggest
that it is major. The Dorian sound which might be expected to result from
this is actually little used in the Fourth Symphony, the composer not
making full use of its possibilities until the Sixth Symphony.

The struggle between C and F sharp in the Fourth Symphony can be
readily traced throughout the work. The strong opening C defines the key
of A as minor, in spite of the frequent F sharps which follow it: nevertheless,
with many repetitions F sharp grows in strength, pulling the tonality
towards G flat (F sharp) major, and a loud dissonant C sharp (page 3,
bar 6) helps to counter the effect of C natural. The prominent new tritone
A-D sharp, which immediately follows the C sharp's firm suggestion that
the key of A might become major (page 3, bars 10 and 11), recurs with
added power later in the work when the tonic major becomes yet more
clearly established. The appearance of C natural (sometimes written as B
sharp) during the following F sharp major passage does little to upset the
hold of the latter key; and at the recapitulation[27] (page 10) the original
tritone, with F sharp given out more strongly than C natural, introduces
A major, the C being sharpened as that key appears. The ensuing A major
section naturally replaces the F sharp-C tritone of page 5 with the new
tritone A-D sharp: this forms a nice parallel to its previous appearance at a

point where A major had taken over from A minor. The brief coda (page 13) reintroduces the loud bass C natural with which the work had opened, and the expected repeat of the opening phrase stops, significantly, short of F sharp so that the movement ends in the minor, the effect of C overcoming that of F sharp (even though the latter note is used in the repetitions of the final phrase) at the very end of the first movement.

The rejection of F sharp is evident in the choice of F major as the key of the second movement: this key has been well prepared by the B flat-A ending of the first movement, and the fact that the tune of the Scherzo begins with a long A (the tonic pedal from the end of the opening movement) also helps to link the two movements in the listener's mind. The repetition of G flat-F (and the drawing of attention to that progression by its manner of scoring) now takes on a new significance, as each attempt to establish F sharp (G flat) is thwarted by resolution onto F. The long coda of the movement begins by attempting to re-establish F sharp, but after a struggle between that note and C, the movement ends on F natural, even if one feels that it has not been clearly established as a tonic: the tonality is much more clearly 'in the balance' here than at the end of the first movement. To this extent the powerful statements of F sharp in this coda have been successful in reducing the importance of C natural.

The growing power of F sharp is seen in the third movement: here the key is C sharp minor so that, just as the F sharp of the tritone was mutated to F natural for the second movement, so here the C natural is mutated to C sharp. Moreover, a key scheme not unlike the progression of thirds used in Sibelius' Second Symphony is also evident here, the keys being A minor, F, C sharp minor and A major (and minor) in the movements of the Fourth Symphony. Nevertheless, the power of C is not destroyed all at once: the movement, indeed, begins in A minor, though the opening A-D sharp tritone in the flute might suggest that there is a certain tendency towards the use of C sharp, since this particular augmented fourth has so far been heard mostly at points where A major has been established. The A minor opening has a further advantage in that it links the movement more readily in terms of tonality to the F major of the Scherzo. C sharp gradually gains in importance, though there are occasional appearances of C natural (and B sharp), some of them quite prominent; and as the note C sharp gains in power, so the statements of the long tune in C sharp minor also get longer and more powerful, and the tritone A-E flat (D sharp), which has always resulted when C is mutated to C sharp, puts in more and more appearances. The long tune itself, growing from the clarinet phrase in the third bar of the movement, gradually ousts the tritone from its melodic line by using perfect fifths as a prominent feature. That the gaining of a firm tonality, the building up of a tune, and the absence of the tritone, go hand in hand is made clear by Sibelius on several occasions, of which the most obvious can be seen in the two bars preceding Letter D (page 33). As C natural appears to upset the C sharp minor tonality, the 'tune' becomes a mere chromatic wandering, and the accompanying fifths (in the violins) begin to turn into tritones.

The Finale begins with a theme that was deliberately foreshadowed at the end of the previous movement (page 36, last bar), and it begins as if in C sharp minor: these two facts help to link the Finale with the slow movement in the listener's mind, and the prominence of C sharp (as well as the appearance of the A-D sharp tritone) further show that C natural is not now the strong force it was earlier in the work. Another point arises here: the conscious linking of each movement of this symphony by tonal means, and by the device of taking over the discussion of the respective merits of C and F sharp in each new movement at exactly the point at which it was left off in the previous movement, shows a growing tendency towards continuous development of the type found in the single-movement symphony towards which Sibelius was gradually moving.

Since A and D sharp (E flat) have been prominent wherever a C sharp has gained the ascendancy over C natural (as well as in a few other places), the keys of A major and E flat are prominent in the Finale; so prominent, indeed, that there is a collision between them, various sections of the music being bi-tonal as both keys strive for domination. The resulting confusion is the cue for the reintroduction of C (in the form of C major, on page 47): the F sharp which formed the original tritone with it also occasionally appears, but it is less powerful when C is present in this movement. Indeed, the repeat of the opening A major section is much shortened in the recapitulation (pages 56f), a fact which amply demonstrates the waning power of F sharp to make the tonic key a major one. The bi-tonal clash between A and E flat in the recapitulation leads to tonal chaos in the coda, in which the rival notes of C, A, E flat and F sharp all strive for ascendancy in a series of grinding dissonances with many clashes between major and minor thirds. On page 66 the glockenspiel pathetically attempts to hail the momentary establishment of A major; but in the end it is the insistence of C natural (with which the work so strikingly began) that forces the movement to close in A minor.

It need hardly be said that the two types of idea examined above do not constitute the only processes which might be discussed in Sibelius' Fourth Symphony; but it will be readily conceded that the composer's handling of these two processes shows a mastery of symphonic style which is quite overwhelming.

Another treatment of the tritone deserves brief mention here, even though it does not occur in one of the symphonies. Sibelius' last major work (excluding the incidental music to *The Tempest*) was *Tapiola*, a tone-poem for which the composer provided the explanatory verse:

Wide-spread they stand, the Northlands' dusky forests,
Ancient, mysterious, brooding savage dreams;
Within them dwells the Forest's mighty God,
And wood-sprites in the gloom weave magic secrets.

Some critics have suggested that the piece ranks as an eighth symphony because of its symphonic nature: others have not found it so. The work does have a musical logic of its own, quite apart from the avowedly programmatic nature which in another sense 'explains' it; and though this need not necessarily be the case in every work which has both 'symphonic' and 'programmatic' elements, the logical growth of the argument in *Tapiola* is interrupted in a way that sets it apart from the symphonies. This does not, of course, make it any less great as a piece of music—Sibelius was not here attempting to write another symphony.

It has been said that *Tapiola* never moves away from B minor, and is monothematic, but this is not quite true: the piece neither begins nor ends in B minor, for one thing, though that key is always felt to be hovering in the background—a kind of tonal back-cloth against which other tonalities occasionally stand out. There is a parallel between the idea of a tonality which is not always obvious yet whose presence is none the less keenly felt to be hovering in the background, and the mysterious presence of Tapiola in the forest. Both are felt as a force, but not always clearly seen (or heard). Thematically, the piece uses the fragments shown in Ex. 57:

Ex. 57a

Ex. 57b

Ex. 57c

These are all closely interrelated: the scalic nature results in the music being largely stepwise. Often, when leaps occur in a part, they are accompanied by the same leap in the opposite direction in another part, so that the result is curiously static (see Figure C, for example).[28] Parallel thirds also play an important part in the piece; but more important still is the strong G sharp which unsettles the B minor tonality at the beginning of the work. The major sixth in a minor key is none other than the Dorian mode, of which Sibelius had already made splendid use in the Sixth Symphony: as I have said elsewhere,[29] that work treats modality in modern symphonic terms. In *Tapiola*, an approach more like that of the Fourth

Symphony is used: from the tonal point of view, the presence of D and G sharp together over a tonic of B provides the problem to be solved, and it is this problem of accommodating the tritone (especially D and G sharp) which sustains the purely musical argument of the tone-poem.

As far as Letter G *Tapiola* is conceived in symphonic terms: the growth of ideas is perfectly logical, and each new development is clearly linked with preceding ideas. The application of the tritone to music in the whole-tone scale, the modes, chromatic scales, and to the harmony are all thoroughly explored in an opening section which bears all the hall-marks of the kind of writing evinced by Sibelius in his symphonies. From Letter G onwards, a scherzo-like section begins which, one assumes, is intended to portray the wood-sprites of Sibelius' quotation. Here the requirements of the programme take over from those of symphonic development, and the steady progress and expansion of ideas slow down. It is not that the unifying elements are not now present: it is just that no significant new development of them takes place here. This is what sets the work apart from Sibelius' mature symphonic style—a comparison with the treatment of the augmented fourth in the Scherzo of the Fourth Symphony will throw into relief the two manners of writing.

After this section, a return is made to the type of music found in the opening of the work. The implication of the augmented fourth in producing a whole-tone scale is now extended: the modal implications are again explored in a passage for divided strings, with many harmonies in octaves (another passage which adds little to the argument in symphonic terms). At bar 359 (just after Letter L) a section begins which acts as a 'development' would in a conventional symphonic work. The whole-tone scale and diatonic tonality are placed side by side, but their opposition creates no struggle of the sort one would expect to find in truly symphonic music. At Letter N (bar 417) the woodwind use x and y in chromatic form and in parallel thirds against a string background in the whole-tone scale: the passage ends with the repetition of two whole-tone scale chords in the brass—but again there is no sense of symphonic drama. A recapitulation of earlier material follows, and a coda begins (at bar 513): here, for the only time in *Tapiola*, a struggle of symphonic proportions ensues. Chromatic versions of y, in divided strings and in parallel thirds and sixths which form frequent augmented triads, rise stormily to a very high pitch, *fff*. Tonal phrases on the brass eventually break through this vast chromatic barrier, which subsides: nevertheless, augmented fourths are still present, as are a few wisps of melody (z) in the whole-tone scale. The final cadence resolves the conflict inherent in the D-G sharp tritone by suggesting that the D must be sharpened to form a perfect fourth in B major.

As a symphonic discussion of the problems posed by the tritone, *Tapiola* cannot rank with the Third and Fourth Symphonies; but this, of course, is not its purpose. The sense of logical growth of ideas which is such a feature of the symphonies can only be found at the start of the tone-poem, after which a certain episodic nature, resulting from the employment of a programme, occurs. The conflicts inherent in the material are explored— modal, tonal, whole-tone, chromatic, harmonic—but the sense of conflict and drama which is a hall-mark of symphonic thought is not really apparent in *Tapiola*. Thematic unity is evident in the use of closely interrelated material, yet other methods of constructing a symphonic work (rhythmic, tonal, etc.) are less apparent than in the symphonies, their place being taken by descriptive passages. The programmatic nature of tone-poems— in this one in particular the evocation of 'atmosphere' as well as of dusky forests and wood-sprites—sets them apart from true symphonies. One should beware of making a value-judgment of the tone-poem on the basis of criteria which are properly applicable only to truly symphonic music: nevertheless, there are clearly identifiable scherzo, development and recapitulation sections in *Tapiola* which give the impression of an approximation to a one-movement symphony, and thus the application of such criteria, in order to elucidate the work's musical logic, is not entirely inappropriate.

The tritone presents a musical paradox: by itself it can easily be used to destroy tonality, yet in certain contexts (as the leading-note and seventh of a dominant chord, for example) it is the interval which most easily leads to the establishment of tonality—yet it does not of itself *state* that tonality. Sibelius, clearly realizing these possibilities, used the identical interval with quite opposite results in his Third and Fourth Symphonies, and its power of suggesting (without actually stating) a tonality in *Tapiola*.

CHAPTER VI

Rhythm

Beethoven's Fourth Symphony

I have already suggested that a connection exists between the material of Beethoven's Fifth Symphony and that of the Fourth, which he was writing at the same time. This connection is a thematic one, and consists of the use of the four-note shape ♩♩♩♩ which is announced very clearly at the outset of each work. Since the main purpose of the present chapter is to examine the use of rhythm in symphonic writing, it will be as well to consider briefly the other facets of composition before proceeding to discuss that topic.

The tonal schemes of the work express very strongly the fact that the first note heard (apart from the B flat tonic pedal) is a G flat: this note (which sometimes appears as F sharp) not only gives the impression that the Introduction will be in the minor, but also begins to replace the dominant as the note which is next in importance to the tonic. Furthermore it is set up in opposition both to B flat and to the usual 'classical' dominant, F, in which capacity it has the function of introducing other keys closely related to itself. When the opening subject of the first Allegro vivace appears in the development section (bar 217) it starts in D major so that the tune itself may begin with an F sharp: and F sharp, acting as a dominant, leads to B major after bar 280. The rivalry between F sharp and F natural as dominant is also evident at the preparation for the recapitulation (bars 280–330). In the slow movement, the presence of G flat gives rise to an E flat minor variation of the main theme which leads to a tonally ambiguous passage (bars 54–60). The struggle between the conventional dominant (B flat in this movement) and the G flat 'substitute' for it is again clear, and forms a nice parallel to the procedures already discussed in the sections on Sibelius' Second and Beethoven's Ninth Symphonies. The dominant chord of E flat (the first violins continuing their stepwise descent onto a B flat, with D natural sounding beneath it in the bass) does not materialize at bar 54, where Beethoven has led the listener to expect it: the listener has this impression not only because the preparation for the recapitulation would normally be a dominant seventh, but also because the music just before this bar seems to be leading to such a chord. Beethoven in fact substitutes a chord of G flat, and the struggle between the two rival 'dominants' is felt in bars 54 and 55, the music in the violins being compatible with either key. The struggle is again felt in bars 59 and 60, where an approach to a cadence in E flat is once more countered by the appearance of a G flat chord. Similar struggles to replace F with G flat occur in the third and fourth movements, often unsettling the tonality for a while: in the third movement, as in the first, G flat is the first chromatic note heard. In the Finale, loud unison B naturals (which result from the interpretation of F sharp as a dominant) fail to establish B major, since the strings immediately reinterpret the B as a leading-note.[1] Beethoven developed this idea further in his Eighth Symphony.

Thematically, Beethoven's Fourth Symphony is very closely built on the shape x: as befits a composer of splendid sets of variations, his inventiveness in handling this melodic germ is remarkable, and is very simple to trace through the work. Various methods of treating x are used: it is inverted, and the order of the notes changes; various counterpoints are written against it, and these counterpoints in their turn are used as unifying devices (one of the most prominent is a rising chromatic scale, another is an arch-shape); new notes are added to the original x shape in order to fill up the leaps; and lastly, a leap is used to replace the stepwise movement between the first two and last two notes of the figure. That such treatments of the motif do not exhaust its possibilities when handled by a master of variation form is evident from the fact that Beethoven used the same four notes in other ways in his Fifth Symphony.

Before leaving the subject of the thematic unity of the work, several other factors deserve brief notice. One of these concerns two passages of the kind often pointed out as examples of Beethoven's ill-balanced scoring, supposedly caused by his deafness—though it must have occurred to many people that a composer with as much experience as Beethoven already had before his deafness became absolute is unlikely to have perpetrated such blunders as some critics attribute to him. The repetition of the opening theme of the first Allegro vivace (at bars 81ff) is given to the 'cellos and double basses, while most of the remaining instruments play the implied harmonic basis of the tune (B flat-E flat-F-D/B flat) in long notes: that this is not a piece of inept scoring is shown by Beethoven's use of the added harmonic material as the skeletal basis of the 'new' theme which appears in the development section (bars 221ff) and which is itself further developed in the recapitulation: the motif recurs also in the third movement (bars 34ff) where again it seems to be too prominently scored—that is, until one realizes its derivation. It seems that Beethoven was in fact using the scoring to draw attention to this thematic link.

The upbeat with which the third movement starts is a reflection of the 'drum-figure' of the opening of the slow movement and the prefatory run which leads into the initial theme of the first Allegro vivace: these figures are in turn derived by inverting the fall from B flat to F which had occurred at the end of the long tonic pedal at the opening of the symphony. The B flat-G flat-F phrase in the strings at this same point (bars 4ff of the first movement) is also used later in the work, for Beethoven makes the shape a feature of several themes, as well as giving it prominence in the development section of the Finale (bars 130ff). A sequential use of this shape in the first movement (bars 46f) develops logically into a descending scale, which in turn provides another unifying thematic element. From this it will be evident that no material in the symphony is wasted: all is logically developed and fully integrated. Further examples are the quaver 'trills' of bars 66ff in the first movement, which reappear at the end of the Trio (bars 64ff of the third movement); the E natural-B natural-C sharp motif of the Introduction (bars 31f), which reappears at bars 64ff of the Finale; and the pentatonic shape F-E flat-C of the third bar of the Scherzo, which is incorporated into the Finale (bars 12f, 26f and 38).

It has become clear in this study that in mature symphonies the opening bars are vital to an understanding of the processes of construction used in the remainder of the work. This is certainly true of Beethoven's Fourth Symphony, where the opening statement of x is immediately repeated in diminution (at a lower pitch). It is this idea of rhythmic diminution (and occasionally the reverse process of augmentation) that provides one of the more important and fascinating unifying devices of the symphony.[2] The most obvious use is that applied to the opening theme x: the minim version is immediately followed by a crotchet one, and a further diminution is evident in the second subject of the first movement (bar 107), where the same shape is played in quavers. Semiquaver and demi-semiquaver versions of the motif are found in the second movement (at bars 18 and 22 respectively), the two being placed close together (just as the original diminution had been placed close to its model) so that the halving of note-values shall be the more readily perceived. The use of diminutions in steadily decreasing note-values as far as this point in the work is quite clear. Such diminutions are not, of course, confined to x in its simple form. The syncopated theme at bars 95–102 of the first movement is immediately repeated at twice the speed in the following bars, and an inexact diminution of the material in bars 135–8 likewise immediately follows its model; the semibreve theme in bars 351–60 is straightway reduced to minims at its appearance in the exposition of the opening movement, though not in the recapitulation. The placing of diminutions immediately after their models at these points yet again helps the ear to identify them as such.

The second movement has its share of diminutions, though (apart from the examples already mentioned)[3] they are treated in a different way, being mostly applied to rhythms within the span of a single melodic line.

The main themes of the movement show the way in which this device works (see Ex. 58).

Ex. 58a

(inexact)

Ex. 58b

The preponderance of dotted rhythms (especially in Ex. 58b, though the final dotted rhythm is written as two semiquavers on the first appearance of this theme) is attributable to the underlying dotted rhythm of the 'drum-figure' that permeates the movement. Ex. 58b is accompanied, also, by a string chord which is gradually built up from the bass to the treble, so that each note is of shorter duration than the one next below it. The idea of diminution within a single melodic line is further developed during the clarinet solo of the second subject (bars 30ff and 85ff: see Ex. 59).

Ex. 59

Here the expected cadence (enclosed in square brackets), mirroring the rhythm of the first two bars, is replaced by one which makes use of a diminution (though not quite exact) of an earlier part of the phrase (marked ⌐——). It will be apparent later that augmentations (as well as diminutions) form part of Beethoven's scheme from the end of the first movement onwards; and the final four notes of Ex. 59, augmented, are immediately made to serve as the rhythm of the following phrase (bars 34ff). Throughout the movement various treatments and lengths of dotted rhythms are placed against the underlying 'drum-figure' ♩ ♪♩♩ ♪♩ .

In the third movement an entirely different approach to the idea of diminutions is evident. This movement is the first 'double sandwich' in Beethoven's symphonies, and it is usually assumed that he extended the ordinary ABA form in order to enlarge the scale of the movement.[4] Yet the Scherzo of the 'Eroica' Symphony shows clearly enough that Beethoven was perfectly capable of writing an extended movement in quick tempo without recourse to further repetition of the A and B sections. The use of the 'double sandwich' here is, simply, the result of applying diminution to the size of the Scherzo itself. At the first reappearance of the Scherzo, Beethoven omits the repeat marks, thus reducing its size by half as compared with its first appearance: by doing this, and by not merely writing a 'da capo' at the end of the Trio, he ensures the omission of the Scherzo's repeats in its second appearance. But such an omission was not in any way unusual, so that, to make the point absolutely clear, Beethoven makes use of the process once more, reducing the Scherzo by a further half (or rather, by roughly half) at its third hearing.[5] Though this is by far the most important use of diminution in this movement, there is one application of the idea to a prominent bass part (at bars 35ff) on the smaller scale evident in the two earlier movements.

There are many examples of small-scale diminution in the Finale: the arch-shaped accompaniment figure at bars 37ff and 45ff is used in a free diminution as part of the second subject (bars 52f), and in yet shorter note-values at bars 327f.[6] As in the first movement, a 'new' theme in the development section of the Finale derives from earlier material: in this instance the theme at bar 131 is taken from bars 4ff of the first movement. Its appearance in the Finale is immediately followed by versions in diminution which omit the semiquaver flourish at the beginning of the theme.[7]

Tovey said of the end of the Fourth Symphony, '. . . by drawing out its opening theme into quavers with pauses, it borrows an old joke of Haydn's, the excellence of which lies in its badness'.[8] This is entirely beside the point, though Beethoven's use of the device is certainly witty. By reversing the processes of diminution so frequently found in the symphony, he draws attention to them, and to the fact that the extremes of diminution have been reached—quicker notes than those used for x in this movement would not have been feasible. Moreover, the use of an augmentation near the end of the movement surrounds the entire work with a frame of longer notes: only the final blustering return to semiquavers stands outside this frame.

The discussion of rhythm in the symphony has so far dwelt on the differences between the movements—on the use of diminution of a portion of one theme in order to create another in the first and last movements, the use of diminutions (and some augmentations) of dotted rhythms against the background of the 'drum-figure' in the second, and, in the third movement, a gradual reduction in the size of the Scherzo with each repetition. The idea of diminution does, of course, run through all four movements; but there are in addition rhythmic connections, also involving diminutions, between the various movements. The first of these links occurs between the Introduction and the Allegro vivace: Beethoven draws attention to the idea, firstly by the repetition of three chords in diminution (bars 34f), and secondly by writing a whole series of chords which become progressively closer together, diminution being applied to the space between them. In the course of this passage (bars 36ff) the change to Allegro vivace is made, and the gradual quickening of pace which results from the diminutions does much to help the smooth transition from the Adagio introduction to the fast main tempo of the movement. The process is reflected several times in the movement; bars 49ff, 191ff and 241ff are only a few examples: the preparation for the recapitulation uses the same idea in a different way (bars 305ff).

Grove remarks concerning the end of the first movement, 'Schumann . . . has noticed that in the eight bars which terminate the movement *fortissimo*, one of the first three is redundant. Schumann's fine ear for rhythm detected this, and he is probably correct, but the error, if error it be, is one which few will feel with him.'[9] Beethoven's music, like that of Viennese classical composers generally, can very largely be felt as being in four-bar rhythmic units. This is not unusual—it is the departures from this general four-bar 'macrorhythm' which tend to be of more interest. Music constructed on classical lines tends to correspond closely to the underlying four-bar macrorhythm at the beginning and end of a piece, and the final chord normally appears at a strong point in the rhythmic scheme—at the beginning of the first or third bar.[10] Schumann's objection is really that Beethoven has ended the movement on a weak bar of the macrorhythm, and that, by omitting one bar of the long B flat chord, he could have ended on a stronger pulse. There are, in fact, good reasons for not doing this. Instead of ending at bar 495 (on the first bar of the macrorhythm) Beethoven adds two detached chords a minim apart, with prefatory runs such as he had used at the beginning of the Allegro vivace; then, reversing the process so often used in the movement, he augments the rhythm so that two more chords, a semibreve apart, round the movement off. This has several advantages: the augmentation draws attention to the presence of diminution in previous parts of the movements; surrounds it, as it were, with a 'frame' of more distantly spaced chords; and also mirrors the idea of three equally spaced chords which have already been a feature of the movement, and which recur in all the other movements. Finally, the ending on a weak pulse of the macrorhythm leaves the listener with the impression that this cannot be the final cadence of the symphony: to this extent the first movement cannot stand alone, and the others are necessary in order to complete the argument.[11]

The second and third movements are linked by another device. The rhythm of the last four bars of the slow movement is slightly unexpected, though not so obviously that their effect is felt other than subconsciously. The arrival of the tonic chord on the third beat of bar 101, with complete silence occurring where one might logically expect that chord to appear— on the first beat of bar 102—gives an effect of hemiola. This slow hemiola is immediately used in diminution to begin the third movement, and the link between the two passages is emphasized by the use of dominant-tonic figures in both places. The link between the slow movement and the Scherzo is similar to that between the first two movements. The use of augmentations, as well as diminutions, in the second movement had been foreshadowed in the closing bars of the first movement. Augmentations can be heard, for instance, at such places as in the brass parts at bars 71f of the second movement (a point which is less clear in the exposition of the piece); the three equally spaced chords used at this point are an important feature of the work, and occur elsewhere in the movement (the theme at bar 34 is a good example).

The third movement again makes use of the three equally spaced chords, and uses them immediately in diminution: the resulting ♩. |♩. |♩♩♩♩↑↑‖ rhythm is often used at cadences to ensure a link—a feeling of 'moving on' —to the following music, since it throws the final chord of a section onto the weak fourth bar of the macrorhythm. This process is itself a diminution of the one at the end of the first movement to which I have already referred: the ending on a weak bar at that point in the work is less strongly felt than in the Scherzo, since the bars at the end of the first movement are much longer than in the one-in-a-bar third movement. With the much shorter macrorhythm of the Scherzo (rather like a $\frac{12}{8}$ pulse, in fact), Beethoven cannot end the entire movement on a weak pulse: this accounts for the additional three bars about which Tovey was led to remark, 'Never have three short bars contained more meaning than the Coda in which the two horns blow the whole movement away'.[12] Although Tovey made no further comment about the nature of this meaning, it is nonetheless quite clear: the three bars simply allow an ending on the strong pulse of the macrorhythm, and the horn phrase is itself a diminution of music it had played eight bars previously.[13]

The third and fourth movements are joined by a link which is partly thematic and partly rhythmic. The Trio closes with a seemingly unimportant figure of B flat-A-B flat-D: the repetition of this phrase many times draws considerable attention to it. Indeed, this motif, which appears in quavers in the Trio, is used in diminution at the start of the Finale (though the shape *x* is worked into the theme as well).[14] A similar paralleling of themes occurs at the corresponding places in the Fifth Symphony, on which Beethoven was working at the same time.

Beethoven's Eighth Symphony

This symphony, often underrated because of its lightweight, humorous nature, was a particular favourite of Beethoven's. Because the work had a cooler reception than the Seventh, Beethoven remarked (no doubt exaggerating a little) that this was because the Eighth was so much better. It is certainly different—it is one of the glories of his symphonies that they are all widely different from each other[15]—though it has seldom been realized how original the piece is, and most people are inclined to reject Beethoven's evaluation of the work, seeing it as an overreaction to adverse criticism. That it might be due to a composer's justifiable pride in a work that solves some novel problems seems just as likely.

The factor that unifies Beethoven's Eighth Symphony is a numerical one—the number three: it is impossible to say why Beethoven should have chosen this somewhat medieval idea, though he could scarcely fail to be aware that the number has, for various reasons, frequently been endowed with mystical qualities. I shall not continually point out the significance of '3'—an awareness of its frequent appearance in the discussion which follows will be sufficient guide to its effect on the work.[16]

Thematically the symphony is based on three figures of three notes: the first of these is a third that turns in upon itself, and which appears in three different forms (see Ex. 60).

Ex. 60

The second melodic formula consists of three notes rising by step (a figure which is sometimes inverted and sometimes extended to four or five notes); and the third is which is gradually extended until it becomes . These figures, found throughout the piece, may easily be traced, and do not need to be enumerated.

The tonality of the symphony is quite often governed by the number three: keys a third apart, for example, are quite common. At bar 34 of the first movement, for instance, the D which has been reiterated from bar 32 onwards is interpreted as a new tonic, a third away from the symphony's key of F. The C sharp at bar 34 acts as the leading-note of D; C sharp assumes much importance later in the work, since not only is it a major third below F, but it can also serve as a pivotal note to the keys of D, D flat and A (all a third away from F) and to F sharp minor (a key with a signature of three sharps). The second subject, though it starts in D, does in fact soon reach the classically correct key of C major (at bar 46): the parallel with schemes already discussed in Beethoven's Fourth and Ninth, and Sibelius' Third Symphonies will be immediately obvious.

A new way of looking at the number three is evident between bars 52 and 58 of the opening movement: here Beethoven for a time uses only minor thirds, superimposed to form various diminished seventh chords. The minor thirds are then opened out into major thirds, and, with an effect not unlike that experienced on coming out of a cloud into the sunshine, the diminished seventh chords are replaced by perfect major triads: the effect is the more striking because of the dynamic markings, which move up from *pp* to *ff*. The same idea is pursued further at the start of the development section (bars 104–40): passages in which the major thirds of the opening theme are made minor ( ) are three times interrupted by loud major chords. After moving to A (not only a third away from the tonic F, but a key with a signature of three sharps), the tonality settles on D, the key in which the second subject had begun, though the tonality here is minor. Many more statements of the opening six notes of the work are now worked into minor triads or are used with all the leaps as minor thirds (bars 144–85), until a crescendo leads up to the tonic major chord which opens the recapitulation at bar 190.

The beginning of the recapitulation is usually quoted as evidence of Beethoven's lapse in scoring due to his deafness: it is often suggested that the tune (in the bass, scored for, cellos and double basses) is given insufficient weight in comparison with the rest of the orchestra at this point.[17] Such an obvious piece of underscoring as this is more likely to be intentional; and in any case, Beethoven was a vastly experienced orchestrator by the time he wrote this work, and is most unlikely to have made such an elementary blunder.[18] There is a good reason for scoring in this particular way, and it is intimately bound up with the logic which runs throughout the symphony. Since the development section has been almost entirely concerned with minor thirds or minor triads, at the recapitulation Beethoven celebrates not so much the return of the main theme (which has in any case scarcely been absent at any point in the development) as the return of the tonic key, and above all the return of the *major* third. The point is made perfectly clear by the fact that, among the instruments not playing the tune, most weight is given to the major third F-A.

This triumphant overcoming of minor by major thirds has an interesting counterpart in the coda of the first movement.[19] Whereas the second subject in the exposition had been in a key a minor third away from the tonic, introduced by a C sharp, here, in the coda, the same foreign note is written as D flat so that it may be reinterpreted as a tonic and introduce a key a major third below F.[20]

In the third movement the tonality is only slightly affected by numerology: although the first chromatic note heard is the pivotal C sharp, it is only in the second half of the Trio that it is used to introduce the key of D flat—and then only briefly. C sharp does, however, have a most important function in the Finale: it appears loudly and unexpectedly (though without affecting the tonality) at bars 16 and 178; at bar 151 the same note is used to move the music into A major. C sharp has its greatest tonal effect in the coda: interruptions by this note (written first as D flat,

then as C sharp) occur three times in quick succession, and attention is
drawn to the third of these interruptions by the fact that the note is played
three times (see bars 372–9). The first interruption leads to D flat (a third
away from the tonic) and in the second, C sharp is taken as the tonic of
C sharp minor (still a third away from F, if considered enharmonically:
naturally, the ear hears the interval as a third). The three C sharps of the
third interruption are taken as dominants of F sharp minor (a key with
three sharps): the natural brass instruments and timpani are, of course,
excluded from this section since they cannot play in such a distant key, and
at bar 391 they enter on what might be taken for a leading-note, E sharp.
But since both audience and orchestra know that the brass and drums
cannot play in such an outlandish key, the note proves to be the tonic of
F major, to which key the music immediately reverts.

With this change back to F major at bar 392, the minor third F sharp-A
of the preceding passage becomes the major third F natural-A, a clear
parallel to the process at the end of the development section of the first
movement, in which F-A flat had eventually become F-A natural: the
triumph of major over minor thirds is evident in both movements. The
prominence of the major third is emphasized in the coda of the Finale
(bars 450ff) in a passage of twenty bars containing (apart from a few Cs
which appear in the bass arpeggio) only the notes F and A, and the device
is repeated for the final thirteen bars of the movement (just as it had been
used to start the Finale).

Before leaving the subject of the effect of the number three on the
tonality of the work, it would be as well to say that, in the Finale, the A flat
of the second subject becomes D flat in the recapitulation: A flat is not only
a third away from the tonic, but also a third away from the expected second
subject key of C major; D flat is likewise a third away from the tonic.[21]

The number three is applied to the rhythm of the work in various ways:
one of the most obvious is the three-fold repetition of phrases which occurs
throughout the symphony. It would indeed be tedious to list all the
melodic fragments which are announced three times, but the most obvious
examples are found in the second subject of the first movement, and the
openings of all the other movements. Other examples are equally instructive—particularly worth mentioning are those in the passage from bar 329
to the end of the first movement (including the 'triple' scoring of the chord
in the pause bar—332—an idea that Beethoven used again to end the
third movement). The use of triple rhythm for an opening movement is
itself rather unusual.

Beethoven's own sketches for the Eighth Symphony lead one to suspect
that he had the number three in mind while working at its composition:
his original sketch for the Finale (shown in Ex. 61) was rejected in favour
of a version of the theme which uses triplets and three-fold repetitions.

Ex. 61

The dotted minims of the sketch—in a place where ordinary minims would be more correct—may well imply that Beethoven thought of the repetition within these two chords as consisting of quaver triplets rather than four quavers: the six quavers necessary for the triplet version may well have caused him to add the dots. The opening quaver triplets of Beethoven's final version of the fourth movement are rather less than satisfactory in that even the best violinists can hope to play these opening chords as written and with clarity only if the tempo is somewhat slower than the composer's marking of 'Allegro vivace (minim=84)': the effect of the number three here has been to produce triplets which are really too short to be distinct. When the woodwind play this theme, they are given triplet crotchets to play simultaneously with the two groups of quaver triplets in the strings: their parts are thus much more easily made distinct.[22] The sketches also suggest that the alteration of the upbeat of the Trio from a single crotchet to three quavers is another aspect of Beethoven's preoccupation with the number three.[23]

One might view the triplets which begin the Finale as an instance where Beethoven allowed his unifying device to overrule the practical considerations of composition and orchestration. In the third movement there is an example of the opposite process—the composer rejecting the dictates of numerology so as to serve a more interesting musical scheme. The sketches show that Beethoven had intended the third bar of the Trio to have the same rhythm as bars 1 and 2, so that there would be three statements of the rhythm of the opening bar (a process found quite often elsewhere in the work). He rejected this scheme, and altered the rhythm of the third bar so as to give greater variety to the theme.

Beethoven applies the same musical idea of 'three' to rhythm on the large scale. At the start of the Eighth Symphony, 'Beethoven, the master of movement, begins with a theme that stops at the fourth bar and is obviously going to be rounded off at the twelfth . . .'[24]. The word 'obviously' in this quotation is ill-advised: to the 20th century ear, now grown accustomed to the published version, it seems perfectly correct. But a contemporary of Beethoven's, hearing the opening four-bar phrase for the first time, would be much more likely to expect either one or three more balancing phrases, making a theme of eight or sixteen bars; the possibility is acknowledged by Beethoven himself when, in the recapitulation, he reduces the theme to two phrases only. The importance to the work of an opening theme of three phrases is made clear by the manner of its presentation. Firstly, it appears without introductory material; secondly, to quote from Robert Simpson:

No. 8 begins with a main theme that is itself a completed ring . . . No previous
Beethoven symphony starts with a self-contained tune . . . It is significant that
when Haydn began a symphonic first *allegro* with a clear-cut self completing
tune, he usually took care to precede it by a slow introduction . . .[25]

This is the crux of the matter. It is important that the tune is heard as being
complete so that it may be clearly perceived as consisting of three phrases.
If the tune were not self completing, this important numerical emphasis
would not be felt; and still more attention is drawn to this triple phrase
structure by virtue of the fact that it is the first musical event of the
symphony.[26]

A most interesting effect of the numerology applied to rhythm on the
large scale can be heard in the Finale. It is well known, and frequently
mentioned by commentators, that the small sonata-form Finale is followed
by a large coda: it is instructive to seek the reasons for Beethoven's use of
this device. 'Beethoven's characteristic rough humour' is often quoted in
this context, but this is only partly the reason. Beethoven, as is well known,
expanded the coda to the point where it balanced the development not
only in size but also in power and importance. The four sections of the
opening movement of his Fifth Symphony are, indeed, almost exactly the
same number of bars in length (though there are repeat marks for the
exposition): nevertheless, it is not essential for a work of art to be precisely
symmetrical in order to give the impression of symmetry. Since in the
Finale of Beethoven's Eighth Symphony the exposition is 90 bars long, the
development 70 and the recapitulation 106—in other words, the first three
sections are roughly comparable in size—the audience, if it expects
anything at all, will be likely to expect a coda of about 70 bars, balancing
the development section. The effect of numerology on the large scale is
evident in the fact that the coda is roughly three times this size—235 bars.
Naturally, this can only be appreciated by the listener if he is clearly aware
of the point at which each of the first three sections of the movement begins
and ends.

Beethoven was, of course, well aware of this, and took immense care to
see that the various sections of the movement were clearly delineated. For
example, he ends the exposition with a firm cadence (bar 90): although
this is in the tonic (F) its effect at this point is more like that of a subdominant. This is very much to Beethoven's purpose. The cadence must be
of obvious importance so as to mark the end of the section with no possibility of doubt; hence the tonic cadence: nevertheless, the cadence must
not be too 'final' in effect, since the listener must also be aware that more
music is to follow—hence the subdominant effect of the cadence. The
development section begins with three repetitions of the opening triplet
chords of a major third F-A: the effect of the numerology could scarcely
be made more evident than at this point. Beethoven then repeats the first

subject (bar 97): it is his normal procedure to begin the development section with the first subject in sonata-form movements where he has omitted the repeat of the exposition. Since this normally gives the listener the impression that the exposition is, in fact, being repeated—a feeling which is only later disappointed—the procedure cannot be used in this particular movement. In order to make quite sure that the audience is aware of the dimensions of the movement, and knows precisely the point at which the new section begins, Beethoven has interpolated the repeated chords of bars 91–6: these make it clear that the development is beginning.

He likewise makes quite clear the point at which the development ends and the recapitulation begins—a passage which Tovey described as 'the funniest return [to the tonic] in all music',[27] even though there is a similar one at bars 70–80 of the third movement of the 'Eroica'. In Beethoven's music the timpani are never chromatic, though in the first movement of the 'Eroica' the tonic and dominant are treated enharmonically at bars 260–71: in the Finale of the Eighth Symphony they have an unusual octave F tuning, partly so that they can play the octave figure quoted on p. 124 above. Since the listener knows that the timpani are never chromatic, and that they will only play the tonic in this movement, Beethoven is able to use them to signal the return of the tonic, dispensing with the more usual long dominant pedal. There is, in fact, a misleading start to the recapitulation: after several bars built around the dominant of A major[28] the first subject appears in that key (bar 151). After a short while only octave Es are left sounding, and these are reinterpreted as the leading-note, changing to the tonic F when the timpani (and the bassoon, added so as to give definition to the timpani notes) enter at bar 157. The octave figure is made prominent so that the point will not be missed. It is now clear to the listener that the tonic has been reached and the recapitulation will begin.

Naturally, the point at which the recapitulation ends must also be evident to the audience if the size of the coda is to be appreciated: for this reason Beethoven ends the recapitulation with a transposed form of the end of the exposition. The big cadence in bar 266 makes the B flat sound like the subdominant it is, so that the ear is aware that more music is to follow. At the same time, its very size and the fact that it mirrors the end of the exposition draw attention to its importance as the cadence which rounds off the recapitulation section. By starting the coda in the same way as he had begun the development, Beethoven makes even more sure that the audience will not miss the point.

Once the use of numerology as a means of unifying the symphony and of governing rhythm on both the large and the small scale is realized, the purpose of the rather ordinary-sounding 'till ready' bars at the beginning of the third movement will be evident: the figure, though it derives thematically from one of the three-note figures quoted on p. 124 above, is also announced three times. Other passages which seem enigmatic or in which nothing apparently happens also take on a new significance when the numerology of the work is understood, and can be shown to result from perfectly logical processes of thought. Beethoven was breaking entirely new ground in using numerology as the basis of a symphonic work. As might be expected of a maturing composer, the unifying processes of this work are much less obvious than in some of his earlier compositions. Here is a clear case of the 'art that conceals art'. As Leonard B. Meyer says: 'To present the complex simply and the convoluted plainly is to meet the most formidable challenge, to demonstrate the highest skill, to achieve the greatest elegance'.[29] Many people have, with justification, remarked on Beethoven's 'rough humour', and on the wit and laughter of this symphony:[30] the use of the number three for purposes of unification and of structural and rhythmic design is, I suggest, yet another typically Beethovenian piece of fun.

Sibelius' Fifth Symphony

The foregoing analyses of Beethoven's Fourth and Eighth Symphonies have shown a preoccupation with the use of rhythmic diminutions and with the number three: both these tendencies find something of an echo in Sibelius' Fifth Symphony, though the handling of them is quite different. The idea of 'three' is evident in the wide use of music in parallel thirds, in triple rhythms, in tonalities a major or minor third apart, and even in the use of three movements. In several places, also, three different speeds—fast, slow and static—are going on at the same time. Several writers have noticed Sibelius' splendid command of movement, and especially his ability to change imperceptibly from one type of motion to another. The First, Fifth and Seventh Symphonies are often quoted as good demonstrations of this ability, but it is in the Fifth that the design of the whole is most clearly governed by rhythm—a point often overlooked in thematic analyses of the piece. This kind of analysis can, of course, help towards an understanding of the work, and a brief discussion of its thematic development may be found in Chapter II. An additional unifying factor is the alternation of two chords (or sometimes two notes). The tonality of the symphony is largely governed by the prominent notes G, G flat and B natural (C flat): that is, the keys used are mostly B major and minor, G, C, G flat and the symphony's tonic, E flat. The G is implicit in the opening bars (where it is a constantly recurring bass note); by contrast B natural is not heard until later, and it results from the prominence of the first chromatic note of the work, G flat, which is taken as the dominant of B.

Of paramount importance to the work is its rhythmical structure: this is complex (no doubt this is why the symphony gave Sibelius more trouble during its composition than any other) and works on several levels. One of these is very much more obvious than the others at a first hearing, and its prominence increases with each movement of the symphony. It consists of the combination of fast and slow motion within a single movement. To take the most obvious example first, the Finale's first subject, a *perpetuum mobile* marked 'Allegro molto' which starts with continuous ♪ movement, is followed by a striding tune in regular minims (a triumphant E flat theme which Tovey, in his usual vivid manner, compared to 'Thor swinging his hammer'): the macrorhythm of the new tune is in strong three-bar phrases to contrast with the indeterminate (or sometimes four-bar) macrorhythm of the first subject. In the slow movement, the two types of motion are presented simultaneously, the main theme in more or less steady crotchets[31] being played against a slow-moving, chorale-like background in longer notes. The contrast of speeds is presented differently in the first movement: beginning like a regular sonata-form movement in 'tempo molto moderato', it gradually quickens until the directions 'presto' and 'piu presto' are reached. The fusion of first-movement form with 'scherzo'—for that is what actually happens here—is the result of a revision of the work, and seems to represent a conscious attempt by the composer to create the same kind of link between the opening and Scherzo as was already present in the two later movements; and the idea of rhythmic contrast is implicit as early as the first phrase of the work, where the first horn moves in crotchets and quavers (apart from its first and last notes), while the three accompanying horns play two chords in very long notes. The splendid fusion in the first movement of the two types of motion into a single whole, complete with recurring motifs and a join between the two sections made so gradually that one cannot tell where the one ends and the other begins, has excited much admiration. Such a technique of moving imperceptibly from slow to fast notes is, of course, essential to the writing of this particular movement if the idea of using the rhythmic contrast is to be a feature: the integration of speeds must be as clear in this movement as it is in the other two if there is to be an overall feeling of unity. If the seams which join the sections were obvious, the two parts of the movement would remain separate in the listener's mind, and thus unity would not be achieved. This view of the first movement is widely held, yet the fact that the Finale reverses the process has not caused nearly so much comment. The overall plan of the symphony resembles an arch—the tempo of the opening movement changes from slow to fast, the second movement combines the two speeds in counterpoint (and at one place in heterophony), and the Finale starts with fast music but ends slowly.

As already mentioned, the integration of first-movement form and scherzo in the first movement of the symphony is the result of a revision. Sibelius actually made three versions of the symphony, the third (which appeared in 1919) being definitive. There were originally four movements, of which the first two are fused in the final version.[32] The first movement originally ended soon after Letter M with an inconclusive cadence on the weakest quaver of the bar. The first two bars of the published score were not present at all in the first version, which in fact began with the six-five chord of the published edition's third bar. The descending scales which are a prominent feature both of the opening and of the passage between L and M were likewise missing from the original version: at M, and until the end of the movement, there were instead two sustained chords on the lower instruments in each bar. The published version shows evidence of some re-scoring, and Sibelius has contracted some passages to make the argument more cogent and concise: in particular, he has cut a large passage (which was originally placed at about Letter F) based on the shape y (of Ex. 62) and string runs like those between Letters F and G. The upper portion of phrase y is less important in several places than in the first version, in which, to take one example, the horns used this phrase very prominently around Letter M before twice plunging down in a very romantic and striking fashion.

The original version's Scherzo opened in a manner very reminiscent of its first movement: a six-five chord was followed by material such as occurs in the published score between Letters B and D (pages 35–9), and then came a quicker version of material similar to that between Letters A and B of the first movement (page 5, published score), given in parallel thirds in the strings. The Scherzo continued with music almost identical to that of the published version's 'Allegro moderato' section (which begins just after Letter N on page 30). The original version had an extra occurrence of the duplet rhythm like that included in the published score at Letter P (page 58), while the passage from J to K was not present. The most striking differences are that the final tonic flourishes of the movement included two loud A flat interruptions on trumpets.

In the slow movement the order of events has been changed slightly: Sibelius did not originally use the string pizzicato tune in quavers, nor was so much made of the slow, chorale-like material. Loud trumpet interruptions, which referred to the close of the original Scherzo, twice led to remote chords in the lower brass—a feature not found at all in the printed score.

The Finale of the first version was strikingly different from that of the published score: it was, for one thing, much more dissonant. For the present purpose it is sufficient to note merely that the final detached chords were originally played against a high B flat violin pedal and a timpani roll; that the speed of the double basses round about Letter E corresponded to that of the horns instead of being much slower; and that the extraneous trumpet blasts (completely omitted from the printed score) were even more tonally remote and terrifying than in the previous three movements. Sibelius was clearly trying to make capital out of the interval of a fourth (it was, in the first version, stated at the very opening of the movement instead of in the second bar): the trumpet blasts surprisingly interrupted the 'Thor's hammer' theme (which did not have the long woodwind tune above it until the recapitulation in the first version). The fourths, in chordal form, played a large part in a long passage which originally occurred between L and M, but which has mercifully disappeared from the score. In performance, the extraneous fourths of the original version sound like the braying of motor horns; and the passage lacks forward motion and purpose.

It is clear that during his revisions of the score, Sibelius decided that his rather crude attempt to unify the work by introducing trumpet blasts of a fourth at various points was misguided, since it is difficult for the ear to follow the logic behind their occurrence and growth in strength. Instead, Sibelius worked towards the revolutionary integration of two speeds in the first movement, and towards the writing of music at various different speeds in the slow movement and Finale: he was evidently aware, consciously or subconsciously, of the importance of the integration of various speeds to the overall design—an importance which in some respects outweighed thematic considerations.

This integration of speeds complements another very important rhythmic feature, in which contrast is likewise implied. This is the contrast between elements on the large and those on the small scale. An example of this is to be found in a rhythmic cell which has short notes at the beginning and end of a bar (or half bar) with longer notes in between—it is a type of dotted rhythm which begins with a 'Scottish snap'—♩ , for instance.

This rhythm, since it combines within itself long and short notes, is a precise reflection on the small scale of the larger integration of slow and fast speeds which is fundamental to the symphony's overall construction. Thus there is an integration of large and small features on both the large and small scales. If (in triple time) two of these rhythmic cells (*x*) occur together, or if the rhythm is, as it were, 'reversed' so that the shorter notes occur in the middle of the bar, then the result is the well known 'hemiola' rhythm ♩ or ♩ . Both these types of rhythm occur very frequently in the symphony (which is, indeed, largely either in triple time or in $\frac{12}{8}$—that is, four 'triplet' beats), and they are clearly implied in the opening phrase on the first horn (see Ex. 62). The figure *y*, besides appearing as marked in the Example, is also evident in that short notes appear between the long opening B flat and the final F which is lengthened by means of a pause: thus once again a figure which itself expresses the integration of large and small appears simultaneously in two different dimensions.

Ex. 62

The difference between x and y is simply that whereas x has long notes (or a single long note) between shorter ones, y has long notes at the beginning and end, with shorter ones between. The two motifs often occur in conjunction in the symphony, either simultaneously or consecutively, though x is by far the more common.[33] There is, in fact, a certain amount of struggle between the two, especially in the opening movement.

These rhythmic figures have an important influence on the tonality of the symphony, rather like the effect of the tritone on the music of the Fourth Symphony, which I have discussed in Chapter V, though in the Fifth the outcome is entirely different. Briefly, when x is the only rhythmic device in use, it has an unsettling effect on the tonality: established keys are replaced by tonal wandering and chromaticism. On the other hand, so long as x has a firm accompaniment in a contrasting rhythm, the tonality remains secure: Sibelius' most important manner of re-establishing a firm tonality (once it has begun to wander under the influence of this rhythm) is to introduce duple time as a contrast to the basically triple time. It is almost as if the composer were maintaining (in this symphony at any rate) that such a duality of rhythm is the natural state of affairs, so that the removal of the contrast results in an unsettled tonality. It follows that much of the symphony is written in such a way that at least two different types of rhythm are used in counterpoint: one might almost argue that it is conceived on two different time-scales. It would be tedious to trace these devices through the work: the reader may easily do this for himself if he so wishes.

The overall arch shape of the work, evident in the change from slow to fast in the first movement, and from fast to slow in the Finale, has already been mentioned. This large-scale application of the arch shape is given a counterpart on the small scale, for both x and y express the shape, and y forms an exact parallel by surrounding shorter notes with longer ones.

Certain other rhythmic features deserve notice. The development of the figure shown in the lower staves of Ex. 8 during the second exposition of the first movement (pages 14ff) provides an example of the gradual transformation of a slow-moving feature into a fast-moving one (a series of measured trills). This slow acceleration is an important element in making the change of pace from slow to fast imperceptible: but the measured trills, although they use short note values, actually create the aural impression of a static background.[34] This method of creating a contrast between fast and slow motion is used again later in the work: in this second exposition the idea serves to point to a musical paradox—that increasing the speed at which a figure is played does not necessarily have a proportionate effect upon the underlying pace of the music. If the gradual acceleration helps the change of pace yet the further development into measured trills produces a static impression, conversely the use of minims for the 'Thor's hammer' theme of the third movement (with a 'static' string background) does not result in a slowing down of pace. This is the other facet of the paradox: just as short notes do not necessarily increase forward motion, so longer ones do not necessarily decrease it.

In the double exposition of the first movement and in the detached chords which end the work we see the result of these paradoxes. The double exposition is necessary so that a large area in slow motion is given at the start of the work before the gradual increase in speed takes place, so that the listener shall be aware that this slow opening is more than merely introductory—it is basic to the entire logic. Furthermore, when the wheel has come full circle at the close of the work, the placing of widely spaced detached chords, apparently divorced from the macrorhythm, serves to draw attention to the return to very slow motion indeed. (The often overlooked 'Un pochettino stretto' of the last 16 bars does not materially affect this slowing of the pace.) This had not been effected by the mere introduction of longer note values, though from Letter N onwards these values had certainly helped in the gradual process of slowing down. The loudness and unexpectedness of these final chords help to maintain the tension which would otherwise decrease with the loss of pace.

In order to end the first movement, Sibelius sets up a very clear four-bar macrorhythm, only to finish on its weak third bar: the rhythm x has been evident in the brass chords of the previous few bars, and it is this rhythm which causes the movement to end on what amounts to an upbeat. Thus, clearly, x, which has been mostly applied on the small scale, is now applied also to the macrorhythm, a treatment which is suggested by the continuous increase in speed throughout the movement, and which is of importance later in the work. Moreover, the ending on a weak bar of the macrorhythm does not sound too final: this is most important to a movement which, in spite of a gradual accumulation of speed and a reassembly of various motifs towards the end, is yet not the Finale: the listener must, of course, be made to feel that this does not constitute the end of the argument.[35]

The slow movement forms the centre of the arch by combining slow motion (in the form of chorale-like music) in the wind with faster music (a set of variations mostly in crotchets and quavers) in the strings. As at the end of the first movement, however, there are in fact three things going on here; the third is a series of long pedals which grow in prominence towards the middle of the movement (pages 79ff) and which are then the cue for the use of a D pedal alternating with the variations theme (see Ex. 63).

Ex. 63

A logical outcome of the process of combining fast and slow motion is
heterophony, a feature heard soon afterwards (see Ex. 64).

Ex. 64

Coming at the very centre of the symphony, this forms an ideal fusion of
quick and slow motion. The two speeds are then separated out again, and
though the final wind phrase of the movement attempts to combine the
crotchet motion of the variations with the slower style of the 'chorale-
music' which has characterized the wind almost throughout, it is with a
surprisingly short note that the movement ends, creating (as in the first
movement) the unmistakable impression that more music is necessary
before the argument is concluded. There is also in this movement a sense of
balance between the various speeds: this helps the listener to identify this
section as the centre of an arch-shape, placed between a movement in
which fast motion overcomes slow and one in which slow overcomes fast.

The rhythm x is used in a new guise in the Finale. After a clear statement
of the figure in the uppermost violin part of the first six bars it is heard only
occasionally until the second subject—'Thor's hammer'—arrives (Ex. 65).
The opening theme of the Finale (which had been foreshadowed at the end
of the first movement) is largely written in ♪s, and it is placed against a
string background which, while using similar note values, yet produces a
static effect since the instruments continually cross between the same few
notes. The use of short note values to produce an impression of slow motion
is evident here, as also in the use of a string tremolando on a single note.
The music moves into a three-bar macrorhythm (overlaid with a six-bar
rhythm), and here the actual moving parts of the horns—that is, those
apart from the upper notes, which are repeated in every third bar—
constitute another version of x (see Ex. 65, in which ⌐   ¬ is used to
show the macrorhythm.)

Ex. 65

To designate this motif x might seem rather far-fetched; nevertheless, it is a phrase whose important movement occurs at the beginning and end of the three-bar macrorhythm, just as that of x in the first movement had occurred at the beginning and end of a bar (or sometimes a half-bar). The use of x in a macrorhythm here, as contrasted with its use in a single bar in the earlier parts of the work, is another indication of Sibelius' concern with quick and slow motion. This concern is also evident in other ways: the bassoons and double basses have the same theme as the horns, but moving three times as slowly.[36] Slower motion still is evident in the upper strings for, as with the accompaniment to the first subject, the parts continually cross each other, using the same few notes, so that the effect is again very static.[37] Furthermore, the application of an idea which had appeared in ♪ note values at the start of the movement to much longer notes at this point is yet another expression of Sibelius' overall design.[38] Sibelius' genius for symphonic construction is very evident here: by writing a subject which returns to the upper notes of the tune in every third bar (see Ex. 65) he fulfils several functions. Firstly, the theme's relationship with x is made clear by confining the essential movement to the beginning and end of the macrorhythm; and, since this is so, it also becomes clear that the general outline of this subject conforms to the motif a shown in Ex. 11. The presence of the upper notes creates in addition a relationship with other important thematic elements; and x is now used in long, instead of short, note values. The theme could also be viewed as a decorated pedal, since it keeps returning to the same notes: pedals and decorated pedals, often providing a static element, have been a feature throughout the work. Moreover, the effect of a slowly swinging pendulum which the subject creates helps Sibelius to begin to restrain the headlong rush of the Finale. Perhaps more important still is the fact that the theme expresses the overall arch-shape of the symphony on two smaller scales: firstly, the music in each three-bar macrorhythm of Ex. 65 is arch-shaped; and secondly, if one ignores the bracketed upper pedal of that Example, it will readily be perceived that what remains is an inverted arch-shape on a somewhat larger scale.[39] Such arch-shapes are characteristic also of other themes in the work.

Just as quicker versions of x tend to be used in counterpoint with fore-tastes of the 'hammer' theme in the first two movements,[40] so in the Finale the theme is accompanied by x in shorter note values (see Ex. 66). Here Sibelius has combined a small-scale version of x with a larger version of y. The result of the presence of various combinations of speeds and rhythms in this subject is that there is a feeling of established tonality.

Ex. 66

The final two pages of the score present E flat in a great blaze of triumph. The six-bar rhythm of Ex. 65 now becomes a two-bar macrorhythm, since the time signature has been altered to $\frac{3}{2}$: thus rhythms that were first applied to the macrorhythm in this movement are now applied to bars. Nevertheless, the change of time signature and gradual ritardando (until the final 'Un pochettino stretto') have the effect of making these devices slower rather than faster: here is another paradox, for the rhythmic feature applied to the bars sounds slower than the same feature applied to the macrorhythm (*groups* of bars). This constitutes a reversal of the processes of the first movement. On the last two pages of the Finale, the various rhythms which have been played off against one another throughout the symphony are combined: the music of Ex. 65, in the trumpets and first and second trombones, extends the rhythm *x* to a hemiola which lasts the two bars of the macrorhythm, while horns and third trombone maintain a

duple rhythm throughout: the string rhythm ♩♩ ♩ ♩ is not only a

version of *x* which also implies the hemiola of *y*, but in addition refers back to the many places in the symphony where the strings play slightly in advance of the wind,[41] a device which may itself derive from the 'upbeat' nature of *x*. The unconventional ending includes within two implied hemiolas a series of chords which are set at wider rhythmic intervals than those which form the hemiolas, again expressing the fast-slow-fast idea which is basic to the symphony (see Ex. 67).

Ex. 67

In effect there is, in this symphony, a polyphony of rhythms. We may call to mind at this point the words of Adrian Leverkühn in Thomas Mann's *Doctor Faustus*:

The degree of dissonance is the measure of its polyphonic value. The more discordant a chord is, the more notes it contains contrasting and conflicting with each other, the more polyphonic it is, and the more markedly every single note bears the stamp of the part already in the simultaneous sound-combination.[42]

Mann's suggestion is useful, for it draws attention to the reasons for another important feature of the work—the dissonant notes. Resolving either up or down, the many examples in this symphony may last a long or short while before the resolution is heard, and may thus draw attention (in the way Mann's composer suggests) to one part or another—or, in this particular work, to one speed or another. The opening of the symphony provides a good example of this. The end of the second bar and the entire third bar consist of a long (though mild) dissonant chord above the E flat pedal of the timpani: this very long dissonance, which resolves by falling, is complemented by the brief ones in the faster moving upper woodwinds (especially in the fourth bar). It would indeed be superfluous to list all the uses of dissonance and differently timed resolutions in the work; but it may perhaps be interesting to examine one use of the device in the Finale.

The Finale begins by introducing an A flat above the tonic E flat—a mild dissonance which resolves only after being held for somewhat longer than the ear might expect; a feature is made of this at the recapitulation in G flat, for at that later stage the long dissonant note is the enharmonic equivalent of one of the most important notes in the symphony (from the tonal point of view), B natural. Long dissonances are also a feature of the tune quoted in Ex. 66, a feature that becomes especially prominent and considerably aids in the building of tension even though the dynamic markings are fairly quiet at its last appearance just before Letter P. So like the final arrival of the tonic has this passage sounded that the wandering modulations which immediately follow it (pages 131ff) must seem to the listener like the application of dissonance to tonality rather than chords, for the expected return to E flat after these modulations is long delayed. Such a use of 'tonal' dissonance, in addition to the more usual type, is most useful to Sibelius at the close of the Fifth Symphony, since it enables him to increase the tension and build a climax without increasing the speed or using more dynamic motifs or shorter note values. Moreover, the application of dissonance to a section of some size, as well as to a single note, provides another way of introducing Sibelius' overall unifying design: the composer may well have remembered this application of dissonance to sections as well as single notes when he came to write his Seventh Symphony, discussed below.

The aspects of the Fifth Symphony so far discussed do not by any means exhaust the possibilities of Sibelius' overall conception. The doubling of melodic lines at various different intervals—large and small—provides another example, and one which plays a considerable part in the tonal construction of the work. For Sibelius, the most euphonious doublings are those at the octave and the third (or the sixth, which is merely an inversion of the third). Within the Fifth Symphony there is much thickening of a part by doubling at these intervals. One might justly argue that such doublings are part of the common currency of the period; yet the attention drawn to them, and the place given them in the symphonic argument, suggest that their use in the work is more than either fortuitous or conventional.

Parallel thirds are first heard in the descending bassoon and horn lines at the opening, and in the woodwind arabesques which follow: many other examples are readily traceable throughout the work. Parallel octaves appear prominently as G major is reached (pages 6ff), though they have already been suggested at the approach to that key (Letter B), at the point where the parallel thirds (with each voice of the pair doubled at the octave) are thinned out to leave pure octaves in the final bar of page 5. The extension of the interval of doubling from a third to an octave is allied to another feature which likewise treats a facet of composition on both the large and small scale. The phrases on the flutes, oboes and clarinets on the first two pages end first with an open fifth harmony (in bars 3f), then with a fourth (bars 5f), and subsequently contract the interval to a third and a unison (in bars 7–9). In bar 10 the interval is one of a whole tone. Sibelius could scarcely have made the point about the use of large and small intervals more clearly than this.

As mentioned above, the doubling of a part in parallel at the interval of a third or an octave is a 'euphonious' sound: it therefore tends to produce a settled feeling. To have doubled a part at an interval of intermediate size—at the fourth or fifth (a common enough procedure with his English contemporaries)—would have produced music alien to Sibelius' style. Yet the settled nature of parallel thirds and octaves needs something more astringent to counter it if the music is not to cloy and lack a sense of argument. Sibelius has found a splendid foil in the tritone, which had already been an important feature of his two previous symphonies. The tritone is used as a harmonic sound in its own right and also as an interval at which a part is doubled. As early as page 6, for example, the rising string passage contains many versions of the augmented fourth (though not at this point in parallel motion). The intervals A-E flat and C-G flat (F sharp) are the most frequently found here, and they give the music an unsettled feeling. A much clearer impression of the struggle between tritones and the more euphonious doublings can be gained from the passage on page 15 of the score: the basses have a double pedal on G and C sharp, while the higher strings move in consecutive tritones (though a third note thickens the interval to a chord) and the woodwind wander above in parallel octaves of indeterminate tonality. When, on pages 18f, parallel thirds reappear instead of the tritones, the tonality settles down.

More instructive still is the wandering chromatic passage which begins on page 21. The music given to the strings at this point consists of two elements: parallel thirds, which are played by the second violins and violas, are surrounded by parallel octaves played by the first violins and 'cellos. The material of both elements is similar—canonic almost—though it is clear that the octaves which surround the thirds continually recoil from the tritones which they make in conjunction with them. The unsettled nature of the resulting tonality culminates in an attempt to establish the tonic chord (E flat, Letter L on page 24), though the brass counter this with their A major chord, a tritone away. This powerful—if somewhat subdued—expression of the tritone affects the music for a considerable time, for even the combination of string parallel octaves and wind parallel sixths does not annul its effect. Indeed, the horn interruptions on pages 26f ensure that the effect of the tritone is not overcome, for they state that interval in a striking set of three quick parallel chords marked *rfz* and *rffz*. Paradoxically, though, it is a series of consecutive tritones which helps to re-establish tonality—not E flat, but B major—on pages 27f: here the augmented fourths played by the trombones have a third note placed beneath them in order to make a series of fuller chords, whose effect is more tonal and less dissonant than that of the previous passage. In the remainder of the movement the tritone is used melodically: indeed, in one place (pages 44f) melodic tritones are played in octaves against a series of rising parallel tritone harmonies in the accompaniment—a combination that produces a very unsettled tonality. The tonic is re-established at the end of the movement by the use of many parallel thirds played with octave doublings.

In the E flat central section of the second movement Sibelius insists that the A should be natural, an effect of the tritone (though slight) which harks back to the statement of the interval in chordal terms during the first movement (page 24). It is as if E flat must not, either in the middle of the first movement or the middle of the second, become firmly established as an undisputed tonic. A parallel to the use of the tritone as a destructive as well as a 'tonal' force, already discussed in Chapter V, is evident in the slow movement: indeed, it has already been briefly mentioned in dealing with pages 25–8 of the first movement. On pages 92–5, E, F and F sharp are tried in turn as the tonic: the establishment of the first two of these keys is prevented by the sudden intervention of loud tritones, though a soft tritone which follows the F sharp version of the main subject is worked into a dominant seventh chord, and leads naturally to the re-establishment of the slow movement's real key of G.

Another parallel with devices already discussed is also evident in the slow movement. Just as the ideal fusion of long and short note values is found in the heterophonic passage, making the movement, as it were, the centre of the arch before the values are separated again in the Finale, so the various doublings at the large and small intervals are also fused in the slow movement. Towards the end of the movement Sibelius combines the various doublings, writing a passage (page 97) in which thirds, octaves and tritones, all used in parallel, are shown to be compatible. The string phrases, in parallel thirds, are doubled out in octaves, while the trombone accompaniment in tritones is provided with a bass part which makes each interval sound more euphonious. Nevertheless, the effect is not one of absolutely settled tonality, for its minor colouring—the wide use of E flat and A

natural reflecting earlier tendencies in the work—conflicts with the
G major which is the real tonic of the movement.

Naturally, one of the main functions of the Finale must be to find a
solution to the problems posed in the earlier movements. Sibelius begins,
therefore, by strongly contradicting the E flat-A tritone with an opening
chord in which E flat and A flat are prominent, and with a first subject
that begins with repeated A flats, eventually descending by step to the
tonic—a shape that had appeared previously towards the end of the first
movement. Nevertheless, A naturals frequently recur later in the first
subject, with chromatic effect but without upsetting the firm hold of the
tonic. This hold is strengthened by the combination of striding parallel
thirds in the horns (Ex. 65) and a woodwind countersubject given out in
octaves (Ex. 66): there is, however, a modulation to C major and back,
occasioned by the appearance of tritones. A short passage of less settled
tonality (pages 113ff) makes prominent use of B natural (C flat), a note
whose importance has already been stressed in dealing with earlier parts
of the work. Its prominence causes it to be taken as a dominant, and an
attempt is made to start the recapitulation of the main theme in E major
(page 118), the long A which would open the tune in this key forming a
tritone with the E flat which has already been sounded in the bass. The E
flat-A natural tritone has, it will be remembered, been a feature of the
work so far; but because the Finale is seeking to overcome the effect of
tritones, E flat is treated as the leading-note of E major, moving upwards
by a semitone. The process is repeated when the tritone E-B flat interrupts,
and an attempt is made to begin the recapitulation in F: at last (page 120)
the recapitulation proper gets under way, in G flat. This key has been
neatly prepared by the previous E (F flat) and F natural; the rise by three
semitones while various keys are tried as the new tonic reflects a similar
device in the second movement (pages 92ff). In the new key the main
theme begins with a repeated C flat (the B natural which has been
prominent in the preceding pages of this movement, as well as in
earlier parts of the symphony). Moreover, when tritones *are* heard in this
subject, the notes used are G flat and C natural (transposed from the E
flat-A natural interval of the version of this tune which opens the Finale)—
in other words the F sharp-C which has been one of the other prominent
tritones earlier in the work.

During the recapitulation the second subject—'Thor's hammer'—is first
heard in G flat, and since this key is so far from the tonic of the movement,
the theme is stated with much less force than previously. On page 126
(Letter N), however, the tonic minor is reached, and the music gains in
power of utterance. There is here a further interaction of doublings at the
octave, third and augmented fourth. The octaves of the original countersubject to this theme remain (see Ex. 66), but the parallel thirds of the

striding tune are replaced by tritones which revolve slowly in the accompanying horn parts, the tune itself being shared between two oboes playing alternately. More power still is gained as the tonic major is reached (page 129) and tritones in the accompaniment are replaced by major thirds, very strikingly used in divided double basses. The striding 'hammer' theme, now in the trumpets, does not use absolutely parallel thirds, and on pages 130 of this subject is written with many tritone doublings in a gradually rising sequence, a most powerful passage which has string octaves pitted against it after a while. It is only when the tritones are replaced by parallel thirds on page 135 that the tonic is firmly regained: the prominent rise and fall of a fifth which is a feature of the tune in Ex. 65 also does much to contradict the tritones in these closing pages. The prominent A flat in the last two bars of page 135 has a similar effect, countering that of the A natural in the tonic key, so evident earlier in the work. For the same reason, the note A flat is prominently sounded in one of the detached chords on the final page. The two final bars consist of a falling fifth, B flat-E flat, in octaves: the interval is one that has already been prominent in the second subject of the movement, and one that also contradicts the tritonal A natural. The three previous chords allude to parallel sixths beneath a B flat which itself is an inversion of the opening B flat pedal of the work, just as the final two notes invert the work's first leap of B flat-E flat. These inversions complete the arch-shape of the symphony.

The shape of melodic phrases provides yet another instance of the working of Sibelius' overall plan. The balance between material which moves largely by step and that which moves largely by leap is most impressive, and can clearly be heard during the 'Thor's hammer' theme (Exx. 65 and 66). Here the part doubled in thirds uses large melodic intervals, whereas the countersubject which uses parallel octaves moves mostly by step. Hence the part doubled at the larger interval uses the smaller steps, and vice versa.[43] Such a contrast of material is characteristic of the work, being clearly evident even in the opening phrases of the first movement. Moreover, it is quite clear that with the second movement the two types of melodic line are fused—made compatible just as are so many other elements of composition in this movement—in a line which uses the largely stepwise main theme, yet continually jumps from the notes of this theme to a pedal D and back (see Ex. 63).

Sibelius' concept of the work as one in which very many facets of composition appear on both the large and small (and sometimes intermediate) scale—the opposing elements being fused in a slow movement which provides the apex to an arch-shape—produces a work which is very close to the concept of total unity: this concept was only reached by serialist composers much later with the strict organization of other elements in addition to pitch. Sibelius' Fifth Symphony shows us a giant

among composers rejoicing in his strength. The sense of well-being which
we feel on hearing the work is due not only to the innate attractiveness of
its material, but also to its sense of balance, its formal perfection and the
perfect integration of every element into the scheme. Moreover, the scheme
itself epitomizes balance in its combination of opposing elements and its
all-permeating arch-shape.[44]

In his Fifth Symphony, Sibelius provides an object lesson in maintaining
a sense of rhythmic flow: such a sense of flow is the only thing that matters
in music, according to Delius.[45] Great symphonies certainly have this
sense, though it is not always easy to define it or demonstrate the ways in
which it is achieved: it is easier to point out where works fail in this
respect.[46] The sense of flow is not concerned merely with 'on-going
rhythm': if it were, an endless series of repetitions of such a tune as that in
the Trio section of the 'Choral' Symphony would prove satisfactory in this
respect. Such a piece would not, however, satisfy the ear because it would
lack the 'on-going' logic—the working out and counterpointing of
tensions, tonalities, themes, rhythms and textures—which we expect of a
symphony. Balance is clearly vital: a sense of flow can be broken by too
much forward motion just as it can by too little. An example of this is the
gigantic first theme of the Finale of Bruckner's Fourth Symphony discussed
above: only by working up slowly to the first statement of this theme does the
piece generate sufficient momentum to carry the subject. The recapitulation of that theme[47] is given without the same momentum being provided
for its preparation, and the scale of the music at this point cannot carry the
subject in nearly such a convincing way as does the exposition.[48]

Although it has often been said that the 'on-going' flow of music is
measured by comparison with human bodily rhythms, the above analyses
would suggest that much more is required. The size of the development,
for example, must match the width and range of tonality, and vice versa—
elements which one does not ordinarily consider rhythmic at all but which,
since they are audible events of some moment taking place on a certain
time-scale, must have an effect on the sense of forward progression. The
handling of tensions—the ebb and flow of degrees and lengths of dissonances, for example—must for the same reason have an effect on the
sense of forward progression, as indeed it does in the Fifth Symphony of
Sibelius: these matters will be discussed more fully in the following
Chapter.

In Sibelius' Fifth Symphony, the flow results partly from the interaction
of several elements, one of which is the use of a 'double time-scheme' at
various levels. The difficulties of handling harmonic rhythm on the vast
time-scales which Bruckner set himself will be remembered from the above
discussion: Sibelius, however, in his Fifth Symphony, overcomes the difficulty in a very simple manner, for the long harmonies are now made to

serve a 'symphonic' function (rather than being a feature which stands apart from other facets of the work), and the rhythms which enliven these harmonies form another part of the same conception. The 'double time-scale' of Sibelius' Fifth was not new, though its treatment was more impressive and thorough than any previous application in music.[49] I shall suggest later (in Chapter VII) that Beethoven's Seventh Symphony may have provided Sibelius with the inspiration for this idea. The counterpoint of two rhythms, brought out by the different lengths of dissonances and their resolutions, helps Sibelius to control tensions and climaxes throughout the work; and it supplies a harmonic background which (as he himself taught) provides an orchestral substitute for the sustaining pedal's effect in piano music. These slowly revolving harmonies do much to provide the characteristic sound of this symphony.

CHAPTER VII

Pace and Tension

The drawbacks of 'paper analysis' have been mentioned in Chapter I. Nowhere does such analysis fail more lamentably than in its sheer inability to cope adequately with the problems of pace and tension, since these elements, by their very nature, are evident far more in the response of the listener than they are on paper. In fact, they are often not evident in the score at all. It follows that pace and tension have been largely overlooked by most analysts. It has already been shown how Sibelius, in his Fifth Symphony, handled these elements within an overall plan. Three of Beethoven's symphonies provide an opportunity for a closer investigation of different methods of handling these two vital elements of composition.

Beethoven's Fifth Symphony

In recent years there has been a certain amount of discussion of what has been described as 'metrical ambiguity' in the development section of the first movement of Beethoven's Fifth Symphony.[1] One interpretation[2] suggests that there is an overlap, at bar 209, of the final bar of a six-bar macrorhythm with the first bar of the following six-bar group. An alternative solution[3] involves (mentally, at least) arranging the macrorhythm in such a way that the bars are at times grouped together in multiples of three plus five. These contradictory views might seem to suggest that Beethoven may have intended the listener to be in some doubt as to which is correct.[4] But these interpretations neglect some important aspects of the evidence provided by the aural impact of the music.

The problem is that there seems to be an extra bar in the development section: this is because the natural four-bar macrorhythm which opens the section with a strong pulse at bar 126 must be altered at some point before the strong pulse at bar 229 (after which four-bar rhythms again become natural); an odd bar has, apparently, to be inserted before the strong pulse of bar 209 is reached. Rhythms consisting of an odd number of bars are by no means unknown in the music of Beethoven's contemporaries and predecessors, and in the present instance it seems to be the *placing* of the extra bar that has created the problem. An investigation of this passage may well show that the problem is not one of apparent metrical ambiguity so much as one of pace and tension.

The widespread discussion of macrorhythm in the movement is a direct reflection of the fact that, with the music moving at a one-in-a-bar pace, the ear naturally tends to hear whole bars as beats, and to organize these bars mentally into larger units, just as beats would themselves normally be organized into bars. Moreover, Beethoven is unable to use his habitual technique of off-beat accentuation within a bar because of this fast pace, so instead he tends to alter accents within the larger organization of groups of bars.

With this in mind, it is obvious that the use of a harmonic rhythm in which each chord lasts for four bars will set up a four-bar macrorhythm, with the stresses occurring on the first and the (slightly weaker) third bars. Such a passage occurs at bars 44–55 of the movement: each change of chord naturally produces a new impulse, so that the mind accepts this regular pulsation as the norm. The natural scansion is as shown in Ex. 68 below:[5]

Ex. 68

The motto rhythm ♪ ♫ | ♩ when it appears in unison is carefully stressed so that the fourth note coincides with a strong pulse of the macrorhythm, and this motto then becomes unmistakable as a metrical unit and can be applied to help define rhythm on the larger scale.[6] The careful treatment of four-bar rhythms at the end of the exposition also strengthens this feeling: naturally, the composer must establish the norm before the ear can readily follow departures from it.

The mind, once conditioned to a certain macrorhythm, attempts to continue its application for as long as possible, until the music makes a change inevitable.[7] Occasional six-bar rhythms do not, on the whole, upset a four-bar metrical pattern, since here the primary and secondary strong pulses merely exchange their functions. An ambiguity between rival means of accentuating a four-bar macrorhythm is created by Beethoven in bars 84–114 of this movement, for instance, until eventually the lighter and heavier of the two strong pulses are reversed. It is when the number of bars is odd (as it is in the development section) that a previously established macrorhythm of an even number of bars is questioned. Beethoven appears to have handled this particular change so skilfully that many analysts have been unable to tell how he achieves it.

An accent, or an unexpected note or chord, may be used to help establish a macrorhythm; on the other hand, such devices could create syncopation against a regular macrorhythm already set up. An obvious example of the latter tendency is the arrival of the expected new tonic chord (even though it is quiet) at bar 63: by introducing harmony after a unison passage, Beethoven shifts the accent forward from a strong to the preceding weak bar, yet without doing it so powerfully as to destroy the macrorhythm itself (the arrows in Ex. 68 show this process). The ubiquitous presence of the motto rhythm ♪♩♩♩│♩ immediately recalls the established metre, a use which amply demonstrates Beethoven's handling of it as a means of controlling the macrorhythm.[8] Previously, too, Beethoven had suggested the shifting of the accent forward (see bar 26—the strong pulse— to bar 29): at that early stage the effect had been mild, sounding more like a feminine ending because of the brevity of the tonic chord as compared with the dominant. The device is immediately repeated: on both occasions the motto rhythm ♪♩♩♩│♩ on dominant and tonic attempts to place the strong pulse on the fourth bar of the macrorhythm, and the second time the rhythm is strengthened by woodwind and horns.[9]

Beethoven now develops the idea of shifting an expected strong pulse onto the previous weak bar, and its next occurrence is not only more intensely stated, but placed significantly at the very start of the development section (see the arrows in Ex. 69):

Ex. 69

The use of the motto theme, whose normal stresses the listener by now recognizes as those shown in Ex. 68, makes this displacement of accent all the more telling. The device here serves an additional purpose: the first four notes of the development section would seem to be in E flat, since not only are they the opening motif of the work played a third higher, but they also immediately follow a big E flat cadence. The sudden twist onto the dominant chord of F minor is made more striking by the use of several devices: by introducing a well-recognized thematic tag, yet with different metrical stresses from those which the ear has come to regard as normal; by using the unexpected sound of an open fifth, omitting the more conventional leading-note (E natural); and by introducing it with the strong pulse on C thrown a bar earlier than expected. The shift of accent is treated with increasing vigour later in the development: firstly, at bars 145 and 153 the upward scales lead to the adoption of a new tonic chord on the (weak) fourth bar of a macrorhythm, though statements of the motto rhythm leading on to the next strong pulse immediately cancel the effect of syncopation which Beethoven has suggested. In bars 171 and 175 the forward shift of accent is stronger because the change of harmony is played tutti just before the strong pulse, the effect being magnified by the fact that in both instances the new chord is preceded by a rest. The accelerating descent of the violas and 'cellos in bars 166 and 167 ensures that the original four-bar macrorhythm remains in the mind,[10] as do the increasingly powerful statements of the motto rhythm—higher than ever before in bars 179f. Next, the arrival of the expected new tonic on the weak fourth bar of a macrorhythm (G major at bar 187 and C major at bar 195) again throws the weight a bar forward, yet the macrorhythm is immediately re-established with strong unison versions of the motto rhythm. The increasingly powerful statements of the 'syncopated-accent' bars and the greater frequency of their appearance thus clearly prepare the ear for the passage which is the main subject of this discussion.

Many analysts have admitted to being puzzled by the antiphonal chords at bars 196–227 and to being unable to tell whence they derive. The statement of the motto rhythm at bars 195–8, given in the same form with which it introduced the second subject, provides the clue, since the chords which follow derive from the continuation of that subject. Beethoven has extracted the harmony (the shape of the viola part is now applied to the top of the chords, as shown by the dotted lines in Ex. 70), and has not included the tune above it or the statements of the motto rhythm in the bass. The antiphonal scoring applied to the chords reflects the changing instrumentation which is applied to melodic lines at several points in the exposition.

As Ex. 70 shows, Beethoven has now shifted the melodic shape of the original viola part forward by a bar: this has the effect of bringing model (second and third bars of Ex. 70b, in the winds) and imitation (fourth and fifth bars, in the strings) closer together, and the arrival of the new (and

anticipated) tonic chord of F minor on a weak pulse places unexpected
weight at that point of the macrorhythm (as demonstrated by the arrows in
Ex. 70b). In order that the device shall have its full effect, Beethoven has
taken great care to ensure that F is felt to be logically the next tonic: thus
he has prepared it with his previous circle of fifths, each new key being
introduced by a statement of the motto rhythm in its second subject form,
as in Ex. 70a. It will not have escaped notice that the shift of accent in
Ex. 69 also introduces F minor; the two passages may well be subconsciously connected, therefore, in the listener's mind. Having yet again
shifted the accent forward, Beethoven maintains his antiphonal treatment
of two chords in strict alternation, so that the ear now begins to regroup the
chords, shifting the strong pulse forward by a bar—an effect which
Beethoven has been preparing since bar 63 (if not bar 29). At the earlier
shifts of accent, the original macrorhythm was recovered at the insistence
of the rhythmic motto; but at the point now reached (bars 195ff) Beethoven uses only the harmonic shape of the second subject, omitting both
tune and motto rhythm: this means that there is no repetition of the motto
to insist on a return to the original macrorhythm. The whole macrorhyth-
mic scheme is thus moved forward by a bar. Nevertheless, with an unexpected chord of G flat in bar 205, the metre begins to assume a pattern in
which that bar represents the strongest pulse: thus, as in bars 84–114 mentioned above, the heavier and lighter stresses of the new metre change
places (see the square brackets in Ex. 71). This exchange is confirmed
when the next tonic chord in the circle of fifths (B flat minor) appears on
the following strong pulse of the new macrorhythm:[11]

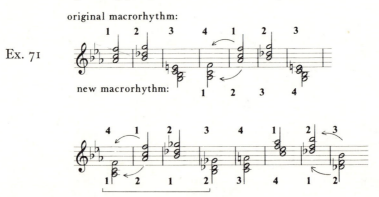

Ex. 71

Beethoven settles the new macrorhythm unmistakably: by repeating the
B flat minor chord in a different instrumentation and at a lower pitch, he
shows quite clearly that the second chord is placed on a weaker pulse than
the first; and the process of scoring in this manner continues. Moreover, as
Schenker has pointed out,[12] the diminuendo is marked to begin with this

lower chord of B flat in the strings: less weight is therefore given to the playing of this lower chord, providing further assistance to the ear in identifying the bar as a 'weak' one.

This is not the end of the matter, for such a process in the development section is likely to have repercussions in the coda. Before dealing with that part of the movement, however, it should be mentioned that the oboe cadenza of bar 268 in the recapitulation is also in some ways connected with the dislocation of accents. Although the bar (marked 'Adagio' for the oboe) as a whole represents only the third bar of a four-bar macrorhythm, the ear hears the cadenza as an elongation of that pulse. By writing a passage which is completely unlike anything the ear expects—virtually a recitative in free rhythm—Beethoven draws attention to this pulse more clearly than he could have done by almost any other means: the additional bars which he added to the pages of his early version of the symphony,[13] for example, do not have the enormous effect of rhythmic extension that this oboe recitative has. The macrorhythm is not, in reality, altered: it is momentarily suspended. The passage between bars 22 and 24,[14] at the corresponding position in the exposition, is considerably more intense than the wistful oboe solo of the recapitulation, and it, too, serves to dislocate the rhythm—yet the effect is by no means so obvious to the ear as is that of the recitative. The arrival of F minor is again the signal for an alteration of macrorhythm in the coda, at bar 389. Here it is an extra bar which is inserted, though Beethoven draws no attention at all to it—it is completely silent, and balances the extra bar in the development section. It perhaps also serves to remind one, even if only subconsciously, of the several points at which Beethoven has added an extra bar to a chord with a pause, so creating five-bar phrases.[15]

The implications of this process are unmistakable: the shifts of accent introduced in the exposition are worked into a climax at the height of the development, where they attain such strength that even the dynamic effect of the motto rhythm is dispersed: in the recapitulation the oboe recitative draws attention to the fact that the whole macrorhythm is, as it were, a bar in advance of its correct position. It does so tentatively and 'senza misura', without reference to the motto rhythm and without re-establishing the original metre. The coda allows its extra bar to re-establish the original macrorhythm, yet without any sense of crisis, for it provides merely an empty bar. Balance is maintained within the movement, yet the symphonic argument is not complete, for the problem has not yet been logically solved. The mind knows instinctively that, though the *movement* ends at precisely the right moment, the *symphony* cannot end here: there must be yet more music to follow, so that the problem can be argued through more fully.

It is now clear that an important facet of this movement is the shifting of an accent forward by a bar to an unexpected weak pulse. Such a treatment of rhythm is naturally more dynamic than the easy-going nature of the contemporaneous 'Pastoral' Symphony:[16] the great and entirely novel dynamic force of the first movement of the Fifth Symphony is largely brought about by the power of the motto rhythm and the logical growth of the changing stresses. This, however, is to see only one of the levels of the piece; and Beethoven's logic is at work on more than one level. Other events in the symphony must also have taken the first hearers by surprise because they happened earlier than expected. A slow introduction might well begin with a pause, but one would scarcely expect two pauses in the first five bars of quick $\frac{2}{4}$ time; moreover, the sudden move to F minor at the beginning of the development, already discussed, must likewise have seemed unexpectedly abrupt and early. The chordal passage with which this discussion has been largely concerned not only starts by altering the macrorhythm, but, by means of sequential extension, repeated minim chords and gradual decrescendo with quiet scoring, subsequently relaxes the tension built up by the forward shifts of expected events. The peaceful nature of these chords (the antiphonal orchestration is here much more restful than the unsettled nature of the changeful scoring of the opening tune) is shattered momentarily by a loud and premature return of the opening motto rhythm which will herald the recapitulation in due course. The minim chords resume after this interruption; but the motto rhythm breaks in again, and it is still premature, for the same motif is repeated several times until the recapitulation proper gets under way.

Some of the tensions of the exposition are resolved in the recapitulation. The uneasy scoring of the opening of the symphony, in which the melodic line is tossed from instrument to instrument (perhaps so that each segment of the phrase can be more clearly identified as consisting of the motto rhythm) is now scored in less fragmentary fashion, and a slow countersubject in the oboe helps to bind the music together in a more tranquil manner. The same premature stop on a dominant chord as had appeared in the exposition recurs in the reprise, though this time it is not interrupted by the loud unison statement of the motto theme in F minor, for the simple reason that to use the figure again after its many repetitions at the close of the development would produce anticlimax. In its place, Beethoven uses the recitative-like oboe cadenza which, as I have already mentioned, does not add anything to the macrorhythm in terms of numbers of bars; instead it suspends the macrorhythm completely. Only a passage lacking regular rhythm and accentuation could fulfil such a function.

If one accepts that the idea of shifting musical events to an earlier point than expected applies to both macrorhythm and length of sections within a movement, it may not be so very fanciful to suggest that the first movement, which is such a short and concise piece for its power, ends much

earlier than one might imagine. Thus, the fact that the second movement
begins earlier than the first audience must have expected helps to throw
unprecedented weight onto the Finale, and the enormous energy and power
of that movement in turn help to balance the conciseness and brevity of the
opening movement.

The various elements of composition are, of course, interdependent: here
the rhythm and the macrorhythm interact with the tonality in a manner
which has all too often been missed. As was mentioned in Chapter III, a
struggle towards C major is evident in each movement of the symphony.
Naturally, in the context of 'flat' keys such as those of the first three movements, C major has a tendency to behave as the dominant of F minor.[17]
Hence the keys of F minor and C major are heard as being in opposition;
at the same time they are in some ways connected. (At bars 90–6 and
273–80 of the Scherzo, for example, there is clearly debate as to whether
F is the subdominant of C, or C the dominant of F.)[18] Beethoven's loud
interruption at bars 22–4 of the opening movement provides an important
statement of F minor, even though the notes used are immediately
reinterpreted as belonging to the dominant ninth of C minor; besides this,
several other syncopations of the macrorhythm in the movement are also
concerned with appearances of F minor. The glimpses of triumph which
appear at the C major passages in the slow movement dissolve towards
F minor (before moving on to A flat) with an indeterminate macrorhythm,
and even the suggestions of F major in the Trio section of the third movement result in the shifting of accents forward by a crotchet. The triumphant
settling of the macrorhythm in the Finale accompanies the reinterpretation
of F as the clear subdominant of C major—as witness bars 6–12 of the
movement. The development section of the Finale sets up A major as a
foil to F minor, yet flat keys (including F minor) are again heard. Once
more the triumphant progress of the 'correct' ordering of rhythm on the
large scale is thrown into disarray, for the preparation of the recapitulation
arrives too soon: this is one of the reasons (but by no means the only one)
for the return of the music of the Scherzo. After this, F again becomes
merely the subdominant of C major, and the large-scale metre marches
steadily on its triumphant way. The chords in the final 25 bars, so often
remarked upon, celebrate the recovery of an unmistakable macrorhythm
which goes hand in hand with an untarnished C major; also, by extending
the final cadence for many bars, they balance in impressive fashion the
many premature events at earlier points in the work. There is here the
sense of final resolution which was absent from the end of the first movement.

The chordal section of the first movement's development raises few problems once this metrical and tonal scheme is understood. C major is almost
entirely avoided until the second subject in the recapitulation: E natural
is omitted from the music of Ex. 69, for instance, so that C major shall not

be given too much prominence at this early point. The C major cadence at bars 194–5 does not establish that key for more than a second, for it is immediately reinterpreted as the dominant of F minor; as so often in the work when the latter key appears, the macrorhythm becomes unsettled. The new macrorhythm becomes regular as the following chords modulate to areas quite distant from F minor (D major and F sharp minor, which are set up to conflict and contrast with it). This is one of the very few places where Beethoven's processes are less perceptible to the ear than they are in the score, and it affords a fascinating glimpse into the working of the composer's mind. As E. T. A. Hoffmann remarked without being able to offer an explanation,[19] Beethoven wrote the F sharp minor chord with a D flat at the top in the winds (though he uses C sharp when the strings play the chord: see bars 215ff). D flat has, indeed, been used at other points in the movement as an indication of an F minor tendency, especially where the presence of an E natural elsewhere in the score might otherwise suggest C major. Bars 76 and 134 of the first movement form a good illustration of this, and the C major section of the recapitulation is immediately cancelled, when the coda begins, by a powerful D flat chord. By writing chords of F sharp minor with D flat in the winds alternating with C sharp in the strings (at bars 215ff of the first movement), Beethoven reveals the debate between flat side keys (primarily F minor) and those on the sharp side of the tonic.

Tovey was exactly right when he described Beethoven as a master of movement:[20] indeed, the evidence presented by Beethoven himself seems sufficiently strong to call for a radical re-examination of the place of rhythm, not only in isolation, and not only for its own sake, but as one of several interdependent elements in symphonic argument and also for the insight it can give into the related aspect of pace.[21] It is difficult to define adequately the concepts of 'pace' and 'tension', largely because they are inherent elements of the listener's response rather than easily isolated facets of composition, such as harmony, tonality or even rhythm. What seems to happen is that the composer presents his listeners with music which contains within itself several possibilities of direction, development and debate. For example, the four-note rhythmic and melodic motif which opens Beethoven's Fifth Symphony creates in the listener's mind uncertainty as to the nature of the tonic and the macrorhythm. The uncertainty which the attentive listener feels causes him to listen for the answers (that is, the resolutions of conflicts and contrasts within the music): he therefore identifies himself with the ongoing tendencies (pace)—whatever form they take—in the music. This very state of feeling could perhaps be properly described as 'tension', but obviously, since response is highly personal, the composer's success in contriving this tension and in communicating it to his listeners cannot be precisely measured. Once we accept the basic principle that music is written to be *heard*, however, we realize that the whole business of pace and tension, though difficult to analyse, is of vital importance in any evaluation.

One of the drawbacks of knowing a piece as well as we know Beethoven's Fifth Symphony is that our perception of the possibilities inherent in the musical material presented to us is blunted. We have heard it so often that we know precisely how Beethoven is going to continue at every point where there are alternative possibilities. We no longer appreciate the existence of such alternative possibilities because we are no longer in the position of an audience that has never heard the work before (nor, indeed, the vast amount of later music). It is one of the great attributes of analysis that, by identifying the questions and pointing out the possible alternative solutions, it can in some measure restore this lost 'innocence' in listening.

Beethoven's Ninth Symphony

The foregoing analysis of Beethoven's Fifth Symphony has shown the symphonic possibilities of rhythm on the small scale and metre on the large scale, and has shown its function in creating and releasing tension. In an earlier part of this book ('Interlude') we have also seen how Bruckner's Fourth Symphony is in some places unsatisfactory because its rhythmic paucity fails to maintain tension.[22] By contrast, a work which deals in exemplary fashion with the idea, on a much larger scale than in Beethoven's Fifth Symphony and with a much greater measure of success than in Bruckner's Fourth, is Beethoven's Ninth Symphony. We could well begin by recalling a passage from Cooper and Meyer's *The Rhythmic Structure of Music*:[23]

> Because more happens in the same amount of time, the pace of the second half of this tune is faster. Our judgments of speed are not absolute. They depend upon what takes place in a given segment of chronological time—on how the segment is filled. Just as one feels that an hour moves slowly as we wait for an appointment or that a play moves slowly or quickly, depending upon the number of events which fill the minutes or hours, so too the psychological tempo of a musical passage depends upon the number of identifiable events or changes which take place in a given segment of time. The absolute rapidity of the stimulus does not determine pace. Notes may follow one another with great chronological rapidity—as they do in a tremolo or in many codas—and yet the music may move slowly or not at all.

One might argue that the whole basis of creating tension through motion is that of setting up a conflict between stillness and forward movement. We have already seen the concept applied to slow and fast motion in Sibelius' Fifth Symphony: we have also seen how the slow rate of harmonic change in Bruckner's *Romantische* necessitates the use of rhythms which attempt to compensate for this rather 'static' harmonic quality. In the 'Choral' Symphony, Beethoven sets up just such a conflict between stillness and motion, treating the idea in several ways and using it to regulate tension. 'Stillness', as I interpret it, can result from several compositional procedures: it can be harmonic stillness, or lack of forward symphonic development; it can be the delay of an expected event, the cessation of music entirely, or a pause (either marked with ⌒ or written out in notes or rests); or it can be the use of continuous repetition, or the use of 'non-rhythmic' music such as recitative or cadenza. In the following discussion I shall refer to passages which contain such stillness as 'symphonic pause' or 'symphonic void'. All these ideas are such as contrast with forward motion, and the forward motion of Beethoven's music can (as in his Fifth Symphony) be made the more striking or the more relaxed by shifting the metrical accents. Nevertheless, the 'pauses' and 'voids' do not necessarily result in a lessening of tension: we shall find instances where Beethoven's handling of such pauses can result in a slow but inexorable increase in tension.

In the 'Choral' Symphony, the process starts at the opening of the work: the spaciousness of the first sounds (the open fifth which hangs for a long time motionless in the air) builds up more tension with every moment that it does not change—for the ear accustomed to music written before this symphony would not expect a work to begin with such a long static harmony. Contrasted with this are the fragmentary descending rhythmic figures of the strings; and the conflict between the two ideas, with the addition of a crescendo, builds up such tension that the first unison state-ment of the main subject in bars 17–20 is so much more intense than it would be if the symphony had started merely with the first subject proper at bar 17.[24] Yet the tension worked up in this passage is made greater still by the shifting forward of changes of harmony so that they come on unexpectedly weak beats of bars 14 and 15, leaving a void in bar 16 which is slightly longer than the ear might have expected. This is the first of many places in the work where the shifting forward of an expected event results in a compensatory 'void' or 'pause' after it.[25] The process is immediately repeated at bars 24–6 of the first subject, where again the unexpectedly early changes of harmony result in a 'written out pause'; and in the close of the D minor statement of the opening theme, where the shifting of accents onto weak beats in bars 31–3 results in a longer than expected $^6_4$ chord over a dominant bass note and in an off-beat arrival of the theme back at the tonic.[26]

So far the 'voids' have taken the form of 'written out pauses'; but another type of void occurs just after the B flat version of the main theme (in bars 55–61). Here the continuous sound is interrupted for the first time, and the logical forward flow of the argument held back by the immediate repetition of the string material in the winds. By 'holding back' for some time this passage also serves to build up further tension which is released in the more continuous forward motion and fast rate of chord change in bars 63f.

Naturally, such an idea is not wasted, for Beethoven expands it soon afterwards, using different thematic material. In bar 106, he leads the ear to expect a firm cadence in the dominant, a quite normal procedure at this stage of a second subject group. The expected cadence is delayed, however, by the repetition of previous material and a new cadence in B major: again, a void is created to follow this shift of expected events, for now Beethoven needs a much longer preparation for his B flat cadence. This preparation, at bars 120–31, is on an F pedal, and consists of many repetitions of a phrase of which one note is in debate—G is sometimes flat and sometimes natural. The reasons for this long dominant of B flat are clear, but it remains true that the effect is that of a pause in the harmonic development of the movement. Such a long 'pause', with crescendo and debate between G flat and G natural, again serves to build up tension slowly and inexorably, and this tension is eventually released in the scurrying demisemiquaver runs in the strings at bars 132–7, and the Bach-like[27] off-beat kick of the other parts.

Since the exposition is not repeated, the beginning of the development section may be regarded as a shifting forward, on a very large scale, of an expected event. If we accept that this, too, necessitates a compensatory feeling of void (on the large scale) later in the development section, we may perhaps see the use of a fugue at bar 218 as the result. Fugue, while not being incompatible with symphonic development, does nevertheless have its own rules of development and tonal logic which are somewhat different from those of the symphony. This fugue is, in essence, an inter-polation of another 'set form' into the development. The effect, to my ears at least, is that of a pause in the forward progress of purely symphonic logic, for such an obvious interpolation of another type of form causes the mind to switch to different principles of construction. This is by no means the same kind of feeling as we experience in the Finale of Mozart's 41st Symphony or his Quartet in G major, K. 387, where the form *as a whole* is more fugal, or even that where fugue is used as one of a set of variations (as in Beethoven's Seventh Symphony). The fugue in the first movement of the 'Choral' is, naturally, fully integrated thematically into the develop-ment section: the subject derives from the main theme, and the Bachian off-beat repetitions of an octave pedal refer back to the shifting of accents and the many pedals elsewhere in the work. Indeed, the whole movement has an intangible Bach-like feeling, partially derived from the restricted use of keys: fugue fits in well with this feeling. I suggest that Beethoven switched to a different kind of musical logic in order to follow through, on the large scale, the idea of 'symphonic pause' or 'symphonic void'. Moreover, the change to dominant-tonic polarity in the fugue contrasts with the general avoidance of this relationship in the movement as a whole, and this interpolation therefore constitutes a stage in the tonal argument.[28] One might also trace a further relaxation of the steady forward movement of the tonal argument of the development section in the sudden change to modal colours at bars 266–73; this again has the effect of a 'pause' in the forward march of the movement.

It has been pointed out that pedals are a feature of the symphony; those in the first two movements have been described as 'tragic', and those in the third as 'joyous'.[29] Pedals form a vital part of the symphony's rhythmic structure, providing one of the elements of 'pause' which throw forward moving rhythms into relief. The working of such devices is clear as the development section begins (bar 162), for there the altered version of the opening of the movement provides a very slow moving harmonic background, the chords changing on weak pulses so that they provide no forward impulse: the idea is pursued further in the work, even during the fugue of the development section.

The coda of the first movement returns to the 'symphonic pause' feeling of the fugal section already discussed, for from bar 469 a version of the fugue subject occurs in a number of repetitions accompanied by a long pedal A: this passage, by its very repetitiveness, holds back the feeling of forward motion. Beethoven breaks away from this 'static' quality by extending the downward triadic string figure to form a long series of thirds (bars 484–9), so encouraging the harmonic movement to start up once more. One is also aware of a similar static quality in bars 513–30, for the two-bar bass ostinato, by its repetitiveness, effectively anchors the sense of forward motion, though this is challenged by the sadly marching canonic fanfares in the woodwind and brass. The conflict here, together with the sound of the chromatically marching bass, builds up tension towards the close, though the expected cadence in D minor is frustrated by the strings, whose expected arrival on the tonic is prevented by the appearance of C natural twice in succession. This not only serves to heighten the expectancy still further, but provides a nice tonal parallel to the rhythmic device already several times mentioned. Just as Beethoven has tended to place chords immediately before the strong pulse, anticipating the main accent, so here the strings twice approach the tonic only to fall short at the last moment. The passage recalls a similar device during the recapitulation, where the 'cellos and basses (accompanying the first theme with new material) twice approach D, but succeed only in reaching C. Indeed, another tonal equivalent to the rhythmic idea at present under discussion is audible at bars 327–38: here the pedal, which is both tonally and rhythmically static, is pitted against antiphonal, partly chromatic scales in the upper parts which, seeking to move away from the tonic, express forward motion both tonally and rhythmically. The intensity of the argument at this point results in a singularly powerful passage.

Beethoven uses the same devices to start the Scherzo. The opening leads the ear to expect a statement of the tonic in bar 7, though the composer shifts it forward to bar 6, leaving a compensatory pause (written out in rests) before the Scherzo proper begins. The fugal opening ensures that no interruption of the progress of symphonic logic is felt here.[30] The shifting of accents forward is occasionally found in the opening section (at bars 55–7, for example, the first violins anticipate the arrival of the main subject by playing a bar in advance of the second violins), and 'written out pauses'[31] are provided in such sections as bars 148–58. The shifting of the beat forward by a bar then logically leads to the habitual shift to macrorhythms of three bars instead of four (and a type of fugal stretto): that this was a conscious change of metre on Beethoven's part is demonstrated by the fact that he marked the passage 'ritmo di tre battuti' (bar 177). The ensuing 'pauses' are filled in solely by octaves sounded on the timpani (bars 195–204) and the four-bar rhythm is eventually restored by using a still closer stretto, entries of the main theme occurring at the distance of a single bar from the point where Beethoven marks 'ritmo di quattro battuti' (bar 234). The conflict between stillness and forward motion is clear at bars 248–51 and 256–9, where the stretto entries in the horns invert the arpeggio of the Scherzo's introduction against a 'written out pause' in the strings. Almost immediately the return of the Scherzo proper is loudly anticipated by the full orchestra—quite a large-scale anticipation that has its repercussions only in the Trio.

The change to duple time at the very close of the Scherzo recalls the similar change in the third movement of the 'Eroica'; but here a more profound logic dictates that octave D leaps should alternate with octave A leaps after two, instead of the expected three, crotchets: thus a further stretto results, again shifting events forward. Such enormous tensions as are generated in the Scherzo by the various types of anticipation are now released in the Trio, which brilliantly exemplifies the rhythmic principles underlying the work by acting as a large-scale 'symphonic pause'. Here the effect of pause is achieved by the use of many repetitions of a theme which, were it not for its great attractiveness and setting in invertible counterpoint, one might be tempted to describe as a five-finger exercise. Just as the fugue in the development section of the first movement takes the listener into a different realm of musical thought in order to retard the pace of symphonic development without slowing the pace of the music, so the inverting of two parts (a technique derived from fugal procedures) slows down the pace of the argument in the Trio. The mere inverting of two contrapuntal voices does not constitute symphonic development as I have understood it in this book. Thus the symphonic thought is not greatly extended here; moreover, the long pedals and multiple repetitions add to the relaxed effect of 'symphonic pause' in defiance of the Presto markings.

One might take the present argument a stage further, in order to suggest why Beethoven reversed his normal order of slow movement and Scherzo in the Ninth Symphony. The listener, knowing no better, might well be surprised to hear a Scherzo when he expected a slow movement: here, on the largest of all scales, is the bringing forward of an event to an earlier place than convention affords it. And at this level, too, release in the form of a certain relaxation is to be gained from the following of the dynamic Scherzo with what is, by any standards, an idyllic slow movement: the Finale certainly could not have fulfilled this function.

The slow movement does fulfil the function admirably, and it does so in part by reversing the common tendency of the two earlier movements, where expected events were anticipated. The dynamic stretti and the contraction of themes and rhythms, so evident in the closing three bars of the second movement, have been the most characteristic feature of the Scherzo, driving it headlong. In the slow movement, the main theme is continually expanded by an 'echo' of the closing notes of each of the first four phrases.[32] This 'echo' does not in any way expand the symphonic argument: it functions as 'symphonic pause', though again one in which rhythmic motion is maintained. It does, however, in most soothing fashion, begin to exorcise the ghost of the Scherzo. The slow movement's introductory two-bar delay has a similar purpose, and in addition provides a dominant-based opening (in the key of B flat) to correspond to the dominant-based opening of the first movement—the very passage that had instigated the entire rhythmic discussion. Another reference to the first movement is found at bars 21–6 of the third movement, where the long chords change in unexpected places, on weak pulses of the bar. The new theme to which this passage leads contains much movement just after the main beat of the bar, which, by providing a feeling of delay and relaxation, goes yet further towards countering the effect of the first two movements. This whole D major subject, moreover, is based on a decorated pedal, anchoring the theme to the dominant and providing an area of restful 'harmonic pause' which does not build up tension.

The varied repeat of the two themes already heard suggests that the movement will be in the form of variations on alternate themes, a form favoured by Haydn. The suggestion of G minor which the original approach to the second theme creates is now firmly taken up at the repeat (bar 65), though the key is made major in order to parallel the previous appearance of the second theme at bar 25. Then, just as D major had led back to B flat at that earlier point in the movement, so here, in a parallel progression, G major leads to E flat. The subdominant key (which is what E flat is in this movement) is one very often associated with relaxation of tension, so that its appearance here has added point. Nevertheless, this passage is not the real return of the first theme, which the listener expects, for it is not in the tonic. The passage beginning at bar 83 is, in fact, an interpolation—a large scale 'symphonic pause'—used to precede the final variation (which only arrives at bar 99). The 'pause' nature of these 16 bars is intensified by their unexpected character—for the first listeners can scarcely have expected to hear a cadenza for the fourth horn, however good the players may have been. The very idea of a cadenza at this period carries with it the idea of a cessation of the flow of the 'argument'; and though this one is not by any means unrhythmical, the device is very much to the point at this stage of the work.[33]

The idea of extension in the slow movement, acting as a foil to the contractions of the Scherzo, is carried on into the coda, that long extension of the close. The fanfares which open the coda (bars 121f, repeated a few bars later) cannot succeed in drawing the music away from its idyllicism, in spite of their insistence that the 'relaxed' E flat tonality be moved toward the more 'dynamic' dominant.[34] Various types of delay are found to counter this dominantwards tendency. Finally, the extension of the dominant seventh beyond the point where its resolution onto the tonic is expected, by means of an interpolated 'cadenza' (bar 151), results in a string of delayed resolutions in the two following bars, and also in an elongated final dominant seventh chord. All these delays and pauses without tension serve to balance the dynamic effect of the Scherzo.

With a caustic dissonance and its somewhat delayed resolution, the opening of the Finale seizes upon the delays of the slow movement and caricatures them violently. The shifting of harmonic changes to weak pulses in this wild opening fanfare leads, as one might by now expect, to another 'void' or 'pause': this takes a form not yet heard in the symphony (though it was not unknown to purely instrumental music), that of recitative. This forms a nice parallel to the 'cadenzas' of the slow movement, likewise associated in the listener's mind with music which normally occurs at positions where the progress of the argument is momentarily halted. This passage of recitative, whose introduction is so logical, also serves to smooth the path for the eventual entry of the voices. As already mentioned, we know that Beethoven gave a very great deal of thought to the manner in which he might introduce the human voice: the careful preparation of 'symphonic pauses' throughout the work is one of the most important means by which he logically achieved his aim.

Beethoven's use of recitative is not the only form of 'symphonic pause' in the introduction of the Finale, for the quotation of the main subject of each of the previous movements can also be thought of in this way. After all, the reintroduction, in virtually unaltered form, of material heard earlier in the work does not advance the symphonic argument. Some later composers

have misunderstood Beethoven's procedures at this point, and in trying to
emulate his mastery of symphonic form, have reintroduced earlier themes
in attempts to make their works cyclical, or have used a theme as an *idée
fixe*, not understanding that such procedures cannot supply a work with
symphonic unity if there is no more profound logic to support it.[35] Beethoven's purposes in the introduction to the Finale are, however, quite clear
and logical, if one has grasped the manner of building up and releasing
tension in the first three movements of the symphony.[36] The very fact that
the themes of those movements are presented in simple, almost unaltered
form, helps to create the enormous 'void' which makes the eventual arrival
of the main subject extremely powerful in spite of its being stated softly. As
in the opening movement, the main subject here is foreshadowed in the
dominant; and partly because it is shifted forward in this way, the statement of the main subject and its first three variations are followed by yet
another compensatory 'pause', in which the introductory material returns
and the human voice is introduced. After the reappearance of the main
theme at bar 241, its frequent repetitions serve to settle the tensions set up
both at the beginning of the Finale and in the earlier movements. The
repetitions here are entirely different in effect from those in the Trio of
the second movement mentioned above, for the greater spaciousness of
the Finale's theme does not cause the feeling of close circular argument
that we experience in the Trio; and the steady progress of the musical
logic is maintained in the Finale by varying the theme, contrasting with
the effect of the mere inversion of double counterpoint in the Trio. In
spite of the resolution of tensions caused by the 'pause' which logically
follows the shifting forward of expected events, the Finale's main theme
itself includes such a shift—in the two final repetitions of the opening motif
of the theme, the first note (F sharp) begins before the main beat rather
than on it. [37] This is entirely consistent with procedures used elsewhere in
the work.

As already mentioned, the use of fugue as a form of variation in a movement which is itself a set of variations does not involve a cessation of symphonic logic in quite the same sense as a piece of fugue occurring within the
development section of a sonata form movement. Indeed, the orchestral
fugue at bar 431 of the Finale, because of its rhythm and speed, sounds
much less academic, less Baroque and much more tumultuous, than that
in the first movement. It is as if the B flat fugue of the Finale were 'resolving' the 'symphonic pause' nature of the fugal passage during the opening
movement's development. Nevertheless, the fugue burns itself out in one
of the most obvious 'symphonic pauses' of the entire work. A series of
repeated octave F sharps throws the main accent onto the weak pulse of
the bar, following the examples of the accentuation of one of the main
themes of the fugue; the 'void' which follows the shift of accent is filled

with three abortive attempts, in various keys, to restart the main subject, while the F sharps continue to accentuate the weak pulse of the bar.

In essence, the second theme of the Finale demonstrates on the small scale principles already mentioned above. Ex. 72 makes clear that the anticipation of the voices by the instruments and the anticipation of the main beat (both marked⌒) lead on several occasions to a feeling of pause (marked ⌒), if only on the small scale.

The very uncertainty of the rhythm here—for the instrumental parts might well be in $\frac{2}{2}$, even though the voices conform more readily to $\frac{3}{2}$—is an obvious result of the shifting forward of accents, and provides yet another form of tension, though mild. Such lack of rhythmic definition can, of course, be very mild indeed, and it is this idea which Beethoven now follows up, for at bar 611 the men's voices, with lower strings and trombones, intone a high passage of rather indeterminate beat, which is then harmonized. There is a stillness about this passage which ties in very well with the static quality of many other 'symphonic pauses' earlier in the work, and moreover gives a splendid rhythmical interpretation to the whirling yet eternally fixed nature of the heavens, as described in the line 'Brüder! überm Sternenzelt muss ein lieber Vater wohnen'. Such a timeless quality as is here described suggests also the religious devotion of the following passage (bars 628–54) with its low, sonorous, organ-like chords, its apparent lack of rhythm resulting from the off-beat anticipations with their subsequent long held chords, and the timelessness of the modal harmonies which Beethoven no doubt considered characteristic of medieval devotion.[38]

In a sense, therefore, we may view this modal passage, like that in the first movement mentioned above, as a pause, though one on a very big scale. There is a prodigiously slow rate of chord change, especially at the end of the passage where the low sonorities float up into the heavens, into the highest ranges of chorus and orchestra. Such passages, as we have seen, are the logical result of the very dynamic forward shift of accents and creation of a following compensatory void. It seems to me that Beethoven is here giving expression to a fundamental truth of life: that is, that what seem to be opposing forces are in fact vital to each other—the fundamental requirement of dynamism and the rest which compensates for it, and without which dynamism could not long endure; the active life and the contemplative; and at its highest level here the tumultuous, intoxicating joy and the inner necessity for meditation and devotion to God. Such an idea is built into the work at all levels.[39]

The joy breaks out again in a triple fugue. Since this is a variation and not part of a development section, combining various ideas from earlier parts of the movement, and since at this point in the work the confining of tonality to a few keys near the tonic does not conflict with the requirement of symphonic logic, it does not have the feeling of 'symphonic pause' so much as of consummation of all the former fugal and contrapuntal devices. In an impressive quiet passage at bar 730, the idea of meditation appears in rather halting fashion, providing a very long delayed recapitulation of the passage at bars 55–60 of the first movement. There is one further large-scale use of 'symphonic pause', a cadenza in the four solo voices at bar 832; this takes over from the slow movement the idea of making what at first appears to be a dominant into a new tonic. The tendency to continuous dominantward movement is clear at this point in the Finale, as is the timeless, 'pause' quality of the cadenza-like vocal writing. Such a feeling of large-scale pause is gradually overcome by the continual B-A repetition following bar 843, a passage which recalls several other 'dominant' introductions earlier in the symphony. The final bars resolve all tensions by celebrating the ultimate regaining of D major (even the previous modal passages being eventually forced to conform) in a rhythm which unmistakably reinforces not only the macrorhythm, but the strong beats of the metre at all levels. Harmonically we have come to an enormous pause on the tonic chord, though these final bars follow a quick alternation of tonic and dominant: the main theme of the Finale is worked into the music at two different speeds (bars 920f), and the metre is strengthened by being simultaneously underlined in quaver (strings), crotchet (woodwind), minim (non-pitched percussion) and semibreve (trombones) note values, as well as finally in triplets (three in a bar being characteristic of several parts of the work). The coincidence of all these types of rhythm with the underlying pulse provides the ideal resolution to the tensions set up in the work because of events which—at various levels—are heard before they are expected.

Beethoven's Seventh Symphony

The foregoing analyses have shown how a composer may use rhythmic devices on the large scale to regulate tensions within a work, but they have not demonstrated the importance of themes which have a 'rhythm-stopping' function.[40] If the feeling of forward motion depends, as Cooper and Meyer suggest,[41] on the number of events which take place in a given segment of time, we still have to decide what constitutes a symphonic 'event'. I have suggested that Beethoven employed a system of 'symphonic pauses', using passages in which no event of importance occurs, or in which there is repetition of material without any sense of development: such passages could be regarded as 'non-events' since they delay or retard the forward motion. By contrast, passages where the symphonic argument is furthered increase the feeling that 'something is happening', that forward motion is being maintained. It seems likely, too, that 'events' which are of no significance to the matter in hand—material irrelevant to the symphonic argument, however striking—will not give a sense of forward motion since the ear cannot relate them to the ongoing logic of the work. The brass fanfare at Letter F (bars 165–8) of the first movement of Bruckner's Fourth Symphony constitutes such a 'non-event', as I have hinted in an earlier discussion.

Because of its use of rhythms which have an 'ongoing' nature—that is, they seem to generate more forward movement which uses the same kind of rhythm in its turn—Beethoven's Seventh Symphony provides a splendid work in which to examine this matter.[42] The symphony demonstrates clearly how, in spite of these 'ongoing' rhythms, motion may be stopped or held in check as well as started or urged on. A simple demonstration of this is found in the treatment of a thematic tag in the third movement. Ex. 73a shows the opening bars of the movement, an 'event' which sets the whole piece in motion and whose first three chords often revive the motion when it shows signs of flagging.

Because of the nature of 'build' in the phrase quoted in Ex. 73a—the rising arpeggio with its increase in tension and gradually thickening chords—we feel it as a real event; yet Ex. 73b is, from the point of view of motion, much more neutral in that it merely repeats the upper line of the first three chords of the movement in various octaves. The fact that the notes are the same precludes the ear from experiencing this as a real event, yet it is not a 'motion-stopping' passage because of the variation in octaves. The effect is neutral; yet Ex. 73c is a clear instance of a motion-stopping passage, for the repetitions of the three notes retard the forward logic by functioning as what I have described above as 'symphonic pause'. There is now no thickening of chords or climbing of arpeggios such as had made Ex. 73a a 'motion-starting' phrase, and no change of octave which would make it merely neutral. Bruckner's mistake in using such a gigantic 'motion-stopping' theme as the horn call on B flat and E flat just after the beginning of the Finale (bars 79ff) of his *Romantische* Symphony will perhaps now be more fully realized.

We can, of course, readily trace other devices which control the amount of motion experienced by the listener in this particular movement of Beethoven's Seventh Symphony, all of which are very simple. A comparison of the passage which leads to the repeat of the Trio's opening (bars 199–206), where the device of hemiola builds tension towards the repeat, with the passage which links back from the Trio to the Scherzo shows a similar horn figure being used without the 'forward moving' hemiola idea: in this latter passage the figure is accompanied by slowly wandering string chords which modulate rather perfunctorily from D to F, and this link, by being the very antithesis of an event, has a 'motion-stopping' effect. Indeed, one might well extend the argument and maintain that the attempt to play through the Trio a third time at the end of the movement is itself 'motion-stopping' because of its very redundancy (for this reason the note-for-note repeat of the Trio at its second appearance is a positive advantage)—hence the abrupt, drily humorous ending of the piece.

The 'motion-starting', neutral and 'motion-stopping' ideas of this movement represent only one type of regulation of motion in a work in which ongoing rhythms are found everywhere. A piece in which 'ongoing' rhythms alone are used could not hope to sustain a symphonic argument, let alone a complete work:[43] the ongoing rhythms of Beethoven's Seventh Symphony are countered and anchored by the more static pedals which play a considerable part in each movement. One can clearly hear the two being held in balance during the debate between them at the link from the slow introduction to the Vivace. The interplay of the ongoing rhythm and the more static pedal (or decorated pedal, which is less static in quality) can be traced through the work, beginning with bar 25. An interesting example is found at bars 205f and 211f of the first movement:

the repeated chords here remind one of Bruckner's brass fanfare in the *Romantische* Symphony just mentioned, though Beethoven's chords, repeated in a dotted-note rhythm, form an integral and intelligible part of the symphonic argument, with pedals being pitted against ongoing rhythms. At bars 268–74 of the first movement the repetitions of the ongoing rhythm gradually dissolve into a pedal which uses that rhythm. The pedal here relaxes tension a fraction by holding back the motion just a little: the single note of the pedal is obviously something of a 'non-event', and by itself would no doubt be 'motion-stopping', but its effect is considerably lessened by the rhythm which typifies forward motion. The conjunction of the two provides a slight symphonic pause before the beginning of the recapitulation at bar 278. Moreover, the pedal does not persist into the recapitulation, for Beethoven replaces it with new counterpoint so that there is more sense of forward motion than in the exposition. The removal of the static pedal results in a yet more tumultuous delivery of the material:[44] pedals only return at bars 301ff, and (with static harmonies) they gain the ascendancy in the first movement's coda, though from bar 401 onwards the ongoing rhythm tries to assert itself finally over the closed, static nature of the pedals. The tension in the coda between pedals (with the slow moving harmonies they imply) and ongoing rhythm accounts largely for its power, and provides most of the force of the musical argument. (From bar 81 onwards in the third movement the same kind of argument is evident.)

In an impressive close to the exposition of the Finale ongoing rhythms batter themselves against a firm static pedal in a passage of great power (bars 114ff). Later in this movement Beethoven recalls the passage in the first movement which had immediately preceded the recapitulation, by again working gradually towards a pedal (see bars 173–97 of the Finale). Naturally, he does not treat this pedal in the same way, but plays on the audience's subconscious recollections of the earlier emergence of the pedal from ongoing rhythms in order to build up an expectation that the recapitulation is about to begin, only to disappoint that expectation.

Beethoven occasionally draws special attention to the presence of pedals or of slowly moving harmonies, so that they shall be given the more force in that part of the symphonic argument which pits them against short note values.[45] He does this by extending such pedals or chords to lengths beyond those which the ear expects: the use of chords of five bars in length, contrasting with the four-bar macrorhythm at bars 98–102, 308–11 and 313–17 of the Finale and the various long pedals which change at unexpected places in that movement's coda (from bar 362 onwards) are examples of this, as is the alternation of two chords in first five, then four, then three bars at various stages of the Scherzo (bars 32ff, for instance).

The interplay of static and ongoing rhythms implied in the work naturally finds a parallel in the note values themselves. The introduction to the first movement clearly contrasts long and short note values, the short notes forming a contrapuntal tracery between the harmonic pillars provided by the tutti opening chords. Indeed, the contrast between minims and semiquavers, so evident in passages like the one beginning at bar 10, is unmistakably built into the opening of the new theme which Beethoven uses in order to draw particular attention to the secondary key areas of C (bar 23) and F (bar 42). This contrast between note values is made the very basis of the second movement, since it consists of variations in which different layers, each distinguished by its own rhythmic nature, are gradually added to the basic pulse. The Finale takes up the point, the contrast of slow and fast motion being played out in the passage around bar 40 and, especially, in the coda from bar 349 to bar 404. It may well have been this symphony that suggested to Sibelius the rhythmic scheme which he worked yet more thoroughly into his Fifth Symphony.

We may perhaps see in Beethoven's employment of ongoing rhythms in his Seventh Symphony a reason for his introduction of a novel tonal scheme (discussed in Chapter III). Hans Keller[46] provides a valuable insight into this matter:

this 'triple time' approach will usually be found either in small composers, or in great composers in their early stages of uncertainty. The reason is that triple rhythms take over part of the task of characteristic invention: other things being equal, an undistinguished idea in triple time will sound better defined, more 'individual', more rhythmic in fact, than one in duple or common time, which forms a more neutral background.

This perceptive comment, though one can scarcely apply it to the 'Eroica', for instance, can indeed apply to the $\frac{6}{8}$ nature of the Vivace of Beethoven's Seventh Symphony: the facile ongoing nature which results is superbly countered by the new tonal colours obtainable from his use of two flat side keys as important subsidiaries to the tonic. It is, indeed, the idea of slow harmonic motion that occasionally serves to draw attention to these important subsidiary keys, as at the beginning of the development of the first movement (bars 180ff) where a 'round' in C major serves to draw particular attention to that key.

The contrast between the static nature of the pedals and the ongoing flow of symphonic logic can be nicely summed up in a single sustained chord—the unstable, unresolved $\frac{6}{4}$ chord with which Beethoven frames the shorter note values of the rest of the second movement. Although other reasons have been advanced in Chapter III for the use of this $\frac{6}{4}$ chord, it may not be taking analysis too far to suggest that this sound is both static (in that the notes do not alter) and yet in a sense 'mobile' in that the ear expects the customary resolution onto the dominant chord. The listener cannot tell when to expect this resolution, and is indeed left with a feeling of frustrated motion because the chord never does resolve. The concepts of forward motion and static pedal are thus united—a stroke of great genius. Familiarity with the work has perhaps dulled our ears to these points, and our knowledge of later music made us ready to accept the $^6_4$ chord as more 'normal' than Beethoven's first audience could have found it. Here, as in the instance from Beethoven's Fifth Symphony mentioned earlier in this chapter, analysis can help us to understand a composer's intentions. These two rare instances—the F sharp minor chord with D flat and C sharp alternating (in the first movement of the Fifth Symphony) and the $^6_4$ chord of the Seventh Symphony—provide features which, for one reason or another, the ear may perhaps miss but which analysis can identify.

CHAPTER VIII

Variations

Nationalism: Sibelius' First Symphony

Those who know the last six symphonies of Sibelius find it difficult to be charitable about the First. It is, of course, hardly surprising that a composer's first symphony will be his least well organized—a work in which dramatic gestures, brass crescendi, sensuous chromatic harmony, long dominant ninths, big tunes and harp arpeggios abound in place of the intellectual underpinning which comes with maturity. After the first movement the seams are all too evident, and Sibelius has difficulty in connecting his ideas and developing his themes: not enough of the music is related to the primary material, which is itself too slender and fragmentary in character to support satisfactorily the large structure built on it. The harmonic language is inconsistent, and the work is tonally unbalanced: the music, as one might expect of a first symphony, is very derivative, Tchaikovsky being an obvious influence. So much is on the debit side; but in spite of this there are some most interesting features, and some fine music, in the work. It also has many facets which point the way forward to the later symphonies, yet it stands firmly rooted in the Nationalist movement.

The Nationalist symphony is one of several types of symphony which derive, in the main, from Beethoven. To be sure, some of Beethoven's predecessors also used themes with a national or folk-song flavour in works of the sonata or symphonic type; but it is only with Beethoven's 'Pastoral' that a new tonal language is evolved which, because it is somewhat 'modal', is able to include folk-like material within its fabric without any feeling of incongruity. (In many earlier works folk-songs tend to provide an extra exotic colour superimposed on the normal tonality, and do not integrate well with it.) This new language gives a certain type of 'pastoral' mood because of its inherent modality, which replaces the more conventional diatonic tonality: the relationships of a major or minor third replace the reliance on tonic-dominant polarity both on the small and the large scale, as I shall point out in more detail later in this chapter. The classic example of this relationship of thirds is the opening of Vaughan Williams' *A Sea Symphony*; but the technique is widely used by Nationalist composers, by comparison with its much less frequent use by those writing in the German symphonic tradition.[1]

Sibelius' First Symphony owes much to Russian symphonies, even though it is also greatly influenced by one of the less thoroughly Nationalist composers, Tchaikovsky. Its treatment of tonality links it with the Nationalist composers, even though (as is usual in Sibelius' music) actual folk melodies are not quoted. The Nationalist treatment of tonality, clearly evident in all movements except the second, is a legitimate extension of that used by Beethoven in his Sixth, Seventh and Ninth Symphonies. Since it marks a stage in the development of tonality towards that used in some of Sibelius' later symphonies, it is essential to examine it in detail.

The work is in 'E minor', though this key is not as clearly stated in the first movement as the title might imply.[2] The slow introduction for clarinet solo scarcely touches E minor at all: it begins (over a timpani roll on B) in B minor, and after some references to G major, it cadences in G minor; the fact that the roots of these keys are a third apart gives the passage a modal flavour. The opening of the Allegro energico, with a high tremolando on G and B natural in the strings, is the more striking by being unexpected: the introduction has led the ear to expect G minor at this point, yet the notes of the tremolando not only suggest G major, but are also compatible with the tonic of the symphony, E minor. The point is clearly made in the tune which appears against them (see Ex. 74).[3]

Ex. 74

The first subject is one of a type which was to become characteristic of Sibelius' melodies—a long note followed by a descending flourish;[4] more importantly for the present discussion the tune cannot seem to decide whether it is in G major or E minor, an ambiguity for which the introduction is directly responsible, and to which the G-B natural tremolo contributes. The ambiguity in turn contributes to the modal sound, since the leading-note of E minor is avoided because of the importance of G major (see Ex. 74). The D natural-E progression which results has considerable implications for the later development of the movement: the avoidance of D sharp in the key of E minor is, of course, typical of Nationalist and other composers who were seeking to avoid the dominant-tonic relationships common in earlier German symphonic music. The discussion of Beethoven's 'Choral' Symphony has already shown how modal traits can arise from this approach. D sharp, when it is heard early in Sibelius' exposition, does not succeed in introducing E minor firmly, and at its first appearance (page 3, bar 1)[5] clashes with the prevailing G chord to produce an augmented triad. This characteristic chord plays a further part in the second movement, yet it is not developed in the thorough manner which Sibelius evolved in his later symphonies.

After a firm cadence in G major, a new subject is announced in B minor and repeated in D minor: this modal progression, typical of Nationalist composers, compels the more attention by virtue of a change of macro-rhythm. The four-bar rhythm, so clearly used up to this point, is now contracted to three bars, coinciding with the transition from B minor to D minor. The timpani, playing the tonic of each of the keys so far used (G, B and D) make it quite clear that the keys chosen so far are built on roots which form the G major triad. By using D minor (reached on page 3, at bar 11) Sibelius avoids the feeling of the dominant key which would certainly result if the major had been used: in a similar way, Beethoven avoided creating a dominant-tonic relationship in the 'Choral' Symphony. The dominant of G major is, for one thing, not the 'correct' key for the second subject of Sibelius' First Symphony, nor is it yet time to proceed to the second subject, so soon after the movement has got under way. The D minor-G major cadence which now results is also of great importance later: the F natural-G progression found in it is one of the more obvious and colourful modal features, and replaces the tonal F sharp-G; it is, of course, an exact transposition of the minor seventh-tonic progression seen in Ex. 74. A new subject enters at this point (page 3, bar 13), and again a tendency towards the 'wrong' dominant, D major[6] is counteracted, the C sharps of the tune being contradicted by a C natural in the harmony, showing a conflict between the modal minor seventh and the more tonal leading-note (see Ex. 75, bar 2).

Ex. 75

This particular conflict is one to which Sibelius referred again in his Sixth Symphony, discussed later in this chapter. Indeed, the resulting sound is one that is heard fairly frequently in the later symphonies, and usually with a similar structural purpose—the pull of two tonal forces in opposite directions. The confusion over the 'correct' key is still apparent in the second phrase of the tune shown in Ex. 75, the leading-note (D sharp) being in conflict with the dominant (D) of the most prominent key so far, and thus the modal and tonal cadences are likewise in conflict. An abortive attempt to establish B minor, the 'correct' dominant (page 4), only leads back to a more powerful statement of the first subject in G, but with a new bias towards the flat side of the key, C major balancing the short excursions to D and B minor which had taken place at the first appearance of the subject.

The alternating chords of F sharp major and C sharp minor give a distinctly Dorian flavour to the bridge passage on strings and harp: these chords were suggested by the D minor-G major cadence (page 3, bars 13 and 14), which in turn was suggested by the 'modal' colouring of Ex. 74. Following the bridge passage is a tune played on the flutes (at Letter E), which is quite clearly in the Dorian mode.[7] Whether or not this new tune is the second subject is immaterial to the present discussion: the new tonality (which, though suggested by the earlier cadence, is now presented on a much larger scale) is of more significance. Sibelius does not use any of the keys which the ear might expect: the preponderance of G major up to this point might lead us to expect a second subject in D; the relative major of the symphony's real tonic (G major, the 'normal' key for a second subject of a minor mode symphonic movement) has been so prominent that we can scarcely expect it to be used, but B minor is an obvious choice. A chord of F sharp, which implies a movement towards B minor, is indeed presented (on page 9), but it is some while before B minor itself is positively stated. The F sharp chord's function as a dominant is counteracted by the series of modal-sounding cadences to which I have just referred: it is clear that, yet again, modal and diatonic methods of handling tonality are in conflict. The listener is briefly reminded of the true tonic, E minor (which, with a C sharp, has now become E Dorian, the modal colouring being carried over from the 'C sharp Dorian' section), before the real second subject, over another F sharp pedal, is reached in a clear B minor (page 12). The music, now marked 'Tranquillo', consists of a short phrase —characteristically introduced by a long note—which is repeated many times in overlapping imitations. The pedal F sharp is a very long one, and the contrapuntal nature of the subject has the effect of stopping the regular macrorhythm: together these two features create an effect of timelessness. The 'C sharp Dorian' flute passage is used in counterpoint after a while, though it is now bereft of its modality, having lost its Dorian major sixth, and it eventually ousts all other material in a long passage of 'cresc. e stringendo' in which the macrorhythm is gradually re-established. At the end of this (page 15, bar 6), the long pedal eventually resolves onto B, a key which has become firmly established by the gradual pruning of the modal elements from the music while the macrorhythm was being re-established in the long stringendo passage. The firm hold of this key cannot yet be shaken by the appearance of the important note G (written as F double sharp) twice in the strings. The importance of this point in the development of Sibelius' symphonic style will be readily appreciated when it is remembered that his Fourth Symphony makes very great use of similar techniques, though the idea is there developed in a much more mature way. The cadence, while using a slow version of the three stepwise notes which are a feature of the work as a whole, defines the key as major: D sharp is then seized on as a new tonic, and the development begins with the brass reinterpreting this note as E flat, and moving quickly into that key, making a prominent feature of the third, G.

Many features of this exposition point the way forward to techniques used in Sibelius' later symphonies. I have already mentioned that clashes between major and minor sevenths (see Ex. 75) and tunes which begin with a long note followed by a downward flourish are quite common. The clear modal colouring—the use of the minor seventh in a major scale, and the major sixth in a minor scale to form the Mixolydian and Dorian modes respectively—is a feature of nearly all the later works; the Dorian mode is especially prominent in the Sixth Symphony. The use of tonalities which lie a minor or major third apart is typical of the Second and the Fifth Symphonies, as of much music by other Nationalist composers. The command of movement and treatment of macrorhythm, though much less striking and less individual, looks forward clearly to the Fifth and Seventh Symphonies; and the use of a series of chords whose outer voices move by chromatic steps (page 5) in opposite directions is also a feature of the Seventh Symphony. Long pedals are found throughout Sibelius' work; and so is the enharmonic treatment of a prominent note for the purpose of changing the tonality. The polyphony of the second subject finds an echo in the last two symphonies; and a harmonic filling-in of horns or wood-wind is characteristic of all Sibelius' orchestration.

More important than all the features mentioned in the foregoing paragraph is the way in which the overall tonal plan of the First Symphony affects the processes of composition. B minor and G major are prominent at the opening, even though the symphony is said to be in E minor. Here, immediately, is one reason for the employment of tonalities a third apart, instead of the 'classical' fourth and fifth. The confusion as to whether G or E minor is the tonic gives rise to the modal colouring of Ex. 74: it is because of the presence of D natural in E minor in that excerpt that various cadences replace the leading-note with a minor seventh. This leads to the C sharp minor and F sharp major chords of the second subject, and so, also, to the presence of the Dorian tune of that subject. The process is a perfectly logical one. So, too, is the process by which C sharp and C natural,

D sharp and D natural are opposed, the confusion between the various rival key centres and between the modal and traditional methods of treating tonality again being the cause. Many of the melodic and harmonic features of the symphony isolated as being also characteristic of Sibelius' later work are thus attributable to the manner of treating tonality in this symphony. These same characteristic features are also related to Sibelius' approach to the problem of symphonic form—and in particular that of tonality—in the other works, even though the problems were never tackled and solved in the same way twice: in this respect, he is similar to Beethoven. In each instance Sibelius has, of course, chosen an overall unifying device—be it tonal, rhythmic or thematic—that is perfectly compatible with the features of his own style. The choice, in his First Symphony, of material that quite naturally leads him to use a 'Nationalist' form of tonality—a somewhat modal scheme—parallels Beethoven's choice in his Ninth Symphony of just such material as would most logically lead to the new view of symphonic tonality which he expressed in that work. In every other symphony by Sibelius the logic is even more compelling than it is in the opening movement of the First Symphony.

Little remains to be said about this movement. Motifs from various themes are developed in a way that suggests later symphonies: the pizzicato passage on page 22 reminds one of the Second Symphony, the chromatic struggle on page 23 is a foreshadowing of many similar passages, especially in the Sixth Symphony, and the opposition of two keys—the dominant of B minor and the dominant of G—is a very small-scale anticipation of similar conflicts in the Fourth and Seventh Symphonies. The recapitulation does not begin with the theme shown in Ex. 74, but with a somewhat expanded form of that in Ex. 75, a theme which is not heard in the development section until its two false arrivals just before the whole tune starts the recapitulation. The recapitulation of the second subject begins likewise with the second theme of the group: the shift from the dominant of G to the dominant of E minor at this point (page 38) is a sound which is very characteristic of Nationalist composers. The second subject (on the long dominant pedal) is, of course, in E minor, and the string figure which at the final cadence of the exposition had used F double sharp, in the recapitulation is altered, logically enough, to conform to E minor (page 46, bars 1–5). But the brass, at the end of the movement, dispute this and move towards G; and the confusion about keys is maintained until the close by several more factors—the final timpani roll is on B (as was the opening one: the timpani have, indeed, never been tuned to the tonic in this movement), the 'cellos and bassoons rise from a low E to G at the end (making use of one of the unifying thematic devices of the work) and the first of the two final pizzicato chords sounds with a G at the top. As in the Second Symphony, the first movement is the most characteristic and the most closely argued of the work. In spite of the Beethovenian heading 'quasi una Fantasia' in the Finale and the Beethovenian power of the Scherzo, this opening movement is the only one in the symphony which stands in the Beethoven tradition of logical argument and symphonic design.

The second movement is in E flat. The important note G of the first movement thus remains as the third of the key; and indeed it is with this very prominently used note that the opening tune begins. As in the previous movement a long G is followed by downward motion, and this is not the only thematic connection: a comparison of Exx. 75 and 76 will show another.

It may be that the chord in bar 2 of Ex. 76 derives from another theme with a chord containing an augmented fifth in a similarly prominent position in the first movement (page 3, bar 1): at that earlier appearance, the presence of D sharp in a predominantly G tonality was the cause, whereas here it is the presence of elements of G major (D, G and B natural) in a predominantly E flat passage. This use of a 'pivotal' chord which links the various important tonalities of the work is an embryonic version of a technique which Sibelius used much more widely in his Second Symphony.[8] It cannot be pretended that the First Symphony's second movement is in any way successful as a musical structure: the seams are all too obvious, the balance of themes and keys uneven (the final statement of the opening tune is much too short to balance the big crescendo and the wide tonal wanderings which lead up to it). Moreover, the lush romanticism of the harmony, with its long ninth chords and sliding chromaticism, and the rather out-of-place fugato, set the movement quite apart stylistically from the remainder of the work.

The Scherzo, even if it is not really 'symphonic', does have a certain amount of rhythmic drive which is quite characteristic of Beethoven, though it is not the sort of movement one finds in Sibelius' later symphonies.[9] The important note G is now taken as the dominant, the movement being written in C major. The use of the flattened seventh, a common feature of the first movement, relates these two movements tonally: the use of tonalities which rise sequentially by step (pages 82 and 83) becomes a feature of several of Sibelius' later symphonies, notably the last two. G major is used quite widely; and the Trio, which reverts to the very romantic feeling of the slow movement, is in the tonic major of the whole symphony, E. The Trio leads into the repeat of the Scherzo by means of another chord which contains an augmented fifth, here linking the tonalities of C and E. The chord is used several times in the Trio, reminding the listener of those heard in the first two movements. Attention is also drawn to the accompaniment on page 101 by a short rising chromatic figure in the 'cellos, which serves no structural purpose: it is, however, very similar to one at the opening of the Third Symphony, which plays a most important part in the construction of that work.[10] Sibelius' favourite augmented fourth also occurs (page 102, an F sharp in a C major chord), providing another foretaste of music to come.

The Finale—basically a sonata-form movement in which the recapitulation and development are telescoped together—is marked 'quasi una Fantasia'. The 'motto' theme which opened the whole symphony returns here, as it does in Tchaikovsky's Fifth Symphony. As in the latter work, the 'motto' theme is very much louder when used in the Finale; and Sibelius, though he does not go so far as Tchaikovsky in transferring the tune to the tonic major, does alter the harmony so that the theme is now very clearly heard to be in E minor, even though there are modulations to G and B minor. This is perhaps the most important point made in the whole movement: one's only regret is that the symphonic struggle does not justify it. One might legitimately expect a considerable amount of discussion to take place before E minor is understood to be firmly established, since G major is so important at the opening of the work; but such a discussion has not been carried through the piece with the determination that warrants the firm statement of the tonic which actually occurs at this point (pages 108f). After an Allegro molto in E minor (in which thematic material only is held in common with earlier movements) the second subject arrives in C major. This tune is in a style very like that of Ex. 76: the chromatic inner parts of the harmony again point forward to the use of a similar device in the Third Symphony, where again it has a structural function. The subject is rounded off by a brass 'chorale', a familiar style in his later works. It is a characteristic of Sibelius' three most popular symphonies—Numbers One, Two and Five—that they all have a 'big tune' in the Finale: this tune, in the First Symphony, does not grow out of the previous material in the way that the tunes of the other Finales do. After a return of the first subject (with much development and a new theme rather like a fast Russian dance in character) the second subject returns in A flat before moving back to E minor by way of a long dominant pedal. The final pages of the last movement are by far the most impressive, and the final pizzicato chords refer back to those at the close of the first movement.

There is evident, in this work, an attempt to write movements which integrate two speeds—an idea which Sibelius handled with infinitely

greater success in his Fifth Symphony. It is the inability to control the two
speeds that, perhaps as much as any other factor, makes the work a failure
from the structural point of view. Russian composers sometimes used a
slower second subject in their symphonies, and Sibelius has copied the
feature: such a manner of writing helps to dramatize the contrast of
tonalities implicit in the opposition of two themes in different keys.[11] It is
not that the change of speed is so very difficult to handle (though a
composer must be careful not to create the impression that an entirely new
piece is starting); it is the maintaining of 'symphonic motion' (discussed in
Chapters VI and VII) which is the crux of the problem. The number of
real symphonic events in a given segment of time is the vital factor, not the
length of the notes themselves. Sibelius' difficulties are evident at various
points in the work, of which the end of the Finale is one of the most obvious.
The slow second subject is no more than a good tune—it contributes
nothing of any value to the argument and thus forms a gigantic 'symphonic pause': the listener merely immerses himself in the gorgeous
sounds, since the argument in no way compels attention. 'Motion' (as I
have understood the concept in Chapter VII) effectively ceases during this
tune; but Sibelius wishes to end loudly (except for the last two chords) and
slowly—an intensely dramatic way of bringing a symphony to its close.
This needs much more control of motion than a composer still beginning
to find his way can have, and he needs a greater weight of forward motion
than he has built up to drive home his final passage. Seeing this difficulty,
Sibelius tries to increase the tension from Letter X with a remarkably fine
passage, but one whose language—because of the power needed to set the
music in motion again—is far removed from that of the foregoing sections.
Comparison of this Finale with the superb one in his Fifth Symphony may
teach one a great deal about the handling of large-scale rhythms in a
symphonic work.

Programmatic Trends: Beethoven's Sixth Symphony

The novelty of a five-movement scheme to a symphony, as opposed to a
divertimento or serenade, is of little moment to the present discussion. For
the purpose of this book, the conflict between the desire to give expression
to extra-musical ideas and the dictates of logical symphonic evolution,
where such conflict exists, is of considerable interest.[12]

I have already suggested that there is a programme behind the music of
the Fifth Symphony of Beethoven, though we do not know what it is: there
are certainly clear extra-musical ideas behind the 'Eroica'. But in spite of
the connection with Napoleon and remarks about 'Fate knocking at the
door', the Third and Fifth Symphonies have programmes of only a very
general nature; there is (so far as we know) no detail to be followed such as

might interfere with the composer's development of his motifs. For it is when music follows a programme too closely that it is most likely to conflict with the type of musical construction I have tried to describe in this book.[13] Beethoven seems to have been aware of this difficulty himself, and the various attempts to formulate his ideas in words before he eventually settled on the phrase 'More an expression of feeling than painting' are well known.[14] If this is a true description of the work, the 'Pastoral' is no more programmatic than the 'Eroica' and the Fifth; but in fact it is not quite true. Beethoven added titles to each of the movements, even though two of his comments had been 'People will not require titles to recognize the general intention . . .' and 'Anyone who has any idea of country life can make out for himself the intentions of the author without any titles'. No doubt the outer movements are indeed feeling rather than painting; but the second movement, developed from a sketch labelled 'Murmur of the brook' and with the note 'The more the water the deeper the tone', is something much nearer to painting, even if one ignores the imitations of bird song (which were not to be taken too seriously, according to Beethoven). The same applies to the thunderstorm,[15] and there are certain imitations of musical events—the peasants' merrymaking and the shepherds' yodelling song, for instance. This was not new—imitation of nature had long been the sport of composers, and (as Grove has pointed out) Beethoven's titles are very similar to those of Justin Heinrich Knecht's *Grand Symphony* of 1784.[16] But Beethoven's feeling that 'all painting in instrumental music, if pushed too far, is a failure' seems to imply an awareness of the fundamental difference between illustrative and absolute music.

Such a difference may cause the upsetting of the logic of symphonic thought; but it does not do so in Beethoven's Sixth Symphony.[17] There is a relaxed feeling about it, evident in the mild pace of the outer movements, the slow rate of chord change, the high proportion of major chords, the numerous repetitions, the tendency to end phrases on weak beats of the bar, and the tendency for the horns and bassoons—when playing a long note— to repeat it on a weak beat. The orchestration helps towards the same feeling—the two muted 'cellos which are the sound of the brook, for example, and the exclusion of the piccolo and timpani from all movements except the thunderstorm (thus setting off that movement dramatically from the others); further touches which contribute to this relaxed feeling are the omission of the trumpet until the Trio of the third movement, and the omission of the trombones from the first three movements. But such an atmosphere is also achieved by means which are the logical result of a symphonic handling of the material, itself chosen with these objects in view; and the atmosphere grows out of Beethoven's handling of it, rather than being imposed on the work, as it were, from outside. This logical growth of every facet of the work is a fundamental principle of symphonic form as I have described it in this book; and another illustration of it might well be worth notice at this point. In the British Isles, the 'Nationalist Symphony' was not a success so long as the national colour was merely pasted on (in a few modal tunes) to the basically German symphonic tradition—in Stanford's music, for example. The successful works are reached only when the whole symphony—not a few melodies only, but all the elements of composition—grow from national roots and are thoroughly integrated (as in the best symphonies of Vaughan Williams).

One very obvious manifestation of such growth in the 'Pastoral' Symphony is the profusion of themes based on triadic figures or arpeggios: the yodelling, 'folklike' style of the 'Shepherd's song' out of which grows the main theme of the Finale[18] should not blind us to the fact that it is the culmination of many of these triadic and arpeggiated motifs. Moreover, the thunderstorm, perhaps the most programmatic passage of the work, uses these devices widely. There is more to the work than this, of course; the arpeggio is such a common figure that it can scarcely by itself provide a sufficient feeling of thematic unity between the movements. Pedals (and tonic and dominant drones) also play their part, as does the frequent movement in parallel thirds—and these features, which are characteristic of folk music, contribute to the pastoral feeling in addition to helping unify the music. The programmatic tendency of all the movements is itself an aid to unity; but all the features so far mentioned are rather 'static', and by their undeveloping nature contribute to the impression of ease which characterizes the symphony. The sense of logical growth must be sought elsewhere.

A thematic motif that occurs throughout the work is a six-note scale, usually descending: developing from the downward scale in the opening phrase of the work, it makes its first full appearance at bars 42f. It has a more prominent rôle in the recapitulation, where it forms part of the new counterpoint to the first subject (bars 300f); and it forms the accompaniment to the opening theme of 'By the brookside', as well as featuring in the final cadence of that movement. It occurs in ascending form in the Trio section of the third movement, and in descending form throughout the thunderstorm, being augmented at the end to form a chorale-like passage. Finally, it becomes a variation of the main tune of the Finale (bars 99ff) and it is particularly prominent in the closing bars (206ff), where it is used in counterpoint, first alone, and then (as in the first movement) as a countersubject to the main theme. We shall see later that this working of themes in counterpoint plays an important rôle in the work. Many other scalic passages in the symphony may also derive from this scale even though they do not fill up the interval of a sixth, for example bars 458f in the first movement, 111ff in the fourth movement, and 227f in the Finale. It will not have escaped notice that D (a sixth above the tonic pedal F) is the

highest, if not the most prominent, note of the opening theme of the work;
the interval of a sixth recurs elsewhere, for example in the second subject
of the first movement (bars 67f).

I have implied that the six-note scale derives from the prominence of the
interval of a sixth in the opening bars of the work: a glance at this opening
reveals several other motifs which are developed throughout the work
(see Ex. 77).

Ex. 77

It will be noticed that the opening four notes of this example are those
which also help to unify the Fourth and Fifth Symphonies, though the
order of them has been changed here: I shall call this figure x in the
following discussion. A relationship between x and the opening is not by
any means clear to the ear, and may be purely coincidental in any case;
but, at the repetition in bars 5 and 6, Beethoven demonstrates a connection
between them by using them in counterpoint. Soon afterwards, by varying
the opening material, the theme itself is used in a form which more nearly
coincides with x (end of Ex. 77). As if this were not enough, the relationship
is made yet clearer at bar 33, when x is played in counterpoint with the
main theme (see Ex. 78).

Ex. 78

This device is extended—and more clearly recognizable—when it is
repeated in the accompaniment to the second subject (bars 67f). Finally,
in the exposition, various thematic threads are drawn together in a single
passage (Ex. 79); here the triadic figure at the top is one of many through-

out the work which foreshadow the main theme of the Finale, while the accompanying figure not only clearly spans the important interval of a sixth (both ascending and descending) but also includes an inversion of the first three notes of Ex. 77, the figure *c* from that example, and an allusion to the shape *x* (see Ex. 79).[19]

Ex. 79

There is an additional feature here—the mild conflict between duple and triple rhythm (the triplets, which occur in the bass, are not shown in the example). Such a profoundly logical development as one sees in this exposition is of a purely symphonic nature, not in any way governed by a programme, even if its effect is one aptly summed up in Beethoven's title.[20]

The use of *x* in contrapuntal combinations with other themes is not nearly so frequent in the other movements: in 'By the brookside', the accompaniment figure which uses the descending six-note scale is given in a variation which uses *x* (bars 7f); this point is made more obvious at the end of the development section and in the coda, where the clarinets and bassoons accompany the figure with very clear versions of *x* (bars 88f and bar 127). There is a clear relationship between this figure and the shape shown in the lower stave of Ex. 79. A similar feature occurs in the first violin cadence figure at bar 39. The prominent horn and bassoon passages in the Scherzo (bars 75f), as well as the rustic music which follows it (bars 93ff, 96f, 105f) and various later passages, also embody *x*; though in the Finale it plays a small part, returning to an accompanying rôle (bars 40f) and appearing almost as if by accident. It is as if the figure so widely used in the Fourth and Fifth Symphonies was still lurking in the back of Beethoven's mind, and acted as a spring-board for the first movement; but other motifs developed from it and these assume greater importance as the work progresses.

By far the most important of these motifs is the interval of a sixth. The open fifth drone which accompanies the beginning of Ex. 77 provides the interval of a sixth between its bass note (F) and the uppermost note of the first violin, D. A range of a sixth is found in many other motifs of the work, the scale passages already mentioned, for example; but there are others. Such phrases as that shown in Ex. 80 also occur frequently in the outside movements;[21] and in the Finale, one such figure is found immediately after a bar in which a leap is gradually expanded until it becomes a sixth (see bars 39f).

Ex. 80

The 'birdsongs' which end the second movement, though not to be taken too seriously, according to Beethoven, nevertheless conform to this outline; moreover, the falling third which suggests the cuckoo occurs quite widely in the work since it is part of x.[22]

Important as these manifestations of the sixth undoubtedly are, they are less so than the tonal use to which the interval is put. The strikingly new use of tonality—the juxtaposition of keys a third apart—is directly attributable to the power of the interval of a sixth (which, inverted, becomes a third) in this work. These new tonal processes are first noticeable in the development section of the opening movement, where they are thrown into relief by the slow rate of chord change. The B flat chord (bars 151ff) is so prolonged as to create the feeling that it must have some structural importance. While waiting for the harmony to make its next move, the attentive mind must wonder in which direction the move will be. Whereas a chord of D minor would be quite a normal choice (since it is the mediant of B flat and the relative minor of the work's tonic), Beethoven chooses instead to move direct to the much more novel and unexpected D *major*. The nature of this harmonic progression is not (as it so often is with the Nationalists) the result of providing folk songs with correspondingly modal harmony, but of the logical development of a different 'folk' element—the opening bass drone together with the tune which rises to the sixth above it. That the resulting harmony should be so like that used by the Nationalists is an extraordinary coincidence, but a most interesting one.[23]

The D major chord is played in a crescendo, instruments being added in layers; they are then gradually pared away, leaving the first violins and bassoons playing a staccato dominant-tonic figure. This time the obvious modulation (to G major) does follow, but Beethoven is careful to conceal the precise point at which it occurs. In fact it happens at bar 191 with the return of the main theme, but it is only after two more bars that G major harmonies gradually begin to accompany the tune. Beethoven has thus avoided both a sense of dynamic change which might accompany a dominant-tonic cadence, and also the drawing of attention to a harmonic progression which is not goverened by thirds or sixths. The earlier progression is now repeated, with a difference: the long G major harmony moves to a chord a sixth away, but this time it is the sixth above, E. As in the earlier progression, the new chord is major,[24] and proceeds to act as a dominant in its own right. Once again Beethoven conceals the precise point at which the modulation from dominant to tonic takes place. The arrival of A major, however, is a signal for the return to clear V-I progressions and to a large-scale circle of fifths which prepares for the recapitulation.

Before the recapitulation can begin, however, the circle of fifths is interrupted at one very important point, for Beethoven leads into F from a chord of B flat rather than one of C. Philip Gossett has shown[25] that this passage caused the composer a considerable amount of trouble, and he has concluded that the replacing of a perfect by a plagal cadence resulted from Beethoven's wish to avoid too dramatic a reappearance of the main subject. The subdominant is, after all, much less dynamic in effect than the dominant.[26] (Indeed, Beethoven again avoids a direct perfect cadence at bars 282–9, inserting a first violin 'cadenza' for the same reason; this takes the place of the pause which had occurred at the corresponding point in the exposition.)

There is more to the subdominant introduction to the recapitulation, however, than has so far been stated. By using the chord of B flat, Beethoven can several times include within the harmony the six-note rising scale F-D. This figure had merely been suggested in the range of the opening of the exposition. Here, however, its increasing importance to the work is displayed in the very definite statement in bars 275ff. This compatibility of the six-note scale F-D and the subdominant chord results in an association of the thematic material with the overall relaxed character of the piece for, as I have already said, such is the nature of the subdominant chord (and key). By choosing to enlarge upon these features at the most dramatic stage of the movement—the beginning of the recapitulation— Beethoven not only draws attention to them but shows that they are the the antithesis of the more normal, dynamic manner of symphonic writing. By introducing this passage with a large-scale circle of fifths which the ear expects to culminate in a perfect cadence in F but by replacing the expected cadence with B flat-F, Beethoven draws attention to the B flat chord. This chord is thus shown to be an event of symphonic importance, yet it is not musically dynamic, and the sense of lyrical flow is not interrupted. Furthermore, by varying the beginning of the exposition, Beethoven lessens the impact of the beginning of the recapitulation (in much the same way that he had earlier concealed his dominant-tonic modulations) in order to reduce its dynamic effect. The contrapuntal additions to the main theme when the recapitulation begins (bars 279ff) are unusual for their date, and give a sense of onflowing logic to replace that lost by the frequent use of a slow rate of chord change and the lack of contrasting minor chords.

The themes of this movement have a strong subdominant flavour which balances the sharp-side nature of the tonalities in the development section. The balance is nicely maintained, and the plagal cadence which leads to the recapitulation neatly recalled, at the end of the coda, where (in bars 497–506) a series of scales ascending from the subdominant to the tonic balances the many descending ones which had started on the sixth degree and ended on the tonic earlier in the movement.

Progressions from a major chord to another a sixth away from it now become a feature of 'By the brookside' (bars 32f, for example: the chords become F and D major in the recapitulation); but in addition there are strong moves in the development section of this movement towards the key on the major sixth (in a long section of G major beginning at bar 58, which is eventually countered by the subdominant) and the minor sixth (G flat at bars 79f). So strong has the pull of the sixth become by the time of the 'Peasants' merrymaking' that the first phrases continually veer between F (the key of the movement) and D major: the slight tonal imbalance of such a scheme is countered by the firm use of the subdominant in the Trio section.

It is with a direct and unexpected move to the minor sixth that the thunderstorm begins, and much use is made in the movement of harmonies whose roots lie a third apart (an idea which derives, of course, from the progressions already heard). Apart from a few passages in the Finale (such as that at bars 95f) transitions between keys a third apart are reserved for the coda of that movement, where (as at bars 182f and 186f, for example) they are quite plentiful. B flat is again used as a foil to D, each of these major keys being a tone away from the dominant: the two areas thus balance each other from the tonal point of view. Attention is drawn to the key of B flat by introducing a new subject in that key at a point where it is least expected—in the middle of the development section (bars 80f)—a device which recalls one used in the 'Eroica' Symphony.[27]

The foregoing discussion has not by any means exhausted the possibilities of development; but sufficient has been said to make clear one very important point. Apart from the birdsongs of the end of the second movement—which are apparently a joke, but which nevertheless fit in with the idea of the prominence of the sixth and the melodic shape of Ex. 80—there is nothing in the work that is not the result of pure symphonic logic. Even if one is inclined to think of the second subject of the first movement as 'Beethoven's Forest Murmurs'—and there is nothing wrong with that—the theme itself is the logical outcome of the previous music.[28] The 'rustic' modality and the relaxed feeling, the gradual growth of triadic themes towards the main tune of the Finale, the connection between tonality and themes, and the fact that the most 'illustrative' movement ('Thunderstorm') itself fits in with all these ideas, should amply demonstrate that the presence of titles and a programmatic idea do not of themselves preclude the writing of a symphony in which all the issues raised by the musical material are thoroughly worked out.

The sense of flow discussed in the previous chapter is not evident in the same way in the 'Pastoral' Symphony as in the works dealt with there.[29] There are very good reasons for this: the sound world of the 'Pastoral' is quite different from that of any of Beethoven's other symphonies. The relaxed nature of things 'pastoral' calls for a less dynamic sense of rhythm and less obviously forward-moving logic than in the other symphonies. For once, we cannot describe the symphony as 'a struggle': it is mostly the expression of happy and relaxed feelings. There is nevertheless an undeniable sense of 'symphonic flow' in the work, and this sense is of necessity treated by Beethoven in a way very different from his usual manner. Joseph Kerman provides a clue to the handling of 'symphonic flow' in the work: 'This was one of those situations in which themes were less important to him initially than other aspects of composition. The first clues were essentially sonorous, not thematic.'[30] It is the peculiar sound world of the 'Pastoral' that compensates for the relaxation of rhythm. At places where there is 'symphonic pause', various ideas assume the foreground of interest. Between bars 16 and 25 of the opening movement the debate between B flat and B natural (an idea to which Beethoven returns in the Finale: see bars 26off, derived from 99ff) comes to the fore, and from bars 67–92 interest is centred on the evocative pre-'Waldweben' scoring and the effect of contrapuntal round. The long static harmonies of the development are enlivened somewhat by the contrast between simultaneous duplets and triplets, and the rescoring of parts of the recapitulation with additional triplet accompaniment figures (which gradually become more prominent as the movement progresses) also helps to maintain interest. The sudden use of a quick rate of chord change at bar 422 of the first movement is another way of emphasizing the reinstatement of the duple notation at a point where the new sound of harmonies changing with every quaver serves to accentuate the important function of the subdominant key.

In the second movement, the unusual sound of the 'Due Violoncelli soli con sordini' provides interest, as do other unusual touches such as the scoring of the tune in octaves at the top and bottom of the orchestra (bars 15ff). These features help to balance the feeling of lassitude which would otherwise predominate; they are helped by the application of arpeggios which are substituted for the previously more normal stepwise motion, combined with the use of hemiola, at such places as bar 29, and by the thicker scoring of the recapitulation with many more counterpoints than in the exposition. Nevertheless, if there is anywhere in the work where the programme has taken over from the symphonic logic, it is here. There is little 'on-going rhythm' or developing logic; it is perhaps for this reason that the second movement is less interesting, at least to my ears, than the others, and seems too long for its material. This is not to say that there is a complete absence of logic, however: the occasional two-bar 'symphonic-pauses' of the movement (beginning with the passage at bars 18ff, which has little to do with the foregoing material) culminate in a 'cadenza' in which Beethoven pauses to listen to the birds. This 'cadenza' has been prepared by many cadences in the movement such as that at bar 40, and the programmatic nature of the birdsong (which has already been shown to have thematic connections with the rest of the work) assumes the foreground interest at the end of the movement.

In the third movement the modal sound and unusual scoring in octaves, the imitation of the wind-band and the 'stamping-dance' nature of the Trio[31] compensate, by the fresh nature of their sound, for the slowness of symphonic pace. Throughout the work, the novelty of the tonal schemes is another means used by Beethoven to compensate for this lack of forward flow in the symphonic argument. At this point we may recall the words of Philip Gossett about the first movement of the 'Pastoral':

The subdominant plays a key role throughout this movement. The opening melody implies a I-IV-I progression, soon after realized harmonically (mm. 9–11) . . . The rare subdominant approach to the recapitulation, then, is both relevant and peculiarly appropriate for the world of the *Pastorale*.

Some characteristics of this world as manifest in the first movement are well known: the scarcity of minor harmonies, the dependence on primary harmonic functions in each key, the appearance of static passages welling up in crescendi and retreating in decrescendi. There is a drastic decrease in the importance of processive tonal relations, normally so characteristic of Beethoven's music . . . In such a world, two moments in the classical sonata design must pose special problems: the transition from the first to the second group in the exposition and the retransition . . . In no other symphonic sonata form movement does Beethoven so underplay the dramatic element of processive motion between the tonal centers of the exposition.[32]

These remarks about the unusual sound-quality of the 'Pastoral' and the importance of the subdominant chord are very pertinent. There is certainly a tendency to concentrate on the primary triads I, IV and V in the work, and these are, of course, all normally major triads so long as the key is major: only in the storm movement do minor triads (and also diminished seventh chords) play a large rôle, and they are the more effective for having been reserved for that point in the work. Such a concentration, in other movements, on *major* triads is much to Beethoven's advantage, for his feelings on entering the country were, as his biographers and his own sub-heading tell us, happy. Beethoven has, indeed, tried to make secondary triads (those on the second, third and sixth degrees) major as well, and to incorporate these into the tonal world of the 'Pastoral', though it is mostly the second and sixth degrees of the scale that he treats in this way. His concentration on major chords in order to produce a happy effect may well provide another reason for changing the secondary triads of the F major scale, which are normally minor, into major ones: in the development section of the first movement, Beethoven makes each of these triads major in turn to produce long passages based on the major triads of

D, G, E and A. Though this reason for using the major form of the secondary triads is programmatic, they are nevertheless, as I have shown above, also the logical outcome of Beethoven's concern with the interval of a sixth.

The major triad on the supertonic is the most important contribution to the special sound world of the 'Pastoral', and it is implied as early as bar 16 of the work. The G major chord here creates a dominantwards tendency—a tendency to movement toward keys on the sharp, 'dynamic' side of the tonic. Such a tendency must, naturally, be balanced, and this provides a further reason for the prominence of the subdominant. The tendency to use 'the dominant of the dominant' (for that is what the major chord on the supertonic amounts to) is so widespread that it is unnecessary to do more than merely mention the fact—such passages as bars 468–74 of the first movement and the final two bars of 'Thunderstorm' (a G major chord used to introduce an F major movement) are among the most obvious examples.

For programmatic, as well as symphonic reasons, the sound world of the 'Pastoral' depends very largely on the incorporation of major-sounding triads into the normal tonal scheme: these express happy feelings, which are both balanced and complemented by the mood of relaxation engendered by the use of the subdominant. The peculiar sound world of the 'Pastoral' largely makes up for the lack of ongoing rhythm, for the symphony has much slow harmonic movement and few of those self-generating ongoing rhythms so characteristic of the Fifth and Seventh Symphonies. This manner of treating symphonic flow and tension is peculiar to the 'Pastoral' Symphony.

The Influence of Renaissance Polyphony: Sibelius' Sixth Symphony

There are two sides to the question of Sibelius' interest in polyphony. On the one hand he greatly admired the works of Palestrina, Lassus and the English Tudor composers;[33] yet on the other he rejected the rather prevalent idea that works written in counterpoint were necessarily greater and more respectable than those which were not, when he said:

The error of our day has long been its faith in polyphony. It has seemed as if people imagined that the whole had become better by placing nonentities on top of each other. Polyphony is, of course, a force when there is good reason for it, but for a long time it has seemed as if an illness had been raging among composers.[34]

Obviously no contradiction exists between these two views provided there is good reason for the use of polyphony: counterpoint, and contrapuntal forms and devices, may indeed contribute to the 'profound logic' which Sibelius so much admired in symphonic writing. There is, nevertheless, another side to this question of profound symphonic logic, too. Sibelius insisted on the importance, first and foremost, of the aural effect of the music, saying of the Sixth Symphony:

You may analyse it and explain it theoretically.—You may find that there are several interesting things going on. But most people forget that it is, above all, a poem.

His view would clearly be that music which failed to interest or please as pure sound would not be saved by solid craftsmanship or brilliance of construction. Implicit in his remark, too, is the idea that 'we murder to dissect';[35] that, once a work has yielded all its secrets and is completely 'explained' it has lost all its interest and thus its value as a work of art. One may question whether this is necessarily so; for a deep understanding of the nature of a work can also have the opposite effect, giving greater depth to our appreciation of the poetry and, by a recognition of the compositional problems solved, a fuller appreciation of the work analysed and of the composer's stature. It is, in any case, doubtful whether all the facets of a great symphony can ever be unravelled within the terms of a single type of analysis, or whether any listener can at a single hearing appreciate all the levels of interest which exist within such a work. It is this multiplicity of levels which makes for great music.

Sibelius' remark about analysis was also intended to refer to a type rather prevalent in his day, which consisted simply of attempting to derive the themes of the various movements from a single melodic germ. Such an analysis has been given briefly in Chapter II; but the thematic view, taken alone, misses the real point of a work, and this no doubt at least partly explains Sibelius' objection to analysis. Commentators have often pointed out that the Sixth Symphony is influenced by Renaissance polyphony—a view that takes us much closer to the heart of the matter: but merely to mention modality and counterpoint—as is usually done—does not give an adequate view of the construction of the piece.

The treatment of modality in Sibelius' Sixth Symphony is quite new. It is not, of course, that modality was new to symphonies—we have already seen how Beethoven, especially towards the end of his life, was beginning to use more and more modal harmonies: it is interesting that he had himself considered writing a symphony based on the church modes.[36] Sibelius had already used modal colour (and especially the sharp fourth of the Lydian mode) in his earlier works. The originality of Sibelius' method in his Sixth Symphony lies in his use of modality not merely to give harmonic or melodic piquancy, but also as one of the means of unifying the work. It is not the Lydian mode that is used here, but the Dorian—a mode that had been quite prominently used in his First Symphony,[37] and which was also implied by the use of the tritone C natural-F sharp within the A tonality of the Fourth Symphony. Not only has the Dorian been the most popular mode used in the Neo-Renaissance music of the early 20th century, but it was also the most popular in the Renaissance itself until modality was replaced by major/minor tonality. The novelty of Sibelius' treatment of the Dorian mode in the Sixth Symphony is, partly at least, that it exactly parallels the classical use of keys: he transposes the same mode to various pitches just as a more classical composer would transpose the major and minor keys, thereby introducing a new unifying element into the symphony.

The opening movement, largely in the untransposed Dorian mode, is followed by a movement in G Dorian,[38] the D Dorian of the third movement is relieved by passages in A Dorian and G Dorian, and the Finale is mostly in D Dorian. This use of the same mode transposed to various pitches in order to replace keys is, as far as I am aware, unique. In the Renaissance, composers did not modulate between the *same* mode at different pitches, and though some pieces changed mode or used a mixture of modes, such procedures were not normal. One of the advantages in replacing the modal system with major/minor tonality at about the end of the 16th century was that the new keys could be used at various pitches, and a technique of modulating between them evolved. At the same time, the peculiarly colourful modal harmonies and melodic formulae became less evident and were replaced by a harmonic and melodic language which was similar for every major key and for every minor key. In his Sixth Symphony Sibelius has used the customary pitch transpositions for a symphony (subdominant for the second movement, and a dominant passage in the third), but by using a mode—the *same* mode—instead of a key at each of these pitches he has contrived at the same time to keep the harmonic and melodic modal colour which had been lost during the 17th century. This novel process is clearly shown at the beginning of the second movement; instead of starting immediately in the new 'key' of the movement (G Dorian), Sibelius modulates into it after starting in D Dorian, the 'key' of the movement which has just ended: the tune of the movement—which begins a little later—also starts as if in D Dorian. This principle of modulating to the key of a new movement after starting in that of the previous one is well known and can be seen, for example, in the slow movement of Dvorak's Symphony *From the New World* and the Finale of Debussy's String Quartet. Sibelius, in the second movement of his Sixth Symphony, is clearly demonstrating the applicability of the principle to modal, as well as tonal, music: the deception as to 'key' at the beginning of the second movement is, indeed, extended to a deception about the rhythm, since the composer starts with what sounds like a slow movement (the sort of movement one might well expect to be placed second) by using chords which are, in effect, the length of a dotted minim, before moving to much shorter note values.

It will already be evident that Sibelius had a liking for Renaissance polyphony, and an examination of his treatment of the Dorian mode in this work makes it clear that he had a deep understanding of it. The popularity and special colour of the mode are partly due to three characteristics—the third, sixth and seventh degrees; in its pure form the mode is a minor scale, but the sixth degree is major and the seventh minor. In Renaissance polyphony, especially that of the late 16th century, which was being rediscovered in the first two decades of the 20th century and with which Sibelius would have been most familiar, this mode was subjected to a certain amount of modification by 'musica ficta'. The result of this was to bring it closer to the modern D minor scale: the sixth degree, under certain conditions, was made minor and the seventh was sharpened in order to form a cadential 'leading-note'. Thus, in the untransposed mode, B natural could become B flat and C natural could become C sharp. The third, F, could also be sharpened to create a major triad at cadences. Since these alterations did not always take place, there was a certain ambivalence in the music between the major and minor forms of the third, sixth and seventh degrees of the mode, an ambivalence which partly accounts for the characteristic cross relations of English Tudor music. Sibelius, being fully aware of these features, used them in the furtherance of the musical argument of his Sixth Symphony.

The ambivalence in the treatment of the seventh degree of the Dorian mode—the fact that C natural (in the untransposed mode) can be altered to C sharp under certain conditions—forms a vital clue to the forces at work on this symphony. At the opening, the mode is used in its pure form, and C naturals are frequent (the first appearance of the violas in bar 3 draws some attention to it, for example); the C sharp which does occur (page 4, bar 5, where > markings draw attention to the chord which contains it) [39] is surrounded by statements of the natural modal form of the seventh, though the two forms of the seventh degree are not at this point brought into conflict. When C sharp is next heard (page 5), we are reminded of the earlier occurrence, since Sibelius writes the same chord as before: it is, in effect, very 'tonal'—a seventh chord, with C sharp in the bass and E, G and B (technically the upper part of the dominant ninth, the root being omitted) above it. By repeating this chord in a crescendo the composer draws attention to it; and while it is going on, the brass and timpani enter with a chord of C major, the C natural of the pure mode contradicting the 'altered' C sharp. Attention is drawn to this clash of chords not only because of the obvious dissonance between C sharp and C natural, but also by virtue of the scoring, since this is the first point at which the trumpets and trombones have been heard. The C major chord is left sounding when the chord over C sharp in the strings and woodwind has ceased, and the ear hears the progression of the bass as C sharp-C natural, even though both notes are, for a time, sounded together. The falling semitone, which I shall call *x* in this discussion, is now taken as one of the most important unifying elements of the work, an element derived from the ambivalence of the Dorian mode already mentioned, and to which clear attention has been drawn by the manner of scoring and of presenting the opposing notes.

The influence of *x* is first evident on page 8 (bars 10ff) as the woodwind reiterate D flat-C, doubling the progression at the third above; as before, constant repetition helps to draw attention to the figure. It increases in frequency until, with C-B natural (in the bass) it introduces the B Dorian tonality (on page 11), where *x* is referred to many times in both the new 'cello tune and in its accompaniment. The growing power of *x* becomes more obvious still in the coda of the opening movement, a rather extraordinary and enigmatic passage which is partly explained by the frequent appearance of this figure. Firstly, two phrases in the horns and lower strings (page 23) end with a Phrygian cadence, the falling semitone being in the bass part; secondly, divided 'cellos make a feature of the figure in a tremolando passage which is rounded off by a long E flat falling to D (again doubled at the major third above) in the flutes and bassoons. The force with which this E flat-D progression is announced (page 24) foretells that it will play an important part in the following movement, though the listener cannot, of course, yet be aware of this. Thirdly, a scalic unison passage in the Dorian mode ends by turning *x* upwards from F to F sharp, so that a balancing sequential phrase begins in F sharp Dorian, again ending with an inversion of *x*. The tonic is regained with harmonies which contradict this rising semitone, since they contain many clear references to

Ex. 81

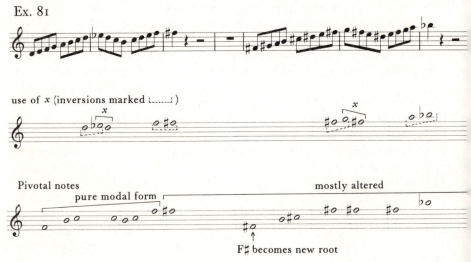

use of *x* (inversions marked ⌐....⌐)

Pivotal notes   mostly altered

pure modal form

F♯ becomes new root

x, and the overall tonal scheme of the passage is D flat-C. After a pause D Dorian is again clearly stated, but in its absolutely pure form, in order to end the movement with the same kind of tonality as had been heard at the opening (some of this passage is shown in Ex. 81).

The second ambivalence in the work is between B natural and B flat: the lack of a B flat in the key signature for most of the opening movement testifies to the purity of the mode, though there are occasions on which B flat replaces the natural form of the sixth degree. The F naturals are also occasionally contradicted by F sharps; and indeed, it becomes quite clear that Sibelius, throughout the movement, is varying the combinations of major and minor third, sixth and seventh in order to create an ever-changing tonal spectrum, even if he returns frequently to D Dorian. The tension of the movement is largely due to these departures from the tonic: since most of them are caused by alteration of one of the three degrees mentioned above, forces are set up to oppose these departures from the norm; either the altered note itself tends to be drawn back towards the pure Dorian mode, or else it forces another note away from the pure modal state. It is, for example, the presence of the altered third (F sharp) along with the altered seventh (C sharp) and the modal sixth (B natural) that leads to the use of B minor (or rather, B Dorian) already mentioned; by contrast, the pure forms of the third and seventh used with the minor sixth (B flat) suggest the passage in F major (page 17). The gradual alteration of the sixth back to the modal state (B natural) during this latter passage leads logically to C major (F natural and C natural also being present) and this involves using one of the very few perfect cadences in the first three movements; from here it is a small step to D Dorian.

The unsettled nature of the tonality, as well as of the music, between pages 9–11 and 12–14 results partly from the continual alteration of the third, sixth and seventh degrees, and partly from the tonal pull between altered and 'pure' forms of these degrees (between, for example, G flat or F sharp and C on pages 9 and 10). It will not have escaped notice that the slow chords which underlie the music of pages 12–14 are themselves governed by the same degrees of the mode as I have already mentioned, given in 'altered' form.

With these points in mind, the enigmatic coda immediately seems somewhat less puzzling. After a considerable debate about the nature of the three 'pivotal' notes (F, B and C), a passage which is largely in unison follows: see Ex. 81. In this example the third, sixth and seventh degrees of the mode (the 'pivotal' notes) are marked on the lowest stave: the occurrences of x which cause these pivotal notes to be altered in one way or the other are shown on the middle stave.

The complex system of forces and counter-balances at work on the movement is well demonstrated by the short passage shown in Ex. 81. The F of the pure Dorian mode, by being sharpened (as it is in the third bar of the example), implies the similar alteration of C to C sharp; the following sequential phrase introduces B flat instead of B natural, since it mirrors the F–F sharp of the original phrase. Figure x, already twice heard in the passage, is then used to alter the D flat (C sharp) back to C and G flat (F sharp) back to F: the B flat becomes natural again by a process which involves the inversion of x (which has likewise already been used several times in this example) and which is in addition suggested by the loud C major brass chord heard just after C natural is regained (x may also be at work at this point, the loud C suggesting B natural instead of B flat). The various stages of the argument are separated by pauses or rests in the music, just as earlier in the movement (pages 12–14) they had been marked by slow-moving chords. As shown in Ex. 81, the pivotal notes, in various forms, provide new tonal centres: at the same time these notes, which begin by being used in a pure modal form, return to this state after a considerable amount of alteration has taken place.

The figure x, as applied to the notes E flat–D in the coda of the opening movement, assumes great importance in the second. At the end of the introductory passage a series of antiphonal chords in alternating combinations of woodwind and harp insist on these same two notes. Repetition is again used to drive the point home: x reappears (page 27, bars 18ff) with the E flats repeated before they fall onto D, and again later (page 30) where the notes involved are D flat and C; in this latter example not only is the progression itself repeated, but each chord consists of repeated notes. Since the second movement is basically in G Dorian, the E flats of this progression become the flat sixth of the mode; but there are many E naturals in addition, to represent the pure mode. The chords which open the movement, however, begin as if in D Dorian (as in each of the first three movements, F is the first bass note), and there is a certain amount of debate about the pivotal notes of D Dorian: F natural and F sharp, B natural and B flat, C natural and C sharp are all heard before the advent of x on the notes E flat and D. The movement does, indeed, have many points at which the listener may well doubt whether he is hearing G Dorian, or D Dorian with a rather strong tendency to use B flat. The pivotal notes of the first movement—F, B and C—are still the subject of debate in the second movement, though only two of them (F and B) provide characteristic intervals of the Dorian mode which I have mentioned above, since the movement is in G Dorian.

As in the first movement, there is continuous change between the major and minor forms of all these notes; but it is clear that, on balance, F sharp becomes much stronger than F natural, so that this movement differs from the opening one in the general use of a major seventh 'leading-note' as opposed to the minor seventh. This is plainly evident in the modal final cadence of the movement, which uses F sharp and E natural in G Dorian. Like that of the first movement, the coda is again somewhat enigmatic, and seems to be conceived in quite a different style from that of the preceding music: this coda, also, looks forward, since a duple-time string figuration which it features seems to foreshadow a triple-time one which frequently occurs in the third movement. The coda's purpose is partly seen in the fact that its key signature varies between G major and G minor; but there is more to it than this. After Letter G (page 35, bar 9), the first two bars have rapid string chords whose common note is E flat: the following two bars use D flat, then bars 5 and 6 use C: x ,using the notes D flat and C, introduces G major, a key also suggested by the prominence of another pivotal note, B natural. G major is suggested in addition by the coupling of the pure modal sixth in G Dorian—E natural—with x when used on the notes D flat and C. At Letter H (page 37, bar 4), E natural is the note common to all the chords; and it is the descent to E flat (the note common to the next series of chords) that moves the music back into G Dorian. Not only does this semitonal progression contribute another version of x, but it also constitutes a debate between the major and minor forms of the sixth degree in G Dorian. Throughout the coda, pivotal notes are common in both major and minor versions.

So far the movements of this symphony have eschewed sonata form, using instead a process of continuous evolution of material rather like that found in Beethoven's late works, even if a certain amount of repetition of material also takes place. In the third movement, Sibelius demonstrates the applicability of his new symphonic modality to sonata form itself—though the movement has no development section and is conceived on

quite a small scale. The opening D Dorian passage has prominent F
naturals in the tune and bass, since one of the functions of the third movement is to overcome the power attained by F sharp in the second (where it
was the leading-note of G Dorian) so as to regain a purer Dorian modality.
In the first subject, B flat and E flat are a momentary reminder of the scheme
of the second movement, though their appearance is fleeting. The second
subject (page 43, bar 8) appears in the dominant (A Dorian), a neat point
since the F natural must now be sharpened, again recalling the power it
had gained in the second movement. A third subject appears in G Dorian,
and consists of a discussion between various elements: the accompanying
chords use B natural and B flat (another pivotal degree) alternately, as
well as a transposition to G Dorian of the opening string phrase of the
movement. Against this, a canonic tune in the flutes and harp is actually
as near D Dorian as G Dorian, though this is a conflict which is not, I
think, audible. Nevertheless, the choice of sonata form for this movement
is governed by the tonal struggle evident in the first two movements. The
third movement as a whole emphasizes the pure D Dorian tendency of the
entire work, but the choice of A Dorian and G Dorian for the second subject group reminds the listener, in the first instance, of the growing power
of F sharp in the second movement and, in the second place, of its G
Dorian tonality. It is, indeed, a loud chord of F sharp minor that interrupts
the progress of G Dorian on page 48, and leads to the recapitulation in
which all three subjects are in the 'tonic'. The loud F sharp minor chord
of the exposition is, naturally, now replaced by one of C sharp minor, so
that the transposition between the modes has resulted in the use of yet
another of the pivotal notes (this provides a further reason for introducing
G Dorian in the exposition, of course), though the end of the movement is
again in the pure mode. As before, this loud interruption sends the strings
scurrying around in a somewhat unsettled tonality before D Dorian is
firmly regained.

In the Finale the far-reaching effects of the initial cross relation just after
the opening of the symphony are powerfully felt in the continual downward semitonal sequences (x) in the strings (pages 66, 70, 78 and 79). At the
great climax of intensity towards the end of the movement, the semitone
progressions are found everywhere—there is scarcely a note on pages 78 and
79 which is not part of either a falling or a rising semitone progression, as
the two forms work against each other. That the struggle has reached its
height here is also clear from the appearance, during these passages, of the
only *fff* markings in the work: the struggle reaches its climax on the *fff*
unison B natural on page 80. This can also be seen as the result of the
working-out of the ambivalence between the major and minor forms of the
sixth, the climax being reached on perhaps the most colourful note of the
Dorian mode, B natural. Sibelius makes the point clear, after all the

previous chromaticism, by relating the note immediately to its scale with a few flourishes in D Dorian. This climax exhausts the influence of both x and B natural; the falling semitone plays no further part in the construction of the symphony, except in a quiet restrospective passage on the last page of the work; here D Dorian becomes C sharp Dorian (page 87, bar 1) for the space of a single bar before moving back by further downward semitone steps towards D Dorian. The introduction of a B flat into the key signature for the final pages points to the fact that B natural, too, has lost its influence; the tonality of the close of the work (though both B natural and C sharp are occasionally touched on) is Dorian with a B flat and a C natural.

The convincing triumph of F natural over F sharp in the third movement means that there is little debate about the nature of the third degree of the mode in the Finale: the last movement starts as if it might be in A Dorian, but, with a few exceptions, it is F natural and not F sharp that is used. Besides providing an element of contrast with the D Dorian of the third movement, this opening also recalls the key of the exposition's second subject in that movement: it thus provides an opportunity to make clear, with many prominent F naturals and some cadences in C (the latter strengthening the claim of the minor seventh against the leading-note), that the F sharp is a spent force. A great deal of tension in the symphony is clearly the result of modal thinking—the working out, in twentieth-century symphonic terms, of the ambivalence of the third, sixth and seventh degrees inherent in the late Renaissance treatment of the Dorian mode.

Other features of the work also derive from Renaissance polyphony. The rising minor scale of five notes which, as I have said in Chapter II, helps to unify the symphony, is none other than the Dorian diapente; and most of the other unifying motifs are also compatible with the diapente and diatessaron of that mode. A feature of some Renaissance music in modes which naturally contain a minor seventh is the use of the triad on that degree of the mode: a well-known example of this is the beginning of Palestrina's *Stabat Mater*. So much was the sound liked that it was sometimes applied to modes which have a major (and not a minor) seventh, as can be seen in the B flat chord which appears in C Ionian, just after the beginning of Weelkes' *Three Virgin Nymphs*. The feature was frequently imitated by late 19th and early 20th century composers who sought to escape from the perfect cadences which are such a prominent feature of German symphonic music: for the Nationalists, the flat seventh was a most useful and appealing alternative to the leading-note. There are remarkably few perfect cadences in Sibelius' Sixth Symphony: writing in a mode which naturally has a minor seventh, he makes use of the type of progression with which Palestrina began his eight-part *Stabat Mater*. On page 6 of this symphony, Sibelius first begins to move away from D Dorian: this he does by means of tonalities which progress downwards by steps of a tone' (C major-B flat major-A flat major), and the importance of this progression is shown by its occurrence at the very point where the music first moves away from the tonic. The idea is several times repeated;[40] the descending scale of tonalities mirrors the descending scale which forms one of the unifying melodic features of the symphony. The progression is used in the chords which accompany the main tune of both the second movement (page 26, flutes, bars 4ff and 10f, for instance) and the third.[41] It forms an integral part of the opening phrase of the Finale, where it also occurs as a series of minor triads (page 65 bar 3-page 66 bar 4) as well as major (page 72 bar 5-page 73 bar 1). This downward stepwise direction of tonalities is twice balanced by upward stepwise motion in the second movement (page 28, bars 6ff, and page 32).

The avoidance of 'leading-notes' through large areas of the symphony is clearly deliberate: almost the earliest major seventh to occur, it will be remembered, was immediately contradicted by a C natural, with far-reaching effects on the structure of the first movement. Apart from the F naturals of the second movement, very few leading-notes occur in the work until its climax near the end of the Finale. It is not until after the fff B natural that perfect cadences begin to appear fairly frequently, and not until the very last page of the work does Sibelius revert to using the minor seventh (C naturals appearing in the two high cadences in the strings on page 87, bars 5f, as well as in the final bars of the symphony). The release of tension after the climax is attributable to several factors, of which the more frequent perfect cadences constitute only one;[42] there is also the use of largely diatonic conjunct motion to replace the chromaticism of earlier parts of the movement, the use of the minor sixth instead of B natural, and the absence of x (as compared with the rest of the work).

The importance of the minor seventh as an element in the melodic and harmonic writing of the work is thus paralleled by an importance of the same degree as a *tonal* centre. The choice of the Dorian mode in this work has involved not only a process of exploring modal colour, but one of frequent modulation to—or harmonic movement towards—one of the pivotal degrees. The parallel between Sibelius' treatment of the minor seventh in this work and Beethoven's use of the major sixth for a similar purpose—and one which also leads to the use of modal harmony—in his 'Pastoral' Symphony, will be plainly evident. One might, indeed, make out quite a good case for Sibelius using the third and sixth in like manner for governing tonal progressions were it not for the fact that such progressions are characteristic of Nationalist music as a whole: nevertheless, such passages as are shown in Ex. 81, pages 12f (where D flat, B flat and F sharp are the roots) and pages 31f (where D, F and A flat are used) seem to justify the view that the third and sixth degrees of the mode, as well as the seventh, play a part in governing the tonality.

In other ways, too, the third, sixth and seventh are important. Much melodic material, for example, is presented in parallel thirds—examples are so numerous that there is no need to quote them. On occasions (as on page 27) parallel sixths are likewise used, and thirds and sixths together occur in a long passage from page 9 onwards. The importance of the seventh is seen in other ways—there are examples of parallel sevenths (on pages 21 and 75 for example) and of sevenths and thirds used together in a parallel fashion (as on page 35), but more frequent are melodic lines which span a seventh (as in Ex. 82, or on pages 18f and 65, for example).

Ex. 82

The seventh plays a most important part in the harmonies used in the work; it is well known that, according to Renaissance theories of composition, any seventh used as a harmony note was required to resolve downwards by step. This idea of resolution is enlarged by Sibelius. The first two occurrences of C sharp (page 4, bar 5, and page 5) both entail the use of a seventh chord consisting of C sharp, G, E and B: on the first of these occasions the chord resolves quite correctly onto D minor, though the second, it will be remembered, was continually repeated in a crescendo until the C major brass chord broke in upon it. The lack of resolution of the chord, and the intensification of the dissonance (in this instance by repetition), are ideas amplified as the music progresses. It is not until page 24 that the influence of the passage is again felt on the harmony (as opposed to the tonality), in the parallel sevenths of the last two bars, which form a series of unresolved dissonances until the powerful dominant sevenths at the beginning of page 22 resolve ultimately onto C major. In the coda, too, the seventh chords in divided 'cellos (page 24, bars 2f) last for many bars without real resolution of the tension they set up; and at Letter M (see Ex. 81) two such chords are used in alternation for a short while before resolution takes place. These facts help to make even more clear the reasons for the use of what has often been thought of as a rather enigmatic coda. The sevenths—derived from the prominence given to that degree of the mode in the symphony—are used in the harmonies to govern the amount of tension; the longer the resolution is delayed or the longer the series of parallel seventh chords, the greater is the tension. Another point will be clear from a study of Ex. 81: *x* itself has its second note transposed upwards by an octave so that the figure spans a major seventh; a nice point indeed, since *x* had in the first place resulted from the introduction into the pure Dorian mode of a major seventh. Sibelius' cross referencing of ideas in this coda is nothing short of astonishing.

To trace the progress of this idea through the remainder of the work is a relatively simple business. The second movement begins with a series of chords which rock gently back and forth between sevenths and consonances; and again the figure x on the notes E flat and D has the second note transposed up an octave so that a major seventh results. The elongation of dissonances by means of repetition is found throughout the movement; and it is not without interest that this is the movement which most concerns itself with the identity of the seventh degree of the Dorian mode. Sevenths—especially descending—are a frequent feature of the melodic lines, especially at points where a rising stepwise figure is made to 'break back' to a lower octave. The coda of this movement, too (from Letter G onwards), uses seventh chords in great profusion, though the direction '*p* flautato' perhaps makes them less striking than some of the previous discords which have long delayed resolutions.[43]

The detached chords in 'double dotted' style in the third movement (pages 44f) consist of an alternation between two seventh chords, though again the quiet dynamic markings keep the tension at quite a low pitch. After the F sharp interruption (C sharp in the recapitulation) it is with a series of longer seventh chords that the tonic is regained. Not only is the length of passages of unresolved sevenths greater in the Finale, but the dynamic markings do not play down their effect as has tended to happen in earlier movements: the gradual lengthening of the dissonance is interestingly shown by comparing pages 66f with the repeat at page 71, in which the dissonant seventh C is very much lengthened before resolution. At several points the dissonances are treated as tonal dominant sevenths, but the resulting circle of fifths keeps the ultimate resolution in abeyance for some time. The many uses of grinding seventh chords culminate, on pages 78f, in a loud chromatic passage of tremendous power: here the ultimate force of the dissonance is felt. If this is so, clearly the time has also come for a resolution of the powerful seventh dissonance in an equally powerful way. Since it was the seventh of the mode that had introduced the idea, there can be only one note on which resolution is possible. This goes far towards explaining the awesome power of the *fff* unison B natural on page 80: the fact that this note is not only the most colourful of the Dorian mode but also involves resolution using the figure x is a guide to the depth of thought that the composer has given to the construction of this work. After such a powerful resolution of all these tensions it is no surprise that, after page 80, unresolved dissonances play no further part in the work (there is therefore no need to use the descending semitone x either, except briefly in retrospect), and that the feeling of the music is much more relaxed. The move towards B flat which immediately takes place shows that the resolution of all the tensions has spent the force of B natural, so that it can play no further part in the governing of tonality. It is for this reason that, though the symphony begins in the pure Dorian mode—with B natural—it ends with a Dorian mode which uses B flat.

The cross relation between C sharp and C natural just after the beginning of Sibelius' Sixth Symphony can now be seen in context: it is one of the most influential events in the work, since *x* derives from it. This figure, with its inversion, expresses the difference between the pure modal form of the three pivotal notes and their altered forms: moreover, *x* is finally the resolution of all the sevenths onto B natural. Since the end of the work uses a modality in which F and C are natural and B is flat, it is evident that the overall power of *x* has been to force each of these modal pivotal notes to the lower of its two forms. Thus the introduction of C sharp into the pure Dorian mode has been resolved: it has not, however, been resolved by a simple reversion to the pure form of the mode, but to one in which the characteristic sixth degree is altered.

Polyphony permeates the symphony, and is evident at even a superficial hearing. By hindsight, it is possible to see how the clue to this manner of construction is provided by the very first notes heard. The opening of the symphony, with its multiple parts, carefully prepared and resolved suspensions, and largely stepwise movement, is clearly derived from the style of late Renaissance polyphony. Many elements which play an important part in the work are foreshadowed in this opening: the very first sound, a major third, is the forerunner of much material which appears in parallel thirds; there is much conjunct writing in the work, especially at the end and in the ecclesiastical-sounding themes which Sibelius liked so much. In spite of these points, the opening sounds unmistakably Sibelian: the cold, high scoring for second violins, the reversing (as compared with Renaissance technique) of dissonance and resolution so that they appear on weak and strong beats respectively, the entry of parts on dissonant notes and the movement of parts in mild syncopation all contribute to the sense of vagueness. Other elements, too, are plainly the result of Sibelius' interest in Renaissance contrapuntal techniques: the frequent use of antiphony, even within the space of a short melody (as for example on page 5, bars 1ff); the use of many-voice polyphony, both imitative and free;[44] the use of canons of various types and complexity;[45] the use of the typically Renaissance device of juxtaposing high and low blocks of sound (as in the opening of the Finale); and also the use of suspensions and resolutions (as on page 5, bars 1ff, and page 86, bars 13f, for example).

The balance of the vocal lines in the works of Palestrina—the way in which upward and downward movement complement one another, in which a leap is normally followed by stepwise movement in the opposite direction, and in which one typical outline consists of a sharp rise at the beginning of a phrase, followed by a gradual descent—is a feature often singled out for praise. In Chapter II it was pointed out that Sibelius' Sixth Symphony has a tendency to use five stepwise rising notes and their inversion concurrently or simultaneously, and a stepwise arch-shaped (or inverted arch-shaped) figure; the balance of such phrases as these is very much akin to that found in Palestrina. Many examples of lines with this type of balance could be given, but the one shown in Ex. 82 must suffice: such a balance as is evident in this work had already been foreshadowed in Sibelius' Fifth Symphony.[46] In his Sixth Symphony, the most perfectly balanced lines of all seem to be kept in reserve for the closing pages of the work, after the great climax of the Finale (page 80), though the balance is foreshadowed by the long canonic lines of the woodwind in the coda of the third movement—lines that are rendered the more effective by being placed after a great deal of staccato writing. As in the first two movements, therefore, some feature of the following movement is foreshadowed in the coda; and the pattern persists in the coda of the Finale which completes the cycle by reverting to the feeling of the opening of the symphony, though with B flat replacing B natural.

The great influence of Renaissance polyphony in this work does not make it any the less Sibelian: indeed, for me as for many other lovers of Sibelius' music, it remains the most appealing of all his symphonies. The composer's diatribe against counterpoint was reported from the year 1936, some thirteen years after the composition of the symphony, and some such reason as the kind of working I have described may well have been in Sibelius' mind when he made the qualification, 'Polyphony is, of course, a force when there is good reason for it'. This 'good reason' is not the most obvious one—the independent contrapuntal lines and Dorian colour—but exists in the symphonic possibilities of the modality. Even remembering that the work is, above all, a poem, one is filled with admiration for the genius who can so thoroughly work out the latent possibilities of such a fossilized concept as the pure Dorian mode; who can see in the ambivalence of intervals within that scale the means of creating and maintaining tension throughout a symphonic work; and who can introduce that ambivalence in a way which at once reminds one of English Tudor music and is yet true to his own musical style;[47] and who, while doing all this, at the same time unifies his work in a unique way by his employment of that one mode. Indeed, one is inclined to wonder whether the composer had his tongue in his cheek when he said, 'You may find several interesting things going on'. Such a treatment not only shows Sibelius' mastery of symphonic development, but is also an eloquent testimony to his knowledge and understanding of Renaissance music: it supplies us, moreover, with yet another symphony in which a single idea governs the total construction.

The One-Movement Symphony: Sibelius' Seventh Symphony

One of the major points made in this study has been that various methods
are used in every symphonic work to unify all the movements. It has been
shown how both Sibelius and Beethoven can use melodic, rhythmic and
tonal devices throughout a work, and indeed build a final all-inclusive
tune from elements which are earlier presented separately. This is, of course,
entirely different from the type of symphony which introduces a 'motto'
or *idée fixe* in the mistaken idea that this by itself constitutes symphonic
integration. In the mature symphonies of Beethoven and Sibelius, the
movements of each individual work all 'belong' to each other without
recourse to such obvious devices. Starting with this 'single-minded'
concept, we may trace the further steps which led towards the single-
movement form of Sibelius' Seventh Symphony.[48] The fusion of the
opening and Scherzo sections of that composer's Fifth Symphony is one
such step, which might well have suggested to him the possibility of even
more extensive development along less 'sectional' single-movement lines.
This development led in part to the single-movement Seventh Symphony,
even though this work was described at first not as a symphony but as a
'Fantasia Sinfonica'. Its claim to the title of Symphony has sometimes been
disputed; but, so long as one defines the term 'symphony' as an orchestral
work in which 'profound logic' unifies 'all the elements', then there is no
reason why there should not be more than the 'normal' three or four
movements (as in Beethoven's 'Pastoral') or fewer, and Sibelius' Seventh
Symphony certainly conforms to this definition. The result may be a short
work, but it is nevertheless very complex.

The Seventh is a total unity, as one might expect of a mature composer
working in the tradition of Beethoven. No bar is wasted; and so, as usual,
the opening is of vital importance to the whole: this includes the initial G
stroke on the timpani. The frequently made statement that Sibelius'
Seventh Symphony opens with a scale of A minor ignores this timpani note,
yet to do so is to misunderstand one of the most important features of the
work. It is an integral part of the rising scale which constitutes the music
of the first two bars and which ends unexpectedly at the beginning of the
third. Much admiration has been expressed that such a simple device as
placing an A flat minor chord after a scale of 'A minor' should sound so
fresh, and (apart from the designation of the scale as 'A minor') one would
not wish to quarrel with this view. It is as if Sibelius had made a chord
which is technically consonant sound like a dissonance because it is so
unexpected: this has an important effect on the work's architecture.

Perhaps it should be stressed that the element of surprise in symphonies
which have 'profound logic' will not sound illogical, but will be subject to
the symphonic argument. Elements which are unprepared, such as the

A flat minor chord at the beginning of Sibelius' Seventh Symphony, must have repercussions later. Surprises are the very essence of the dramatic: they are 'real events' in the sense that I have understood them in this book; yet they must not sound incongruous or outside the work's logic, or they will cease to be real events and take the listener's mind away from the argument.[49]

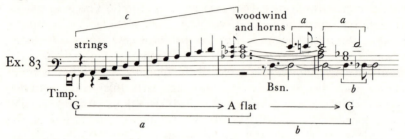

Ex. 83 includes most of the elements on which the music is based; though it does not show that the double basses play the rising scale a quaver later than the rest of the strings. The effect is one of continual upward resolution of a dissonance, a device for which there are good structural reasons.

In Ex. 83 the most striking motif is the scale (*c*), and this is certainly a feature of considerable thematic (and occasionally tonal) significance in the work: the semitone D-E flat at the top, and more especially the harmonic underpinning of G-A flat provided by the initial timpani stroke and the unexpected chord of bar three, are in some ways more important. The rising semitones soon afterwards become a series of suspensions which resolve by step upwards, and this feature is balanced by the downward stepwise resolution of the parts underneath it. These are technically only partial resolutions, however; there is a weakening of dissonance, rather than a move from dissonance to consonance such as would constitute complete resolution. Nevertheless, the aural effect of these bars is one of suspensions followed by resolutions. I shall refer to the upward step as *a* (whether it is a tone or a semitone, and whether or not suspension is involved), and to the downward step as *b* (with the same provisos). Motifs *a* and *b* provide most of the essential material for the work, since the scale (and it inversion, which is frequently used) includes both, and the tonality is strongly governed by the G-A flat progression. The C flat contained in the A flat minor chord in bar three likewise has tonal implications for the rest of the work: as so often happens, this first 'chromatic' sound plays an important part in the design of the piece.

At the time of writing his Sixth Symphony, Sibelius was much interested in Renaissance music, an interest which profoundly influenced almost every detail of that work, but one important Renaissance feature which is not fully explored in the Sixth Symphony is dissonance. This element is so important to Renaissance music that several theorists have described the stylistic features of 16th century composers mainly in terms of their treatment of it. Briefly, there are two types, unessential (that is, passing-notes and returning-notes, the nota cambiata, etc.) and essential (that is, suspensions). It is the latter type of dissonance that we are concerned with here. To reduce the matter to its essentials, a dissonance (a second, fourth or seventh, or their octave transpositions) in Renaissance music must be prepared by being present as a consonance on the beat before the sus-pension, and be resolved by step downward on the beat afterwards. The resolution may be a simple one of a downward step, or an ornamental one which first moves to another note before moving to a step lower than the dissonant note (see Ex. 84).

Ex. 84

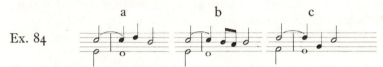

Sibelius was well aware of these formulae, since he had a great love of this music; and a symphonic discussion of the treatment of suspensions is found in the Seventh Symphony. The Seventh thus forms a counterpart to the Sixth, which likewise reinterprets old means and formulae in a new way. There are certain important differences between the Renaissance treatment of dissonances and that bestowed on them by Sibelius. For one thing, Sibelius is not in the slightest concerned with the preparation of a dissonant note, nor, for another, can he see any reason why such a note should necessarily resolve downwards.

In the work there is a continual pull between upward (*a*) and down-ward (*b*) resolutions: either may be a tone or a semitone, though *b* is usually a tone. A struggle is maintained as to whether sevenths and ninths should resolve using *a* or *b*, or whether they should resolve ornamentally by using some such formula as that shown in Ex. 84a. This latter formula, for Sibelius, constitutes a resolution in two directions at two different points (earlier and later): the Renaissance composers, however, were quite clear, because of the music's underlying pulse and the need for a dissonant note eventually to fall by step, that resolution only occurred with the final note of the formula. The diffused resolutions in Sibelius, and the listener's consequent uncertainty, contribute greatly to the sense of forward motion and the fluidity of the work. The struggle between *a* and *b* is maintained from bar three, where the C flat is introduced (see Ex. 83) until the very last chord of the work, where that note is resolved: we hear *a* first and last, nevertheless, since the upward resolutions begin as early as the double bass entry in the first bar.

I have suggested that *a* (in the shape of the G-A flat progression at the beginning) has an effect on the tonality: this is clear as early as the third and fourth bars. The experience of the Fourth Symphony, however, has led Sibelius to link rhythm with tonality. In the first two bars, the tonality is firm and is accompanied by steady crotchet movement: the introduction of the A flat minor chord in bar three causes the tonality to become uncertain, and the rhythm correspondingly unsteady. All this is clear in Ex. 83.

Enough has now been written about the first few bars to make it evident that the music of the work is closely integrated. Now that the separate elements have been isolated, it is necessary to illustrate their use and effect throughout the work: nevertheless, considerations of space dictate that this discussion be confined to the most vital features.

The passage for the solo trombone (page 9)[50] is one of three which mark high points, or points of reference, in the work (see Ex. 85): all three occur in the key of C, the first and third in the major, and the second in the minor.

Ex. 85

The suspensions here (with the dissonant note always a D, and mostly resolving downwards) are very clear: the solo trombone entry on a ninth, with its delayed resolution downwards, is a feature of this music on each of its occurrences. What also becomes clear is that the progression from simple suspensions (in the first two bars of the example) to ornamental ones whose resolution is long delayed (in bars 3 and 4 of Ex. 85) is paralleled in the symphony as a whole.

The tonality of the music which leads up to this passage betrays the influence of *c*, as well as of the G-A flat and D-E flat motifs. Of these last two, the G-A flat motif perhaps assumes the greater importance tonally. Throughout the work, the note G is used, basically, to define the tonality as C major, of which it is the dominant. The use of this note rather than C itself to represent the key is perhaps evidence of Sibelius' familiarity with modal theory, and especially that concerned with Gregorian psalm-tones. Thus, on the whole, returns to the note G involve returns to C major. The A flat tendency is set against this, and passages governed by the note A flat (or G sharp) provide tension by taking the music away from the tonic (see Ex. 83, for instance). Returns to G often occur by way of A flat, so that the effect is one of a 'tonal' resolution using the shape *b*: nevertheless, there is a balancing tendency to use a rising approach to G (from F sharp, using the shape *a*). The two approaches are often found in conjunction (as at page 8, bar 1. See also Ex. 86). The frequent establishment of the note G and the key of C by using F sharp as an approach (as at page 6, bar 1) often involves Sibelius' favourite augmented fourth chords.

Just as the dynamic markings at the beginning of Beethoven's First Symphony were not fortuitous, so neither are those at the beginning of Sibelius' Seventh. The crescendo through the opening scale up to the *fz* E flat (bar 3) throws such weight onto the note that one suspects it of having some important structural function, especially as Sibelius has led us to believe that the bar will begin with an E natural: the *fz* markings emphasize the element of surprise. E flat does, indeed, have an important tonal function in the work, as a force which can only be counterbalanced by E natural: hence the crescendo marks in the double bass part extend to the E natural in bar one, to be immediately followed by decrescendo markings. The insistence on the natural form of E in the basses is given greater weight by the fact that these instruments drop out when the E flat is sounded in bar three. The dynamic markings have evidently been made with great care.

The events so far described lead inevitably to the realization that the idea of 'dissonance' is being applied to the work at several levels and to several different facets; the chords (or, perhaps more accurately, the part-writing), the tonality and the rhythm. The first of these, which consists of resolutions of dissonances at various different speeds, upwards or downwards, simply or ornamentally, has already been alluded to briefly, and can easily be traced through the work: examples are very numerous indeed. The idea is, however, extended so that 'resolutions' can take place as a new dissonance occurs (as can happen in Renaissance music, too), or a whole series of dissonant chords may follow each other, delaying the eventual resolution.[51] (See the music on either side of Letter E, for example.) A 'dissonance' may be created and 'resolved' within a series of repeated chords which are themselves technically dissonant (pages 17f). This is only one of several new treatments of dissonance which Sibelius employs in this work: the result, as compared with the simple resolution of a dissonance, is an increase in tension. This is evident, too, where the same note has more than one apparent resolution: in Ex. 86, for instance, the dissonance (all dissonances are marked*) which begins the bar can be heard either as resolving (resolutions are marked +) with the C major chord in the second bar, or at several earlier points in the first bar, because of the continual downward steps of the upper part. (Various other possibilities also occur, as will be seen from the example.) This use of resolutions on both the large and small scales—an idea perhaps lurking in the back of Sibelius' mind because of his treatment of a similar idea in the

Fifth Sympnony—can be extended. In Ex. 87, the mildly dissonant first
chord of the second phrase may be heard either as resolving on the following chord or (on the large scale) with the final chord of the phrase.

Ex. 86

Ex. 87

Such larger scale resolutions may be viewed as a reinterpretation of the
'ornamental' ones of Ex. 84. Ex. 87 shows another reinterpretation of
Renaissance dissonance treatment, for the first phrase comes to rest, not as
one would expect, on a consonance, but on a dissonance (though mild) :[52]
in a sense, therefore, the rôles of consonance and dissonance are reversed
for a short while at this point. Further, the listener may well feel that this
$\frac{6}{5}$ chord, since it is made a point of repose, can act both as a consonance
and as the dissonance it technically is: thus in the second phrase of the
example the return to a similar chord (bars 6 and 7) may be felt as a point
of repose, though not consonant. (The points in question are marked
+----→+ . Inevitably, one recalls two things—the FACD chord of the first

bar of page 4, which forms the immediate resolution of the opening dissonances quoted in Ex. 83, and also the manner in which Sibelius had caused the consonant A flat minor at the work's opening to sound dissonant because of its unexpectedness: it is clear that in this work the composer is exploring the nature of consonance and dissonance and the relationship between them. Dissonances may, naturally, be strengthened, multiplied or lengthened in order to increase the tension: obvious examples are to be found on page 50 of the score, and at the modulation into E flat on page 54.

Sibelius makes tonal use of the same ideas, for departures from the key of C (and especially from the note G) constitute what may be called 'tonal dissonance': the farther from C major tonally, and the longer the passage concerned, the greater is the effect of 'tonal dissonance'. Sibelius never remains so long away from the key of C that its function as the main tonal background is forgotten, though he does on one occasion discussed below approach the idea of establishing an alternative tonal centre quite firmly. The 'tonal dissonances' are resolved by returning to G (a note often strengthened with a preceding F sharp) and thus to C major. This is well illustrated by pages 44–9 of the score: the fact that this passage is surrounded by octave Gs draws attention to its function as a 'tonal dissonance', and its large scale is evident when it is compared with Ex. 83. The three solos for trombone (see Ex. 85) constitute powerful statements of the 'tonally consonant' key of C (though the second states the minor form). As Robert Simpson has put it, 'Themes are always more easily noticed than tonalities':[53] it is for this reason that both Beethoven and Sibelius draw especial attention to important tonalities or stages of the tonal argument by introducing at the same time new or important themes.

Digressions away from C and from the note G are often governed, in some way or another, by A flat. With this in mind, it becomes evident that the Renaissance-like passage on pages 5ff has several purposes. It establishes the main tonality, so necessary because the opening has been more concerned with postulating the ideas of tonal, chordal and rhythmic dissonance than with establishing a key centre: in doing this, it draws attention also to the importance of F sharp in strengthening the note G and to the more subsidiary importance of E flat (the note towards which the opening scale of the work had led). The polyphonic passage also emphasizes the main thematic material, and includes (in the second violins, either side of Letter B) a phrase used in association with the three solos for trombone. The thematic material announced here also alludes very clearly to the leap of a fifth (rising at first, though often it falls later in the work), a thematic counterpart of a vital tonal tendency in the symphony. This is the tendency, already mentioned, for the key of C to be represented by its dominant: Sibelius makes it quite clear in bar 3 of the work that E flat stands in a similar relationship to A flat (see Ex. 83). Further than this, though, G has its own dominant (D), which is the dissonant note featured in the trombone solos (see Ex. 85, where it will be noticed that the whole axis C-G-D controls the greater part of the trombone melody);[54] and E flat (as a key) is often stressed by the use of its own dominant, B flat. There are, in fact, two tonal axes at work in the symphony, but whereas C-G-D—the consonant tonal axis—is important, the other, A flat-E flat-B flat, although present as a 'dissonant' tonal axis, is not so strongly evident in the music: if it were, it would be inclined to replace the C-G-D axis as the tonal consonance. Just as Sibelius had a tendency to reverse the normal rôles of consonance and dissonance during the music quoted in Ex. 87, so by using this same theme (pages 53–5) first in B flat, then in A flat and finally, after a long drawn-out dissonance, in a very settled E flat (Letter T) he follows precisely the same procedure with regard to tonalities. It is because of the very settled nature of the theme used, because of the long-delayed resolution which occurs at its beginning, and because the secondary axis has been well prepared in the preceding bars that the technically 'dissonant' key of E flat actually sounds consonant at this point. Moreover, Sibelius has also prepared for the consonant sound of E flat here by making a C major version of the same tune (Letter R, page 50) sound more dissonant by applying a stronger-sounding and longer dissonance to the $\frac{6}{5}$ chord and by giving the theme a somewhat unsettled introduction. Yet again the composer has related the chordal and tonal treatments of dissonance: this link between chordal (or, perhaps, polyphonic) dissonance and 'tonal' dissonance parallels that between the thematic material (a and b) and the treatment of tonality. The mind returns again to the 'dissonant' effect of the intitial A flat minor chord, a small-scale foreshadowing of this larger-scale feature.

The departures from the main tonality mentioned in the foregoing paragraph have a tendency to lengthen as the work progresses, so that tension is increased: to compensate for this, returns to the note G are given with corresponding weight, as can be seen by comparing page 5 with pages 64–8. (The passage between the two G's on page 5 also provides an illustration of the way in which the scoring—here the 'coll punto e veloce' of the strings—can emphasize the tonal dissonance.) E flat (the dominant of A flat) grows in power through the work, forcing the second trombone solo to be in C minor (instead of C major). Nevertheless, the trombone itself avoids stating the third, always at this juncture resolving its ninth dissonance downwards onto C: the sombre effect of this passage is heightened by the avoidance of F sharp (normally a harbinger of G and the tonic major), by the alteration of C to a chromatic scale, and by the low pitch of the scoring. Nevertheless, in spite of the recovering of the tonic major, the third and final trombone solo does not constitute a complete resolution, since the key of E flat with its prominent note B flat causes

'tonal dissonance' immediately after it (page 74). Indeed, the music is
battered by the conflicting claims of this E flat and the F sharp-G repetitions in the strings just before Letter Y. (The passage is an amplified
version of the end of the first trombone solo. The third solo is in a sense
continued, after the tonal dissonance on page 74, with more of a feeling of
resolution, in the four bars preceding Letter O, though with a horn solo
replacing the trombone.) The two detached chords in the violins (on page
74) point to the struggle between the tonalities governed by G (as shown
by the presence of F sharp in the chord) and those governed by B flat.
There is an interesting parallel here with the development section of the
first movement of Beethoven's Fifth Symphony, where the struggle (as
mentioned in Chapter VII) is more visible than audible. The F sharp and
B flat (on page 74, perhaps recalling the similar feature at Letter G, and
perhaps also Letter I) of Sibelius' work sound like a chord of F sharp
major, giving the impression of great distance from C (and thus of considerable 'tonal dissonance'); yet the implied struggle between the F sharp
(which refers to the tonal axis C-G-D) and the B flat (which represents the
subsidiary axis) is very clear when one reads the score.

By his handling and mixing of these various types of dissonance,
Sibelius controls tension. Two features may stand as an illustration of his
manner of working. Firstly, similar material recurs at four bars before
Letter N and Q and thirteen bars after Letter U, in the keys of E, A flat
and C flat respectively. The last of these acts more powerfully as a 'tonal
dissonance' (for it is farthest away from C major), and results in a considerable amount of music in tonalities closely governed by C flat towards
the close of the work. Secondly, at Letter Z the big unison E (following a
loud B) is necessary to counter the E flat-B flat axis of so much of the
subsidiary material, and it is followed by a tonic chord, C major (the
progression is an inflation of the earlier one quoted in Ex. 86. See also the
three bars before Letter N, and page 38). This C major chord, though,
contains a seventh—B flat again, which leads to another statement of E flat.
This dominant seventh chord, not very dissonant tonally, is announced
with the utmost force; yet the F sharp-B flat chord mentioned above,
which, being further from the tonic, constitutes a greater tonal dissonance,
is quietly scored by comparison. In a sense, therefore, the force of the two
'tonal dissonances' is balanced, though they are very different in sound.

The rhythm of the work can itself give an effect of 'dissonance' when it
moves unevenly or out of phase with the main pulse. This is evident in
many places, and is well illustrated in Ex. 83 (where the regular 'consonant' rhythm of the opening two bars becomes unsettled and thus 'dissonant' in the following passage) and between Letters Y and Z. The idea of
'rhythmic dissonance' or consonance is used to strengthen or oppose the
other types of dissonance and resolution in the symphony. It follows from

this that the unity of the work is governed, as it had been in Sibelius' two previous symphonies, by a single idea.

The single idea of consonance and dissonance, when applied to the tonal procedures of the work, inevitably requires that only one key area—C major—be felt as the ultimate consonance. Sibelius must, therefore, confine the tonal background to this one key, and this points clearly to the use also of a single continuous movement, for the normal scheme of related keys in a work in several movements would necessitate resolution in several key areas, and thus weaken the point of the whole argument. On the contrary, the form and design of Sibelius' Seventh Symphony are dictated by the very nature of the material chosen. It will be clear from this that I am among those who regard the work as a true symphony— one of the most tightly integrated of all symphonies.

Although the Seventh Symphony is a single-movement work, it nevertheless includes sections which correspond to the different types of movement traditional to the symphony—scherzo and slow movement, for example. Indeed, these different styles could scarcely be more clearly unified than by being fused into a single movement: in order to achieve this result, the joins between the sections must be imperceptible to the listener, just as those in the first movement of Sibelius' Fifth Symphony are. Moreover, the return of certain thematic elements and the gradual expansion of simple suspensions to ornamental (or longer) ones gives a strongly unified feeling to the piece.

The final resolutions—one down (b) and one up (a)—take place against the final tonic chord of the piece. By being slow they draw special attention to themselves, the long dissonances resulting in a greater sense of repose when they eventually resolve; moreover, they cause no ambiguity about the point of resolution. Indeed, these final resolutions 'resolve' all the partial and ornamental ones, and all the various ambiguities of dissonance in earlier parts of the work. The D-C resolution (b), which refers especially to the trombone solos, resolves the fifth above G onto the tonic. The final B-C (a) replaces the F sharp-G which had so often established the note G earlier in the work, and it now yet more clearly emphasizes the tonic chord: moveover, the B-C figure resolves the C flat in the A flat minor chord of bar three (the other two notes of that chord having been resolved onto C major already on the last page of the score). Thus the first dissonant tonal sound, which in a sense set the symphonic argument in motion, is the last to be resolved, and the very distant key area of C flat, which had been prominent at pages 59ff (and is perhaps also referred to in the F sharp-B flat chord of page 74) is at last overcome. In overall shape, the work expresses 'resolution' of the important dominant tendency, too, for the final C major chord stands as the ultimate goal of a symphony that had begun with a G stroke on the timpani.[55]

The Seventh was Sibelius' last symphony: he promised an eighth, and eventually said that it would be performed after his death. No such work has ever come to light, and it seems most unlikely that such a piece was written, especially in view of the fact that Sibelius wrote little music of any kind in the last thirty years of his life. It seems that the composer had worked out the piece in his mind, but could not capture it on paper in a manner that satisfied him.[56] One may ponder on the reasons for his inability to produce his eighth symphony. So convinced and excellent a symphonist is unlikely to have lost faith in the form: it is more likely that, with the Seventh Symphony, he had reached the *ne plus ultra* of symphonic form as I have understood it in this book, and as I believe he understood it. The composer himself is quoted as saying:

Composing has been the guiding line in my life, and it is still so. My work has the same fascination for me as when I was young, a fascination bound up with the difficulty of the task. Let no one imagine that composing is easier for an old composer if he takes his art seriously. The demands one makes on oneself have increased in the course of years. Greater sureness makes one scorn solutions that come too easily, that follow the line of least resistance, in a higher degree than formerly. One is always faced with new problems. The thing that has pleased me most is that I have been able to reject. The greatest labour I have experienced, perhaps, was on works that have never been completed.[57]

He had achieved the highest possible integration: not only had formal unity been carried to the point where the movements were fused together, but the notes were so tightly governed by a single unifying principle that none was unrelated to the overall scheme. The use of a tone-row to integrate music yet more fully would not have appealed to Sibelius, even though it could have been used without producing atonal music;[58] and extra-musical ideas—such as a programme—would be more inclined to loosen, rather than tighten, the purely musical structure. Sibelius had indeed written what was, for him, the symphony to end all symphonies.

Coda

An examination of the symphonies of Sibelius makes it possible to trace the various patterns of development which run through them. Briefly, the rudimentary use of a pivotal note and a pivotal augmented triad in the First Symphony blossoms into a much more developed form in the Second, where the pivotal notes themselves constitute the pivotal augmented triad. The enharmonic treatment of pivotal notes in the Second Symphony is found again in the Third, and the key scheme of the Second Symphony, in which tonalities move round a 'circle of thirds', reappears in the Fourth, both works sharing the idea of using as pivotal notes those which help to define the tonalities as major or minor. An obvious connection between the Third and Fourth Symphonies is the use of the tritone to govern the tonality; the interval is also used for structural purposes in the Fifth Symphony. The importance of rhythm, so closely bound up with tonality in the Fourth Symphony, is further stressed in the Fifth, where it becomes still more vital. The 'counterpoint of rhythms' in the Fifth Symphony leads to a counterpoint of notes in the Sixth: in the latter, the modal nature of the first two symphonies returns. The application of modal ideas to symphonic tonality, and the consequent looking back to the polyphonic composers, may well have provided the initial idea for the use of other Renaissance techniques in the Seventh Symphony; whereas the concept of 'tonal dissonance' had been foreshadowed in the Fifth. Moreover, the idea of treating elements on various different time-scales in Sibelius' Fifth Symphony recurs in the Seventh, where it is applied to dissonances and resolutions.

From the Second Symphony onwards there is a tendency to obscure the outlines of the separate movements: the Scherzo and the Finale run together in the Second Symphony, there is a small amount of quotation of themes between the movements of the Third, and a very careful link between the tonalities of the various movements in the Fourth Symphony. The Fifth Symphony—which the printed score describes as 'in one movement'—creates an arch shape in which the three separate sections are made to hang together by the rather unexpectedly abrupt endings of the first two 'movements'; and the Sixth provides a foretaste of each new movement in the coda of its predecessor. Clearly the one-movement Seventh Symphony was the logical outcome of these processes.[1]

A similar pattern of development could easily be traced through Beethoven's symphonies: the most striking development might well be the gradual evolution of a kind of 'progressive tonality' which accompanies Beethoven's search for an alternative to the classical dominant key: the expansion in size of his symphonies in any case demanded an expansion of classical tonality. The process continues, of course, in the works of Sibelius, and there are, naturally enough, other parallels to be drawn between the works of these two men.[2] The compatibility of the chosen thematic material with the tonal scheme, and the thoroughness of the working-out of the tonal implications of that material, would certainly be among these parallels; so would the contribution of all the elements of composition (rhythm, orchestration, harmony and so on) to the argument. In more concrete fashion, the processes at work in Sibelius' Second Symphony— the 'circle of thirds', the prominence of B flat in D tonalities, the conflict of 'axial' and conventional tonality, and the countering of a continual flattening of keys by a corresponding sharpening in the Finale—are found also in Beethoven's Ninth Symphony. Beethoven himself considered writing a symphony based on the church modes: whether or not Sibelius knew this, and whether or not he was influenced by such knowledge, his Sixth Symphony is just such a work. Moreover, the conflict and balance between 'stasis' (pedals, in the main) and ongoing rhythm in Beethoven's Seventh Symphony is vital to Sibelius' Fifth: the 'new tonality' based on third and sixth relationships in the 'Pastoral', too, finds an echo in the 'new tonality' based on the minor seventh in Sibelius' Sixth Symphony. It will not have escaped notice that the rhythmic upsets in the opening movement of the 'Eroica', which accompany the wide tonal excursions, find something approaching a parallel in Sibelius' Fourth Symphony.

Sibelius was of the opinion that the form of a work was a necessary consequence of the musical content.[3] The greatest symphonies of Beethoven and Sibelius demonstrate the principle that the form and the material chosen are as one.[4] As Robert Simpson has said, '. . . in all art the form itself is the expression of the content'.[5] In great symphonies, none of the material is wasted ; or, to view the idea from another angle, the unity of each work is complete, and derives from the total integration of all the aspects of composition. Both Beethoven and Sibelius state the problem set by each symphony in clear terms at the outset: in both, the first 'chromatic', sound is likely to prove of structural importance. Both use one overriding means of unification—or, to put it another way, both set one particular kind of problem—in each new work: never do they repeat themselves. Seen from this point of view, Ferdinand Ries' remark that 'In writing his compositions Beethoven often had some special object in mind, though he

often laughed and scolded about musical tone-paintings, especially those
of a more trifling nature'[6] takes on great significance. Certainly there may
be programmatic tendencies—as in the 'Eroica' and 'Pastoral' Symphonies;
but these do not interfere with the purely musical processes of thought. In
an illuminating passage comparing Sibelius with Beethoven, Santeri Levas
makes the following observation:

> ... the works of Sibelius were described as programmatic and at the same time
> compared with those of Beethoven. Sibelius found this description funda-
> mentally inaccurate. He said: 'One could have said of Beethoven—if one abso-
> lutely insists—that he wrote programmatic music. For his point of departure was
> always a specific idea, whereas I . . .' The sentence broke off. Sibelius noticed
> that he had trodden on dangerous ground, and changed the subject.[7]

This somewhat frustrating passage seems to justify the view taken in this
book that the symphonies of both men consist primarily of a highly logical
musical development, but that those of Beethoven contain, on a few
occasions, programmatic elements in addition.[8] Sibelius himself maintained that his symphonies were absolute music, containing no programmatic elements.[9] 'Profound logic' there may be in the works of both
Beethoven and Sibelius; yet both have great 'foreground' appeal also.
(Like many an artist, Sibelius preferred to forget the labour of composition
once a work had been completed, and immersed himself instead in the
'foreground'.) The implications of rhythm are explored by both, and the
implications of modal harmony in a symphonic work are likewise explored
by both; but these parallels need not blind us to the tremendous differences which also exist between the two men.

The opening chapter of this book posed the questions: 'How does a
composer ensure that the separate movements or sections of a work belong
together, so that they cannot be interchanged with portions of other
works?'; 'How is it that the themes of a symphony cannot be played in any
order and still achieve the desired result?'; and 'How does a composer
manage to weld the diverse types of music required of a symphony—
scherzo, slow movement, and so on—into a logical whole?' We must now
return to these questions in order to see what answers can be given.

An examination of the expansion of classical tonality has taken up a
large part of this book: it is a facet of symphonic writing which is of paramount importance, and which is all too often neglected in favour of
thematic analysis. Themes, it has been said, are more easily noticed than
tonalities: both Beethoven and Sibelius learned to use a new theme (or
some special thematic treatment) in order to draw attention to some
tonality or other. Both themes and tonalities have their place: indeed, both
help to provide answers to the questions asked. It is one of the supreme
marks of genius in both Beethoven and Sibelius that each symphony is so

very different from the others: even if the basic thematic formulae are the same (as in Beethoven's Fourth and Fifth Symphonies) the rhythmic and tonal treatment is entirely different. The gradual progress towards a tonal goal in Beethoven's Fifth Symphony is quite a different idea from the use of diminutions and the pull of the minor sixth degree in his Fourth. Even though thematic links exist between the two, to substitute any movement of either for one in the other symphony would interrupt the logical growth of rhythm and tonality. Tritones are found in Sibelius' Third and Fourth Symphonies; yet there can be no interchange of movements since the building of a new kind of 'expanded diatonicism' in the Third is quite opposed to the destructive nature of the tonality in the Fourth. Clearly, then, any explanation of 'unity' which takes only thematic material into account is unsatisfactory.

The handling of tonality by both composers explains why themes cannot appear in any order: and the gradual diminution of note values in Beethoven's Fourth Symphony and the gradual expansion of intervals in the Fifth make it imperative that the first and second subjects of those symphonies appear in *only* that order. In Sibelius' Second Symphony, the growing and waning power of B flat (and indeed of F sharp) is a vital ingredient of the argument, and the order of events cannot be changed without upsetting the logic of the discussion.

The answers to the first two questions also provide the answer to the third: obviously there must be some distinction between the movements of a symphony, and hence the material, though unified by various means, must be different. This is so self-evident that it scarcely needs spelling out. Even Sibelius' Seventh Symphony has identifiable sections which approximate to the types of music found in a conventional four-movement symphony; and the conventional four-movement symphony, such as Beethoven's Seventh, has a logical progression of rhythms, tonalities and themes which, different as the movements are, binds them together and keeps the musical argument in suspense until the Finale. Such a method of working also explains why many themes are changed on repetition: such is the power of the argument of these two composers that themes can only appear in a different light after the development section. Such an alteration is parallel to the change of character of protagonists in a tragedy as opposed to the more 'static' caricatures found in some comedy. This helps to explain why, for example, so few of the repeats in Beethoven's Fifth Symphony are exact.

The complexity of thought shown by both Beethoven and Sibelius is astonishing: the ability to handle and develop various types of motif, and at the same time to write music which will appeal at several levels, is the work of pure genius. It may well be impossible to appreciate all these levels at once; but it is their depth which gives these works their lasting interest.

It is indeed impossible to identify all the implications of any one of these symphonies until one knows it thoroughly; and I cannot hope to have drawn attention to more than a few facets of each of these works.

Many great composers have founded 'schools' of composition—pupils and admirers who were so impressed by their achievements, so full of admiration for their style, that they tried to emulate them and copy their methods and mannerisms. One of the greatest compliments that one can pay Beethoven is that he did not found a school—he founded two, or possibly even three. The classical forms and symphonic logic, which have formed the subject-matter of this book, were copied by Brahms and, as I have tried to show, by Sibelius. The large-scale 'romantic' symphony of Bruckner and Mahler looks back to such devices as the horn-calls of the 'Eroica', the opening string tremolandos of the 'Choral', and the rhythmic drive of the Seventh Symphony. The modal harmony towards which Beethoven was moving at the end of his life, and which was an important feature of the 'Pastoral' Symphony, became a hallmark of Nationalist composers (Dvorak and Borodin, for example); the appeal to 'national consciousness' (or perhaps 'subconsciousness') as opposed to the intellect is not characteristic of Beethoven, though it is certainly evident in Sibelius' First Symphony (and in *Kullervo*): the appeal to a national collective past in such Nationalist works may make them more viable for that nation, but possibly less 'international' in appeal. The use of a programme for Nationalists as well as other symphonic writers (Berlioz and Tchaikovsky, for instance) may also look back to Beethoven. I have suggested that the prominent sixth degree of the scale, as it appears in the 'Pastoral' Symphony, leads through Mendelssohn and Wagner to the Impressionists. Even the use of the human voice in symphonic music has been copied, especially in the 20th century. Few symphonies written after Beethoven's day have been untouched by his spirit.

These influences show the many ways in which Beethoven expanded the symphony: interest in his works has never waned, and this perhaps is because Beethoven can be all things to all men. This book has dealt with one aspect of the symphonies only—the aspect which appealed most to Brahms and Sibelius: other aspects have been dealt with at length by other writers—but it is an index of Beethoven's greatness that there are these several levels at which his work can be appraised. Sibelius, too, has had his followers, though his works have gone through a period of neglect; but perhaps the greatest compliment that can be paid him is to show that his symphonic works can stand comparison with those of Beethoven.[10]

It is possible to explain at length what happens in a good symphony, but it will always take more space to do this than the music itself takes. Good symphonic writing, like good poetry, is so condensed that the tale cannot be told more concisely; and in music, words cannot in any case either tell the whole tale or capture its essence. Sibelius' comment on his own Sixth Symphony might well apply to any of the works discussed in this book:

'You may analyse it and explain it theoretically.—You may find that there are several interesting things going on. But most people forget that it is, above all, a poem.'

BIBLIOGRAPHY AND ABBREVIATIONS

The following books and articles are referred to in the foregoing chapters. They are identified in the notes by author and an abbreviated title: these are listed below in alphabetical order of author.

Abraham, *Sibelius*. Abraham, Gerald (ed.). *Sibelius, A Symposium.* Oxford University Press, 1952.

Arnold, *Beethoven*. Arnold, Denis, and Fortune, Nigel (eds). *The Beethoven Companion.* Faber and Faber, 1973.

Barrett-Ayres, *Haydn*. Barrett-Ayres, Reginald. *Joseph Haydn and the String Quartet.* Barrie and Jenkins, 1974.

Below, *Beethoven 7*. Below, Robert. *Some Aspects of Tonal Relationships in Beethoven's Seventh Symphony.* Music Review, xxxvii, 1976.

Cherniavsky, *Sibelius*. Cherniavsky, David. *Special Characteristics of Sibelius' Style,* in Abraham, *Sibelius, q.v.*

Cone, *Composer*. Cone, Edward. *The Composer's Voice.* University of California Press, 1974.

Cooke, *Music*. Cooke, Deryck. *The Language of Music.* Oxford University Press, 1962.

Cooper, *Rhythm*. Cooper, Grosvenor and Meyer, Leonard B. *The Rhythmic Structure of Music.* University of Chicago Press, 1960.

Deane, *Beethoven*. Deane, Basil. *The Symphonies and Overtures,* in Arnold, *Beethoven, q.v.*

Eliot, *Letters*. Haight, Gordon S. (ed.). George Eliot, *Letters.* Oxford University Press, 1954–6.

Forbes, *Beethoven 5*. Forbes, Elliot (ed.). *Beethoven's Symphony No. 5 in C Minor.* Norton Critical Scores, 1971.

Forbes, *Thayer*. Forbes, Elliot (ed.). *Thayer's Life of Beethoven.* Princeton University Press, 1967.

Fujita, *Middlemarch*. Fujita, Sieji. *Structure and Motif in 'Middlemarch'.* The Hokuseido Press, 1969.

George, *Tonality*. George, Graham. *Tonality and Musical Structure.* Faber and Faber, 1970.

Gossett, *Beethoven 6*. Gossett, Philip. *Beethoven's Sixth Symphony: Sketches for the First Movement.* Journal of the American Musicological Society, xxvii, 1974.

Grove, *Beethoven*. Grove, George. *Beethoven and his Nine Symphonies.* Dover Publications, 1962.

Hill, *Sibelius*. Hill, William G. *Some Aspects of Form in the Symphonies of Sibelius.* Music Review, x, 1949.

Hines, *View*. Hines, Robert Stephan (ed.). *The Orchestral Composer's Point of View.* University of Oklahoma Press, 1970.

Hyatt-King, *Mountains*. Hyatt-King, Alec. *Mountains, Music and Musicians*. Musical Quarterly, XXXI, 1945.

Imbrie, *Beethoven*. Imbrie, Andrew. '*Extra*' *Measures and Metrical Ambiguity in Beethoven*, in Tyson, *Studies, q.v.*

Johnson, *Sibelius*. Johnson, Harold E. *Sibelius*. Faber and Faber, 1959.

Keller, *Mozart*. Keller, Hans. *Wolfgang Amadeus Mozart*, in Simpson, *Symphony, q.v.*

Kerman, *An die ferne*. Kerman, Joseph. *An die ferne Geliebte*, in Tyson, *Studies, q.v.*

Kerman, *Quartets*. Kerman, Joseph. *The Beethoven Quartets*. Oxford University Press, 1967.

Kerman, *Sketches*. Kerman, Joseph. *Beethoven Sketches in the British Museum*. Proceedings of the Royal Musical Association, XCIII, 1966–7.

Kirby, *Pastoral*. Kirby, F. E. *Beethoven's Pastoral Symphony as a Sinfonia Caracteristica*, in Lang, *Beethoven, q.v.*

Lam, *Beethoven*. Lam, Basil, *Ludwig van Beethoven*, in Simpson, *Symphony, q.v.*

Lang, *Beethoven*. Lang, Paul Henry (ed.). *The Creative World of Beethoven*. Norton, 1971.

Layton, *Sibelius*. Layton, Robert. *Sibelius*. Dent, 1965.

Levas, *Sibelius*. Levas, Santeri. *Sibelius, a Personal Portrait*. Dent, 1972.

Lockwood, *Beethoven*. Lockwood, Lewis. *Beethoven's Sketches for* SEHNSUCHT (WoO 146), in Tyson, *Studies, q.v.*

Mann, *Faustus*. Mann, Thomas. *Doctor Faustus* (transl. Lowe-Porter, H.T.). Penguin Books, 1949.

Mann, *Schenker*. Mann, Michael. *Schenker's Contribution to Music Theory*. Music Review, X, 1949.

Meikle, *Eroica*. Meikle, Robert B. *Thematic Transformation in the First Movement of Beethoven's Eroica Symphony*. Music Review, XXXII, 1971.

Meyer, *Explaining*. Meyer, Leonard B. *Explaining Music*. University of California Press, 1973.

Meyer, *Ideas*. Meyer, Leonard B. *Music, the Arts, and Ideas*. University of Chicago Press, 1967.

Mies, *Sketches*. Mies, Paul. *Beethoven's Sketches: an Analysis of his Style based on a study of his sketch-books* (transl. Mackinnon, Doris L.). Dover, 1974.

Palmer, *Impressionism*. Palmer, Christopher. *Impressionism in Music*. Hutchinson University Library, 1973.

Parmet, *Sibelius*. Parmet, Simon. *The Symphonies of Sibelius*. Cassell, 1959.

Reti, *Sonatas*. Reti, Rudolf. *Thematic Patterns in Sonatas of Beethoven*. Faber and Faber, 1967.

Rosen, *Style*. Rosen, Charles. *The Classical Style*. Faber and Faber, 1971.

Sayers, *Maker*. Sayers, Dorothy L. *The Mind of the Maker*. Methuen, 1941.

Schenker, *Beethoven 5*. Schenker, Heinrich. *Beethovens Fünfte Sinfonie*. Universal Edition UE 26306, reprint of 1969.

Scherchen, *Music*. Scherchen, Hermann. *The Nature of Music* (transl. Mann, William). Dobson, 1946.

Simpson, *Beethoven*. Simpson, Robert. *Beethoven's Symphonies*. BBC Publications. 1970.

Simpson, *Bruckner*. Simpson, Robert. *The Essence of Bruckner*. Gollancz, 1967.

Simpson, *Nielsen*, Simpson, Robert. *Carl Nielsen: Symphonist*. Dent, 1952.

Simpson, *Symphony*. Simpson, Robert (ed.). *The Symphony*. Penguin Books, 1967.

Somfai, *Haydn*. Somfai, Laszlo. *The London Revision of Haydn's Instrumental Style*. Proceedings of the Royal Musical Association, c, 1973–4.

Sonneck, *Beethoven*. Sonneck, O. G. *Beethoven, Impressions by his Contemporaries*. Dover, 1967.

Strunk, *Readings*. Strunk, Oliver. *Source Readings in Music History*. Norton, 1950.

Thorpe Davie, *Structure*. Thorpe Davie, Cedric. *Musical Structure and Design*. Dobson, 1953.

Tippett, *Aquarius*. Tippett, Michael. *Moving into Aquarius*. Paladin, 1974.

Törne, *Sibelius*. Törne, Bengt de. *Sibelius: a close-up*. Faber and Faber, 1937.

Tovey, *Analysis*. Tovey, Donald. *Essays in Musical Analysis*. Oxford University Press, 1959.

Tovey, *Beethoven*. Tovey, Donald. *Beethoven*. Oxford University Press, 1944.

Truscott, *Sibelius*. Truscott, Harold. *Jean Sibelius*, in Simpson, *Symphony*, q.v.

Tyson, *Studies*. Tyson, Alan (ed.). *Beethoven Studies*, Vol. I. Oxford University Press, 1974.

Walker, *Analysis*. Walker, Alan. *A Study in Musical Analysis*. Barrie and Rockliff, 1962.

Walker, *Criticism*. Walker, Alan. *Anatomy of Musical Criticism*. Barrie and Rockliff, 1966.

Weingartner, *Music*. Weingartner, Felix. *Weingartner on Music and Conducting* (transl. Newman, Ernest; Crosland, Jessie; and Schott, H. M.). Dover, 1969.

Wood, *Sibelius*. Wood, Ralph. *The Miscellaneous Orchestral and Theatre Music*, in Abraham, *Sibelius*, q.v.

NOTES

Introduction

1. The reader may consult any standard edition of Beethoven's symphonies: the publishers of Sibelius' works discussed in the text are given in footnotes at the appropriate points.

2. Sir Michael Tippett has made this point in Hines, *View*. It is because the present book seeks to demonstrate the workings of symphonic logic rather than to provide a complete guide to the symphonies of Beethoven and Sibelius that *Wellington's Victory* and *Kullervo* (a symphonic poem in several movements) are not discussed here.

1 Exposition

1. '... the symphony is my real element', Beethoven is reported to have said: see Mies, *Sketches*, p. 162. In Mann, *Faustus*, p. 63, we read 'Music was actually the most intellectual of all the arts, as in no other, form and content are interwoven and absolutely one and the same'.

2. See Cherniavsky, *Sibelius*, p. 141.

3. See Meyer, *Explaining*, pp. 68f, and Cherniavsky, *Sibelius*, pp. 156ff.

4. See Levas, *Sibelius*, p. 59. Johnson, *Sibelius* (pp. 48 and 94) suggests that some of Sibelius' views represented carefully thought out stock replies which he considered suitable for public consumption: among these he notes Sibelius' comparison of his music to the wings of a butterfly.

5. The terms 'foreground' and 'background' are not used here with the meanings attached to them by Schenker.

6. Walker, *Analysis*, pp. 26ff. See also Tippett, *Aquarius*, pp. 110ff: and the quotation from Mendelssohn in Cooke, *Music*, p. 12.

7. See Meyer, *Explaining*, pp. 4f. Taking the argument further, a mere description of technical processes is insufficient: to make a literary comparison, the *fact* that Iago is a villain is less important than the *effect* this has on the plot of *Othello*. (See Meyer, *Explaining*, p. 6.)

8. See Chapters V and VI. I am deeply grateful to Dr Robert Simpson for drawing my attention to the problem, and for discussing it with me. See also Rosen, *Style*, pp. 36 and 40.

9. The smaller the number of notes used in 'thematic correspondences' within a work, the more questionable does their use as a unifying device seem. See Meyer, *Explaining*, p. 74, in this connection.

10. There is, of course, monothematicism before Beethoven: see, for instance, Rosen, *Style*, pp. 37f.

11. Such views of unity and inevitability have sometimes been questioned: see Meyer, *Explaining*, p. 147.

12. Grove, *Beethoven*, p. 179.

13. Levas, *Sibelius*, p. 61: the 'compulsion' is discussed on p. 81 of that book. Meyer, *Explaining*, pp. 21f, suggests that composers' statements about music—either their own or that of other composers—may not always be reliable.

14. Walker, *Analysis*, passim. See also Meyer, *Ideas*, pp. 266f, 277.

15. The exception which proves this rule for each composer will be found in the discussions of Beethoven's Fifth Symphony (p. 154 of this book), and of Sibelius' Seventh (p. 211).

16. Tovey, *Analysis*.

17. See Robert Simpson's two introductory Essays in Simpson, *Symphony*.

18. One may learn much from all forms of analysis without accepting any single one in full; as is pointed out in Cooper, *Rhythm*, p. 146, 'It is probably very rarely, if ever, that a method of musical analysis is wholly wrong. It is often true that it simply goes too far.'

19. Keller, *Mozart*, pp. 76f.

20. The openings are quoted in Keller, *Mozart*, p. 72.

21. Lam, *Beethoven*, p. 160.

22. Compare Mann, *Faustus*: 'Hear? . . . If by "hearing" you understand the precise realization in detail of the means by which the highest and strictest order is achieved, like the order of
the planets, a cosmic order and legality—no, that way one would not hear it. But this order one
will or would hear, and the perception of it would afford an unknown aesthetic satisfaction.'

23. See the discussion in Meyer, *Explaining*, pp. 23f.

24. Levas, *Sibelius*, p. 83.

25. Moscheles says that Beethoven avoided all musical discussions, only occasionally explaining
matters to his pupil Ries (Sonneck, *Beethoven*, p. 91). Schlesinger suggested that Beethoven should
write an essay on symphonic form; see Forbes, *Thayer*, p. 959.

26. 'He can do everything, but we are still unable to understand all that he does', said Schubert
of Beethoven. See Scherchen, *Music*, p. 77. Nevertheless, E. T. A. Hoffmann's article on the Fifth
Symphony (1810) says, '. . . it is particularly the intimate relationship of the individual themes
to one another which produces the unity that firmly maintains a single feeling in the listener's
heart. In the music of Haydn and Mozart, this unity prevails everywhere. It becomes clearer to
the musician when he discovers a common bass pattern in two different phrases, or when the
connecting of two movements makes it obvious . . .' See Forbes, *Beethoven 5*, p. 163.

27. Sonneck, *Beethoven*, p. 22.

28. Parmet, *Sibelius*.

29. Fujita, *Middlemarch*, p. 7. Incidentally, George Eliot was also aware of the necessity of
integration in a novel: 'I don't see how I can leave anything out,' she wrote, 'because I hope
there is nothing that will be seen to be irrelevant to my design . . . I . . . think of refining when
novel readers only think of skipping.' (Eliot, *Letters*, Vol. 5, pp. 168f.)

30. Walker, *Criticism*, pp. 83f. See also Walker, *Analysis*, pp. 129ff; and Tovey, *Analysis*, Vol. I,
p. 68.

31. In this respect see Tippett, *Aquarius*, p. 15.

32. Sonneck, *Beethoven*, p. 152. Beethoven's advice was not to use a piano when composing: see
Forbes, *Thayer*, p. 683. He took care to enquire about the acoustics of the auditorium before
beginning a work for a particular hall: see Forbes, *Thayer*, p. 677.

33. Sonneck, *Beethoven*, pp. 146f: further corroboration for these points can be found on pp. 25,
127 and 171. Lewis Lockwood and Joseph Kerman suggest that Beethoven did not always work
in this way: see Tyson, *Studies*, pp. 122 and 150.

34. Levas, *Sibelius*, p. 88.

35. Levas, *Sibelius*, Chapter 10: especially pp. 92, 101 and 104.

36. Sayers, *Maker* (especially Chapter 3, *Idea, Energy, Power*) also confirms that 'the idea' of a
piece and its working-out occur in the head, and that the commital to paper is a more mechanical
process of getting this idea into a tangible form. The element of 'inspiration' which provides the
idea is described partly by a quotation from Browning's *Abt Vogler* (see Sayers, *Maker*, p. 22),
Beethoven must have composed the opening movement of his tenth symphony in his mind, since
he played the movement to Holz on the piano; see Forbes, *Thayer*, p. 986.

37. Sayers, *Maker*, especially Chapter 5, *Free Will and Miracle*.

38. Meyer, *Explaining*, p. 75.

39. Barrett-Ayres, *Haydn*, p. 193.

40. Kerman, *Quartets*, pp. 186 and 226.

11 The Thematic Approach

1. Elements of thematic unity can be found also in Haydn: see Barrett-Ayres, *Haydn*, pp. 61,
72, 134, 181, 193 and 308. Compare also Simpson, *Bruckner*, p. 90, 'Themes are more easily
noticed than tonalities'. See Kerman, *Quartets*, pp. 66 and 276.

2. See Deane, *Beethoven*, p. 295. Sibelius said, 'You may find thematic connections in my
symphonies when you study them. I myself call these the "symphonic necessity" because I am
more the medium than a cerebral type of man. Especially when regarding my first symphonies,
a cerebral study would hardly give a key to them. What is needed there is the "Boy's mind".'
(See Johnson, *Sibelius*, p. 158. See also Weingartner, *Music*, p. 286.)

3. Naturally, a composer sometimes draws particular attention to thematic transformations: an example of these can be found in the Finale of Tchaikovsky's Serenade for Strings.

4. Breitkopf & Härtel's Partitur-Bibliothek Nr. 3323.

5. Sibelius himself, however, denied that he built his themes out of small fragments. See Levas, *Sibelius*, p. 88.

6. Hill, *Sibelius*.

7. I use the word 'movement' to refer to the three distinct sections of the work, even though the title-page describes it as 'in one movement': see Chapter VI, note 44.

8. The last five bars of p. 59 of the miniature score (bars 11-15 after Letter P) contain the seed of both themes in the last movement.

9. Meyer, *Explaining*, p. 71, shows similar thematic correspondences in Brahms' symphonies: see also p. 67 of the same book.

10. See Parmet, *Sibelius*, pp. 78f.

11. It is clear that Sibelius considered thematic correspondences unimportant. See Parmet, *Sibelius*, pp. 78f, 81.

12. See Tovey, *Analysis*, Vol. 1, pp. 38ff.

13. See Cone, *Composer*, p. 97 for an analysis of the purpose of this cadenza.

14. The fact that Beethoven's sketches contain a different theme for a projected purely orchestral Finale need not concern us, since it is not known how Beethoven would have handled this motif had he used it in such a version. Although he used the theme in his Op. 132 Quartet, his handling of it in this piece can give no clue as to the way in which he might have used it in the 'Choral', since the requirements of these two works are very different. (The sketch is transcribed in Grove, *Beethoven*, p. 330.) The unreliability of sketchbooks for the purposes of analysis is mentioned in Meyer, *Explaining*, p. 23. See also Kerman, *Quartets*, pp. 329f.

15. On this point see the splendid passage in Kerman, *Quartets*, p. 194.

III The Expansion of Classical Tonality (1)

1. See the discussion in Mann, *Schenker*, especially pp. 11f. Meyer, *Explaining*, p. 91, draws a distinction between works 'having form' and 'being a form'. See Kollmann's discussion of sonata form (from his *Essay of Practical Musical Composition* of 1799, quoted in Barrett-Ayres, *Haydn*, pp. 94f). A splendid introduction to the workings of the tonal system can be found in Rosen, *Style*, pp. 23-9.

2. One can find the process foreshadowed in the final pedals of Renaissance motets, where the 'tonic' and 'subdominant' chords alternate below (or around) a held tonic note. The closing pages of Handel's chorus 'Let their celestial concerts all unite' (*Samson*) and Haydn's 'The Heavens are telling' (*Creation*) are extensions of this idea, which comes to a culmination in the coda of the first movement of Beethoven's Ninth Symphony.

3. As Barrett-Ayres puts it, we accept *spaciousness* as a characteristic of symphonies. (See Barrett-Ayres, *Haydn*, p. 83.)

4. See, for example, Haydn's String Quartet in C, Op. 74, No. 1.

5. See Rosen, *Style*, pp. 112f.

6. This point is implied in the writings of Schenker: see, for example, the discussion in Mann, *Schenker*, p. 13.

7. Though Kerman (in *Quartets*, pp. 13f) has drawn attention to Beethoven's growing interest in counterpoint—for its own sake—at this stage of his career.

8. See Meyer, *Explaining*, p. 212.

9. Similar conflicts can be found elsewhere in Beethoven (for example in the opening movement of the Fifth Symphony, bars 342-5 and 354f) as well as in Sibelius.

10. As Kerman says, 'The last "neutral" Symphony was the Second, in D, which was composed over a relatively long period, from 1800 to 1802. D major was the traditional key for a vigorous symphony. Beethoven simply produced an especially good and notably brainy example.' (Kerman, *Quartets*, p. 117.)

11. Kerman, *Quartets*, p. 158, points out that in slow introductions it was customary to introduce a feeling of mystery after the initial clear statement of the tonic. See also Somfai, *Haydn*, pp. 166f.

12. To have followed this precept would in any case have shown a tendency to repeat the devices of the First Symphony, as it were 'in inversion'.

13. Haydn had already used the word 'Scherzo' in place of 'Menuetto' in his Op. 33 String Quartets (see Barrett-Ayres, *Haydn*, p. 311). As Barrett-Ayres remarks, 'Haydn had already pioneered many of the formal techniques usually accredited to Beethoven' (ibid., p. 299).

14. A characteristic shape of many Baroque fugue subjects.

15. 'If *I* write a symphony an hour long it will be found short enough' was Beethoven's answer to criticisms that the work was too long: he suggested that it should be played at the beginning of a concert, before the audience had grown weary. See Forbes, *Thayer*, p. 376; also Kerman, *Quartets*, p. 101.

16. See, for example, Meikle, *Eroica*, p. 205.

17. Macrorhythm is discussed in Chapter VII.

18. Sibelius, as will be shown later, used a similar device with quite different intentions and results.

19. Mies, *Sketches*, deals with aspects of the 'Eroica' Symphony on pp. 13, 40, 70, 84f, 134 and 187.

20. One is reminded of Schenk's description of Beethoven's improvisations (see Sonneck, *Beethoven*, p. 15): 'My ear was continually charmed by the beauty of the many and varied motives which he wove with wonderful clarity and loveliness into each other . . . and anon, leaving the field of mere tonal charm, boldly stormed the most distant keys in order to give expression to violent passions . . .' The splendid passage dealing with this part of the development section in Cooper, *Rhythm*, pp. 137–40, should be consulted by the reader.

21. Mozart had already introduced a new theme in the development of his 'Hunt' Quartet (among others).

22. As Basil Deane points out (in Deane, *Beethoven*, p. 292), the final dissolution of the rhythm of the main theme was an idea which occurred to Beethoven only after he had tried several more conventional endings. Kerman, *Quartets*, p. 345, says that thematic breakdown was a favourite device of Beethoven's second period; and Hans Keller, in a broadcast, pointed out that music had never *disintegrated* like this before—Mozart's 40th Symphony, for example, rebuilds again after the disintegration.

23. One of the main problems posed by the gigantic first and second movements of the 'Eroica'—that of adequately following them on a similar scale—is mentioned in Kerman, *Quartets*, pp. 65f.

24. A similar kind of rhythmic change to duple time (in this instance by placing the secondary accent at an unexpected point in the bar) had occurred in the first act of *Don Giovanni* ('Giovinette che fate all'amore').

25. A process which was nearly exactly repeated when for a time he used the Trio of his Second Symphony in his sketches for the 'Choral'.

26. The modulation from G minor to the dominant of E flat is present in all the sketches: see Mies, *Sketches*, p. 139.

27. Probably suggested by Mozart's normal use of a penultimate slow variation.

28. A concept discussed below: see Chapter VII.

29. This work will be dealt with in Chapter VI.

30. Even Beethoven's early sketches showed this tendency towards C major: see Forbes, *Beethoven 5*, pp. 120, 122.

31. E. T. A. Hoffmann mentioned the possibility, Scherchen, *Music*, p. 170, did likewise, Schenker denied it (see Forbes, *Beethoven 5*, pp. 153 and 167). Hoffmann's article, written in 1810, remains one of the finest commentaries on the work.

32. Throughout the argument, indeed, the figure has a tendency to get higher and to be presented more strongly.

33. One might compare the concentration of this exposition with that evident in Shakespeare's mature plays and the later sonnets. (Cf. Arnold, *Beethoven*, p. 505 fn.)

34. As Schmitz points out (Mies, *Sketches*, p. 91) this also draws attention to the most important melodic and rhythmic motto.

35. Early sketches do not use A flat on nearly such a large scale. See, for instance, Forbes, *Beethoven 5*, p. 126.

36. Haydn had already re-introduced the theme of the Minuet into the Finale of his Symphony No. 46 in B major.

37. Basil Lam, in Simpson, *Symphony*, Vol. I, p. 160.

38. See also Kerman, *Quartets*, p. 119.

39. The most obvious parallels with battle and victory are mentioned by many commentators: see Deane, *Beethoven*, p. 297, for example. Kerman, *Quartets*, p. 243, says that the issue of the symphony is 'defiance'.

40. Simpson, *Symphony*, Vol. I, p. 142. See also Below, *Beethoven 7*.

41. Kerman, *Quartets*, p. 171.

42. Meyer, *Explaining*, pp. 142–4 (and p. 180) provides an analysis of themes from the first movement.

43. Though some preliminary sketches begin in A. See Mies, *Sketches*, p. 81.

44. Forbes, *Thayer*, p. 527, points out a resemblance between the tune of the Trio and an Austrian pilgrimage hymn.

IV The Expansion of Classical Tonality (2)

1. See Kerman, *An die ferne*, pp. 156f.

2. See Kerman, *Quartets*, p. 239, on writing without dominants. See also Rosen, *Style*, pp. 382f.

3. The expansion of tonality in this direction forms an interesting contrast with Sibelius' procedures in his Third Symphony, discussed below.

4. Perfect cadences are not, of course, avoided merely because Beethoven is postulating a tonal scheme which replaces, on the large scale, dominant relationships with keys a third apart. It is not my intention to suggest that Beethoven ceases to use the dominant chord.

5. The written-out change of key signature within a movement was not quite new to symphonic music, for it had already appeared in two major-key Finales, those of Beethoven's Fifth and Seventh Symphonies.

6. The figure, incidentally, inverts the B flat—A motif *x*.

7. This device was later copied by Brahms in his Fourth Symphony.

8. This provides an interesting example of Beethoven making a virtue out of necessity—the trumpets and drums were, of course, limited as to the number of notes they could play.

9. See Tovey, *Beethoven*, p. 14.

10. This device was copied by Brahms in the first movement of his Second Symphony.

11. A similar manner of working can be found at bars 8of and 345f.

12. The whole passage recalls two similar ones in the Seventh Symphony.

13. Haydn had already written a minuet as the second movement in some string quartets, though it was normally placed third in his symphonies: see Barrett-Ayres, *Haydn*, pp. 65 and 343.

14. The development of the subject from two separate themes is shown in Mies, *Sketches*, pp. 73f.

15. Because its arch-shape was ideal for Beethoven's purpose, he used the Trio of the Second Symphony in this place until he had evolved the music of the Trio of the Ninth proper.

16. Compare the schemes shown by Meyer, *Explaining*, pp. 168–70.

17. The second theme was originally in A. See Mies, *Sketches*, p. 175; also the discussion of the evolution of the opening theme at pp. 97f.

18. Basil Deane maintains that different criteria for formal coherence must be applied to a movement containing a text setting as opposed to a purely instrumental movement (*Beethoven*, p. 311), though this is not necessarily so, as is demonstrated by this Finale, where the formal criteria applied to the earlier movements are equally applicable.

19. The original text of Beethoven's sketches for the recitative, which clearly rejects the music of the first three movements, can be seen on pp. 891–4 of Forbes, *Thayer*. See also ibid., p. 451 for a discussion of the introduction of voices into the Choral Fantasia. See also Mies, *Sketches*, pp. 145f. Haydn's Sinfonia Concertante in B flat for oboe, bassoon, violin and 'cello, introduces recitative at the opening of the Finale.

20. This point also helps to explain the angular tenor part of bar 260 and the augmented leap up from B flat to F sharp (both, in a sense, pivotal notes) in the alto at bar 634.

21. This does not happen all at once, however, and the B minor of bar 204 is immediately destroyed by the appearance of B flat in the melody; and the semitone drop (B natural–B flat) is carried a stage further, down to A (*x* being yet again used for modulation).

22. Kerman, *An die ferne*, p. 154, suggests that the growing complexity of the variations fits in

with 'the ambivalence in respect to simple and complex utterance' which is a feature of Beethoven's later music.

23. Note, too, how the chorus prolongs many dominant chords (bars 915f, for instance).

24. In Simpson, *Symphony*, Vol. I, p. 173.

25. Schenkerian analysis would see this overall progression from the dominant to the tonic as a significant feature, but such a view would be an oversimplification of the real functioning of tonality in this work.

26. See, for instance, Forbes, *Thayer*, pp. 895f. Nielsen wondered whether Beethoven used a choral Finale because he was afraid he could not succeed with a purely instrumental movement (see Simpson, *Nielsen*, p. 84).

27. Sonneck, *Beethoven*, p. 127.

Interlude

1. Robert Simpson has shown this in Simpson, *Bruckner*.

2. All references are to the edition produced by Leopold Nowak (Vienna, 1953).

3. The minor sixth is a very 'romantic' and evocative interval: its use for expressive purposes in the late Renaissance is very widespread. One might also instance its frequent use in connection with the plagal cadence in major keys during the Romantic period.

4. Tovey, *Analysis*, Vol. II, p. 73. See also Chapter III above, p. 63 and note 9.

5. In some early versions of the Finale only the rhythm of Ex. 35, and not the shape, is used.

6. Bruckner used the rhythm but not the notes in earlier versions. Their function is, as Robert Simpson remarks in *Bruckner*, p. 89, that of stopping the rhythm.

7. Compare Simpson, *Bruckner*, p. 128.

8. The point is discussed in Simpson, *Bruckner*, pp. 96f.

9. The point is well discussed in Simpson, *Bruckner*, pp. 99f.

10. Robert Simpson has shown that a similar difficulty exists in the Finale: see Simpson, *Bruckner*, pp. 99f. See also, in this connection, Cone, *Composer*, pp. 126f; and compare Cherniavsky, *Sibelius*, p. 172.

v The Expansion of Classical Tonality (3)

1. See Rosen, *Style*, p. 33.

2. The idea may have come originally from Beethoven's Quartet in B flat, Op. 130. See Kerman, *Quartets*, pp. 311f.

3. Meyer, *Ideas*, p. 259, suggests that much analysis does not take into account chord relationships on a large scale.

4. Sibelius said, 'I am a slave to my themes and submit to their demands': see Johnson, *Sibelius*, p. 97; pp. 97 and 98 of Harold Johnson's book give details of programmes which various people have tried to impose upon the work.

5. Levas, *Sibelius*, pp. 82f.

6. References are to the miniature score published by Breitkopf & Härtel, No. 3323.

7. The use of B flat-A as a link is another reminder of Beethoven's 'Choral' Symphony.

8. The terms 'exposition', 'development' and 'recapitulation' may not be wholly satisfactory for a movement such as this, yet they are the only ones in use in English, and are employed here for that reason. Brahms had already shortened the recapitulation of his own Second Symphony by combining two themes, which had appeared separately in the exposition, in contrapuntal combination.

9. There is here yet another parallel with Beethoven's 'Choral' Symphony.

10. Layton, *Sibelius*, p. 35f.

11. While agreeing with the findings of such writers as Hill (*Sibelius*), I hope to show that thematic analysis is, by itself, an insufficient guide to the working of the composer's mind and to the various forces at work in the symphony.

12. The score referred to is the study score of Sibelius' Third Symphony, Eulenberg No. 531.

13. 'The older I grow, the more classical I become', Sibelius said to Törne (see Törne, *Sibelius*, p. 86).

14. Dr Roger Bullivant has made the interesting suggestion that the C-D-E-F sharp progression

it an unconscious inversion of the one at the opening of Beethoven's Leonore No. 3 Overture, where F sharp is also reached from C in order to move into B minor.

15. E flat minor (p. 15) also results from interpreting F sharp as G flat.

16. In this passage B sharp is, of course, the enharmonic equivalent of C—a fact to which I shall not continuously draw attention. However the note may be written for notational convenience, the real point is that the ear still hears the struggle as being between B and C.

17. There is also in the second movement a passage (on pages 38–9) in which the bass of the opening of the first movement's development section (pages 10–11) is recalled.

18. Abraham, Sibelius, p. 22.

19. It is a nice point that the tritone (when incorporated into the dominant seventh chord, for example, or used with similar effect) can also be used to establish tonality: that is the function of the interval in Sibelius' Third Symphony, just as it is in Beethoven's First.

20. The references are to the study score published by Breitkopf & Härtel, No. 3326.

21. Johnson, Sibelius, p. 128, notes that although the score marks the part 'glocken', 'Finnish conductors, with Sibelius as their authority, insist that the part . . . should be rendered on the glockenspiel'.

22. Parmet, Sibelius, pp. 149f, concludes that the composer attacked by Sibelius cannot have been Schoenberg, on the grounds that Schoenberg's first revolutionary work (Three Pieces for Piano, Op. 11, 1909) was not taken seriously by most people.

23. Levas, Sibelius, p. 74.

24. Johnson, Sibelius, p. 183.

25. Ibid., p. 29, mentions a different programmatic possibility.

26. Törne, Sibelius, p. 101, ventures to suggest that the Fourth Symphony was Sibelius' own favourite.

27. The movement is in a very highly condensed sonata form.

28. References are to the miniature score published by Breitkopf & Härtel, No. 3328.

29. See Chapter VIII below.

VI Rhythm

1. The parallel with the tonal scheme of Sibelius' Third Symphony discussed above is obvious.

2. Haydn foreshadows this treatment very briefly in his String Quartet Op. 33 No. 3 in C (see Barrett-Ayres, Haydn, p. 169.) He also used ideas from the Introduction of some of his later symphonies for development in the body of the work.

3. The descending scale in the flutes and oboes which accompanies the version of x in bar 22 is itself a diminution of Ex. 58a.

4. Mozart's Clarinet Quintet (K. 581) had already used a 'double sandwich' Minuet and Trio form, though with different Trios. See also Kerman, Quartets, p. 106.

5. See also Mies, Sketches, p. 55.

6. Beethoven had already used a similar correspondence of themes in his First Symphony at the same point as the first two mentioned above.

7. Further diminutions are found at bars 165–8 (rhythmically altered from bars 66–9) and 173–4 (from the previous four bars.)

8. Tovey, Analysis, Vol. I, p. 37.

9. Grove, Beethoven, p. 110.

10. A famous exception is the end of Mozart's Haffner Symphony.

11. Kerman, Quartets, p. 126, also remarks on a tendency to write an inconclusive end to a movement in order to provide a better link.

12. Tovey, Analysis, Vol. I, p. 37.

13. The horns had also been prominent at the end of the slow movement, and to a much lesser extent, at the end of the first movement too.

14. Meyer, Explaining, pp. 218–22 has provided an analysis of this subject.

15. The same point was made by Sibelius when he said, 'Each of my seven symphonies has its own style, and their creation in every case took a lot of time.' See Levas, Sibelius, p. 87.

16. References to features which are used thrice in this and other works may be found in Mies, Sketches, pp. 46, 48, 50ff and 55. A rhythmical analysis of the first movement of this work can be found in Cooper, Rhythm, pp. 188f: see also pp. 177f.

17. See, for example, Weingartner, *On the Performance of Beethoven's Symphonies* (transl. Jessie Crosland) in Weingartner, *Music*, p. 171.

18. This view is supported by the opinion of Cipriani Potter: 'Some judges are of the opinion, that his misfortune had considerable influence upon his writings, and that it contributed to their complexity, particularly his later production; but it would have required a much more extended period than was allotted to him, to have caused him to forget the powers or genuis of an orchestra' (Sonneck, *Beethoven*, p. 110). As late as 1823 Schulz reported that Beethoven 'was desirous of ascertaining, for a particular composition he was then about, the highest possible note of the trombone . . . . He then told me, that he had in general taken care to inform himself through the different artists themselves, concerning the construction, character, and compass of all the principal instruments' (ibid., p. 151). Such a man is not likely to have been careless about his use of these instruments.

19. The coda was originally 34 bars shorter. Beethoven extended it so as to include material from the second group as well as the first (Arnold, *Beethoven*, p. 305).

20. The use of the opening motif in the final cadence seems to have been an after-thought: see Kerman, *An die ferne*, p. 139.

21. At bar 436 one more attempt to establish a key a third away from F—A minor—is immediately contradicted by a tonic cadence.

22. I am most grateful to Mr George Biddlecombe and Mr Hugh Maguire for invaluable assistance with this matter.

23. See Mies, *Sketches*, p. 7.

24. Lam, in Simpson, *Symphony*, Vol. I, p. 149.

25. Simpson, *Beethoven*, p. 51.

26. It has become clear throughout this study that the opening moments of a Beethoven or Sibelius symphony (with the possible exception of the First Symphonies) are of vital importance to an understanding of the constructional processes at work in the composition as a whole.

27. Tovey, *Analysis*, Vol. I, p. 66.

28. A key a third away from the tonic, and with a signature of three sharps.

29. Meyer, *Ideas*: the final sentence.

30. There is, in addition to the processes outlined in this discussion, the alleged connection between the second movement and Mälzel's invention of the metronome. See Forbes, *Thayer*, pp. 534f. Kerman refers to the work as a classical evocation of the type Beethoven sometimes turned to throughout his life (see Kerman, *Quartets*, p. 362).

31. The variations of this theme use mostly quavers.

32. Scores of the first and second versions of the work are not available, though the first version has recently been performed: the following discussion is based on hearings of a tape recording of this performance, kindly given to me by Robert Simpson.

33. In an interesting passage on page 25 (just after Letter L) of the first movement, Sibelius draws particular attention to the presence of *x* by his placement of stress signs in the horn and woodwind parts. All bars and page references in this section are to the miniature score published by Wilhelm Hansen, No. 2103b.

34. The effect is rather like the visual effect of watching an accelerating wheel: there comes a point where it rotates so rapidly that to the eye it seems motionless.

35. Compare the first movement of Beethoven's Fourth Symphony, discussed above.

36. Parmet, *Sibelius*, pp. 83f, notices the movement at two speeds without mentioning its deeper implications: Sibelius, as usual, would not be drawn into discussing such matters of construction.

37. This is one of the few places in the work where the strings move more slowly than the wind.

38. The device has been well prepared by the music which the composer used to end the first movement: from page 59 onwards the various thematic segments used include the 'hammer swinging' theme, as well as music moving in longer notes.

39. It is worth noting that the change to the firm three-bar macrorhythm is carefully introduced by the first four notes of Ex. 65 (with a final E flat) in the same note values but in combination with a four-bar macrorhythm just before the beginning of the second subject: it occurs in the bass at page 104, bar 8 to page 105, bar 2. The device helps Sibelius to move from quick to slow motion with similar ease to that with which he accomplished the opposite transition in the first movement.

40. One of these foretastes, the one which occurs in the double basses in the second movement, was added to the final version of the symphony, apparently as an afterthought.

41. Pages 9 and 133 of the score are good examples of this.

42. Mann, *Faustus*, p. 75.

43. Notice also how Ex. 65 juxtaposes leaps with stepwise motion.

44. Throughout this discussion I have described the work as if it were in three separate movements (in the sense of 'large-scale section', not 'motion'): this is a useful way of referring to the various sections since the work does fall into three distinct and separate parts, yet the title page of the printed score describes the symphony as 'in one movement'. The progression towards a single-movement symphony is evident not only in this work but in certain facets of the Sixth Symphony (notably the reference at the end of one movement to ideas contained in the next) as well as in some of Sibelius' earlier works. Sibelius deliberately creates the feeling that neither of the first two movements of the Fifth Symphony completes the sense—by ending on a weak pulse of the macrorhythm in the first movement, and by ending on a very brief tonic chord in the second.

45. See Palmer, *Impressionism*, p. 145. Nielsen put the same idea another way: see Simpson, *Nielsen*, p. 201.

46. As Robert Simpson remarked during a conversation I had with him, some works which survive all other types of analysis can fail in this respect.

47. Study score, ed. Nowak, p. 138.

48. Robert Simpson's observations on another Bruckner symphony are very much to the point: see Simpson, *Bruckner*, p. 70.

49. Russian composers had sometimes used slower movement for a second subject, and the idea is basic to Dvorak's *Dumky* Trio. Earlier than these are very many applications in such pieces as chorale preludes (and such later manifestations of that style as the slow section of Smetana's *Vltava*), cantus firmus pieces, dialogues (such as the second section of *Lamento di Ninfo* from Monteverdi's *Madrigali Guerreri e Amorosi*) and variations by colouration or divisions.

VII Pace and Tension

1. Schenker, *Beethoven 5*, Tovey, *Analysis*, Vol. I; Imbrie, *Beethoven*.

2. Schenker's, given in the essay quoted in note 1.

3. Andrew Imbrie's, given in the essay quoted in note 1.

4. Imbrie does, indeed, suggest that Beethoven intended the listener to feel a sense of ambiguity.

5. The solution given by Andrew Imbrie in Ex. 6 of his essay goes against the tendency shown in Ex. 68 of this book: the appearance of an unauthorized accent on the horn note of bar 62 in Imbrie's Ex. 6 strengthens his case. Both Schenker and Tovey agree that the natural scansion is that shown in Ex. 68 of this book.

6. The rhythm does, of course, occur in weaker positions, too, especially in passages consisting of continuous quaver movement: however, the loud unison versions and the isolated statements are normally accented as shown in Ex. 68.

7. Andrew Imbrie makes this point in his essay quoted in note 1.

8. The motto rhythm is also used for a similar purpose in the subsequent movements.

9. I owe to Robert Simpson the additional idea that an overlap of macrorhythms is possible at this point, the pause causing a shift forward of the strong pulse by a bar in the following manner:

bar	22	23	24	25	26	27	28
macrorhythm	4	1	2	3	4	1	2
					1	2	3 etc.

10. A feature pointed out by Schenker, *Beethoven 5*, p. 11.

11. The G flat–A natural leap in the upper parts also indicates that such a regrouping is correct because of the placing of the unexpected A natural on the lesser of the new strong pulses: see Ex. 71.

12. Schenker, *Beethoven 5*, p. 18.

13. Bars 5, 24, 128 (though this bar restores an original three-bar cell to one of four bars), 252, 482. See Forbes, *Beethoven 5* pp. 15, 130.

14. Added to an earlier version of the score: see Forbes, *Beethoven 5*, p. 130.

15. Subconsciously, because the pauses which occur at those points where bars are inserted tend to ensure that the rhythm is not heard as a strict five-bar one.

16. Here we may compare Robert Simpson's comment (in Simpson, *Bruckner*, p. 183)—'the tension created [by Bruckner] is of the opposite kind from Beethoven's: the latter crowds his idea fiercely upon the expectations, while Bruckner's tension results from what is essentially a delaying action.'

17. The countersubject to the A flat tune of the second movement, with its slow progression from E flat, via E natural (part of a C major chord) to F and back illustrates this perfectly.

18. Something of the same kind may well be traceable in the continual plagal cadences in the coda of the first movement (bars 455–67, for instance). It is interesting that such a progression is hinted at in Mann, *Faustus*, p. 49.

19. E. T. A. Hoffmann, quoted in Forbes, *Beethoven 5*, p. 155. The purely optical effect of the music is, according to Mies (*Sketches*, pp. 184 and 186), of importance to Beethoven. Schenker, *Beethoven 5*, in his large-scale analysis of the movement, hides this point by rewriting D flat enharmonically (see opposite p. 6).

20. Tovey, *Analysis*, Vol. I, p. 35 (discussing the Fourth Symphony): see also ibid., pp. 39f.

21. I am most grateful to Robert Simpson for kindling my interest in these processes.

22. Kerman, *Quartets*, pp. 326f, makes a good point about rhythmic continuity in Beethoven's Op. 131 Quartet.

23. Cooper, *Rhythm*, p. 66. This quotation states the problem admirably. Obviously tempo and metronome marks affect the music in performance, but the present discussion is concerned with the various levels of pace which are, at least to a certain extent, independent of the overall tempo and relative to each other.

24. The opposite view is quoted in Arnold, *Beethoven*, p. 518.

25. Indeed, the opening might be regarded as the 'first subject' appearing prematurely, the subject not being heard until D minor is reached.

26. The dominant chord is omitted entirely, partly because of the rhythmic upset, but partly also so that the first theme shall not sound too 'closed' a form in its own right, with too final a cadence. We must remember, too, the conflict of dominant and 'substitute dominant' discussed in Chapter IV, which is another reason for not overstressing the dominant chord here.

27. Rosen, *Style*, p. 385, makes the point that Beethoven's music shows little of Bach's influence, in spite of his great respect for and knowledge of his music.

28. This tonal argument is discussed in Chapter IV.

29. See Lam, in Simpson, *Symphony*, pp. 163, 165 and 172, for instance.

30. Contrast with this the effect of the fugue in the development section of the first movement, discussed above.

31. 'Written out' in the sense that the sign ⌒ is not used, the necessary rest (or sometimes notes) being written into the score.

32. Mies (*Sketches*), p. 102, points out that such irregularity of bars was a feature not found in the sketches for the movement.

33. Further reasons are given in Chapter IV for the inclusion of the horn cadenza.

34. It is generally accepted that motion towards the dominant is more 'dynamic', and motion towards the sub-dominant more 'relaxed'.

35. Glaring examples of this can be found among Rheinberger's Organ Sonatas.

36. Other reasons for Beethoven's manner of writing in the introduction to the Finale are given in Chapter IV.

37. The elongation of the F sharp has tonal significance, too: see Chapter IV.

38. In this connection see Kerman, *Quartets*, p. 254.

39. We may well wonder whether such feelings gave rise to the idea which governs the whole construction of Sibelius' Fifth Symphony, discussed in Chapter V.

40. See, for example, Simpson, *Bruckner*, p. 89.

41. See above, p. 164.

42. It is, indeed, this pervading use of ongoing rhythms that led Wagner to characterize the symphony as 'the apotheosis of the dance'.

43. One has only to imagine Rimsky-Korsakov's *The Flight of the Bumble Bee* as the basis of a symphonic argument to see how impossible such an idea is.

44. We may note, too, that the 'symphonic pause' of bars 77 and 80 (each an echo of the end of the previous phrase) of the first movement are omitted in the tutti repeat (bars 98 and 100) where more power is called for.

45. The importance of pedal E's is noticed in Below, *Beethoven 7*.

46. Keller, in Simpson, *Symphony*, p. 57.

VIII Variations

1. The special colour of these tonal progressions based on thirds also at times attracted other types of composer—witness, for example, the scheme of Debussy's Prelude 'La Cathédrale engloutie'.

2. The timpani begin this movement tuned to a G major triad.

3. Sibelius perhaps shows the same influence as Bruckner did at the beginning of the *Romantische*—the influence of the beginning of Beethoven's 'Choral' Symphony: nevertheless, Sibelius' tonal language, melodic shape and command of movement are quite unlike Bruckner's earlier adoption of Beethoven's idea.

4. It is often said that the theme is like the main theme of the first movement of Borodin's First Symphony, though this is merely a paper likeness: the two are entirely different in effect.

5. References are to the miniature score published by Breitkopf & Härtel, No. 3325.

6. 'Wrong' because it is the dominant of the prominent key of the opening, and not of the tonic, E minor.

7. I shall refer to the mode as 'C sharp Dorian' or 'E Dorian', etc., according to whichever note is the Final.

8. Chords of this type occur quite often in the second movement of the First Symphony.

9. The Scherzo of the Second Symphony is the nearest to it in style.

10. See Chapter V: and cf. also the top part of the bass stave in Ex. 76.

11. Cf. George, *Tonality*, p. 173, and Reti, *Sonatas*, p. 138. We can see something of this differentiation of subjects in the character of themes in D minor and B flat in Beethoven's 'Choral' Symphony.

12. See E. T. A. Hoffmann, in Strunk, *Readings*, pp. 776f. Also Kirby, *Pastoral*, pp. 103ff.

13. The application of a programme after the composition of the music is, of course, another matter.

14. They can be seen in Grove, *Beethoven*, p. 191.

15. A storm scene had become conventional in Italian opera by the late 18th century. See also Kerman, *Quartets*, p. 173.

16. See also, in this connection, Forbes, *Thayer*, p. 436; ibid., p. 438, mentions the village band which seems to have suggested certain features of the third movement.

17. As F. E. Kirby has conceded (*Pastoral*, p. 121): 'The Pastoral Symphony, then, *is* a symphony.'

18. Hyatt-King, *Mountains*, points out that Beethoven quoted a Swiss 'ranz des vaches' melody known as 'Rigi' tune at the opening of the Finale. This quotation does not affect the symphonic logic since it is integrated with the argument, not 'pasted on'. It has sometimes been maintained that other themes, too, are borrowed from folk material: see, for instance, Grove, *Beethoven*, pp. 194, 212.

19. The thematic unity of the work is confirmed by Philip Gossett, in Gossett, *Beethoven 6*, pp. 262ff.

20. One further use of x in a new contrapuntal combination with the other motifs occurs in the 'wind-band' passage of the coda of the first movement (bars 476f).

21. In this connection see Gossett, *Beethoven 6*, pp. 262f. See also Kirby, *Pastoral*, p. 118.

22. Gossett, *Beethoven 6*, p. 268, suggests that Beethoven decided to end the first movement with this interval after working out the second movement.

23. Beethoven became even more interested in the modes, and used modal sounding progressions more widely towards the end of his life. See Forbes, *Thayer*, p. 984.

24. Basil Deane has pointed out (in Deane, *Beethoven*) how infrequent minor chords are in this movement.

25. Gossett, *Beethoven 6*, pp. 253ff.

26. I have already pointed out that movement towards the dominant (and other keys on the

sharp side of the tonic) is generally regarded as being 'dynamic' in effect, whereas movement towards the subdominant (and flat-side keys, which balance those on the sharp side) is considered to be more restful. See, for instance, Cooke, *Music*, pp. 81f, and George, *Tonality*, p. 20; see also Rosen, *Style*, p. 382. Some writers prefer to use 'bright' for sharp-side keys, and 'dark' for those on the flat side.

27. The 'flat-side' nature of this passage is intensified by Beethoven's modulation back towards the tonic by way of even flatter keys, so that no dominantwards feeling shall result from F following B flat.

28. The prominent use of the sixth degree of the scale in passages such as that shown in Ex. 80 reminds one strongly of the use of this interval (and the $\frac{6}{5}$ chord) in later Impressionist music: see, for example, Palmer, *Impressionism*, pp. 51, 94. The line of influence from Beethoven to Wagner might well be traced through such pieces as Mendelssohn's *The Rivulet*, Op. 16, No. 3.

29. Cf. Kerman, *Quartets*, p. 161.

30. Kerman, *Sketches*, p. 91.

31. Kerman, *Quartets*, p. 201.

32. Gossett, *Beethoven 6*, p. 253.

33. See Johnson, *Sibelius*, pp. 160f.

34. Quoted by Ekman: cf. Cherniavsky, *Sibelius*, pp. 151f.

35. See, for instance, the remarks in Levas, *Sibelius*, pp. 80f, and in Parmet, *Sibelius*, p. 85. Compare Palmer, *Impressionism*, p. 240, note 2. 'Apparently no one was more astonished by these revelations of highly complex tonal relationships and the evolution of 'germ' motifs than the composer himself. Musical vivisection was so completely foreign to his way of thinking that he frequently protested that his admirers were attempting to turn him into a cerebral composer, whereas in reality he regarded his symphonies as "poems" ' (Johnson, *Sibelius*, p. 192).

36. See Grove, *Beethoven*, pp. 326f.

37. Sibelius also used the Dorian mode in the First Humoresque for Orchestra, Op. 87b of 1917.

38. Transpositions of the mode will be referred to by stating the Final first: thus G Dorian refers to the Dorian mode transposed up a fourth from D to G.

39. References are to the miniature score published by Wilhelm Hansen, No. 3343b.

40. For example, p. 8, bars 3–6: p. 10, bars 4–7, and p. 12, bars 3–7, where the progression is extended. There is a shorter example on page 11.

41. Page 41, violins and flutes, bars 5–7; p. 43, violins, bars 1–3, and many other similar runs, mostly in the strings.

42. The freshness of the appearance of perfect cadences in the opening theme of the Finale itself results from the infrequent occurrences of the cadence in previous movements.

43. At a point of relaxation from the sevenths, on p. 37, Sibelius introduces the other two 'pivotal' intervals of the mode, first using the woodwind in parallel thirds, and then in sixths.

44. There are many examples, for which two must stand: p. 4, bars 2–6, and p. 30, bars 7f (violins and violas).

45. A canon 3 in 1 in the strings (p. 10) in which each part is thickened to a third; a canon 4 in 2 (p. 8); a canon by dimunition (p. 12, bars 2f); and a canon with augmentations at two different speeds (p. 38, bars 6f); and these do not exhaust the list.

46. See Chapter VI.

47. As Harold Truscott reminds us: see Truscott, in Simpson, *Symphony*, pp. 80f.

48. This form, in a sense, already existed in the symphonic poem.

49. We may make a literary comparison here, and say that the 'innocent' reader of *Emma* may feel surprise at the marriage of Emma and Mr Knightley; but in fact, a careful re-reading of Jane Austen's novel shows that this is precisely the end towards which the whole work has been geared.

50. All references are to the miniature score published by Wilhelm Hansen, No. 2426b.

51. A technique explored by Sibelius in his previous symphony: see above.

52. The $\frac{6}{5}$ dissonance which is quite mild at this point in strengthened and lengthened to create more tension later in the work (page 50). The reasons for this are given in the text, below.

53. Simpson, *Bruckner*, p. 90.

54. It will be noticed that the music of Ex. 87 also revolves around the C-G-D axis.

55. Such a resolution has already been hinted at on several levels: the opening G of Ex. 87, for instance, could be held to 'resolve' onto C in either the following bar or the last bar of that quotation. It is, of course, the overall 'resolution' of G onto C that results in the final 'resolution' of F sharp–G onto the ultimate B–C.

56. See the discussion in Parmet, *Sibelius*, Chapter 8; and in Levas, *Sibelius*, Chapter X.

57. Quoted by Karl Ekman; see Wood, *Sibelius*, p. 45.

58. Britten's *The Turn of the Screw* is a fine example of a tonal work integrated by a twelve-note row.

Coda

1. See Ralph Wood's remarks (Wood, *Sibelius*, pp. 43 and 47) about the degree of logic in Sibelius as compared with Brahms, Dvorak and Tchaikovsky; also Cherniavsky, *Sibelius*, pp. 155f. Delius said of Sibelius, 'A lot of his work is too complicated and thought out . . . . The English like that sort of thing . . .' (See Johnson, *Sibelius*, p. 131.)

2. Sibelius' admiration for Beethoven is discussed in Levas, *Sibelius*, pp. 61ff. See also Cherniavsky, *Sibelius*, p. 151, and Törne, *Sibelius*, p. 46.

3. Levas, *Sibelius*, p. 74.

4. See Thorpe Davie, *Structure*, pp. 12f: '. . . the author is convinced that great music exists only where significant musical material is allied to the form which *for itself* is the right one . . .'

5. Simpson, *Nielsen*, p. 14.

6. Sonneck, *Beethoven*, p. 53.

7. Levas, *Sibelius*, pp. 62 and 63.

8. Kerman, *Quartets*, p. 136, remarks that schematic plans in Beethoven have an aesthetic end.

9. Levas, *Sibelius*, p. 84.

10. I would not support Cecil Gray's contention that Sibelius is the only true symphonic composer after Beethoven.

INDEX